Fanfare for a City

Support for this book was generously provided by the AMS 75 PAYS Endowment of the American Musicological Society, supported in part by the National Endowment for the Humanities and the Andrew W. Mellon Foundation.

The publisher and the University of California Press Foundation also gratefully acknowledge the generous support of the Constance and William Withey Endowment Fund in History and Music.

Fanfare for a City

MUSIC AND THE URBAN IMAGINATION
IN HAUSSMANN'S PARIS

Jacek Blaszkiewicz

UNIVERSITY OF CALIFORNIA PRESS

University of California Press
Oakland, California

© 2024 by Jacek Blaszkiewicz

Library of Congress Cataloging-in-Publication Data

Names: Blaszkiewicz, Jacek, 1988- author.
Title: Fanfare for a city : music and the urban imagination in Haussmann's Paris / Jacek Blaszkiewicz.
Description: Oakland, California : University of California Press, [2024] | Includes bibliographical references and index.
Identifiers: LCCN 2023026014 (print) | LCCN 2023026015 (ebook) | ISBN 9780520393479 (cloth) | ISBN 9780520393486 (ebook)
Subjects: LCSH: Music—France—Paris—19th century—History and criticism. | Opera—France—Paris—19th century. | Street musicians—France—Paris. | Urbanization—France—19th century. | France—History—Second Empire, 1852–1870.
Classification: LCC ML270.8.P2 B53 2024 (print) | LCC ML270.8.P2 B53 2024 (ebook) | DDC 780.944/36109034—dc23/eng/20230605
LC record available at https://lccn.loc.gov/2023026014
LC ebook record available at https://lccn.loc.gov/2023026015

Manufactured in the United States of America

33 32 31 30 29 28 27 26 25 24
10 9 8 7 6 5 4 3 2 1

CONTENTS

List of Illustrations and Musical Examples vii
Acknowledgments ix

Introduction 1

1 · Baron Haussmann's Musical Imagination 21

2 · Fanfare City: The Expositions universelles 42

3 · Urban Planning Lessons from the Café-Concert 77

4 · Street Music: Between Regulation and Liberation 111

5 · Street Cries: Constructing the Old City 146

Epilogue 180

Notes 189
Bibliography 215
Index 229

LIST OF ILLUSTRATIONS AND MUSICAL EXAMPLES

ILLUSTRATIONS

1. The inauguration of the boulevard du Prince-Eugène, 1862 *2*
2. The Palais de l'Industrie, 1855 *51*
3. Closing ceremonies of the 1867 Exposition universelle *72*
4. Edgar Degas, *Le Café-concert aux Ambassadeurs*, 1876–77 *83*
5. Gédéon, "La Tragédie au café-concert," 1867 *88*
6. "Un Café-concert aux Champs-Élysées," 1867 *92*
7. Honoré Daumier, "Le Joueur d'orgue de Barbarie," ca. 1860. *123*
8. Cover of *La Chanson des rues*, 1850 *126*
9. Illustration for "Ferraille à vendre! Chiffons!," 1855 *154*
10. Registration medallions for street vendors, ca. 1860 *161*
11. The inauguration of the boulevard Haussmann, January 15, 1927 *185*

MUSICAL EXAMPLES

1. Hector Berlioz, *L'Impériale* *54*
2. Hector Berlioz, *L'Impériale* *57*
3. Camille Saint-Saëns, *Les Noces de Prométhée* *67*
4. Gioachino Rossini, *Hymne à Napoléon III et à son vaillant peuple* *70*
5. Henry Marx, *Eh! Lambert!!* *119*
6. Antoine Elwart, "Paris!" *133*
7. Casimir Ménétrier, "Le Flâneur" *137*

8. Léo Delibes and Antoine Vialon, "Le Code fashionable: Chansonnette" *141*
9. Peuchot, "Ferraille à vendre! Chiffons!" *155*
10. Jean-Georges Kastner, *Les Cris de Paris*, orchestral interlude *166*
11. Jean-Georges Kastner, *Les Cris de Paris*, hawkers' interjections *170*
12. Jean-Georges Kastner, *Les Cris de Paris*, "rage aria" *171*

ACKNOWLEDGMENTS

In the world of academia, single-authored books are forbiddingly called "monographs." While writing this text necessarily relied on long periods of solitude, in particular during the COVID-19 pandemic, *Fanfare for a City* would not exist if not for the patience, brilliance, and generosity of the people and institutions that I have the privilege of acknowledging here.

This project began during my doctoral research at the Eastman School of Music, University of Rochester. My dissertation advisor, Ralph P. Locke, helped me shape my diffuse thoughts about music and urban space into a coherent thesis. He has remained a thoughtful editor, advisor, and mentor in the years since we have both moved on from Rochester. Holly Watkins and Robert Doran offered their unsurpassable knowledge of aesthetics and philosophy as members of my dissertation committee. The faculty and my fellow students at Eastman have influenced my thinking on sound, culture, history, pedagogy, writing, and countless other topics, allowing me to function as a professional academic and teacher today. I would especially like to thank Michael Anderson, Gabrielle Cornish, Melina Esse, Roger Freitas, Sarah Fuchs, Lisa Jakelski, Lauron Kehrer, Ellen Koskoff, Jennifer Kyker, Patrick Macey, William Marvin, Mary McArthur, Honey Meconi, Darren Mueller, Trevor Nelson, Austin Richey, Megan Steigerwald-Ille, Jane Sylvester, and Alexis Van Zalen.

Research for this book was made possible thanks to the M. Elizabeth C. Bartlet Fund from the American Musicological Society, the Richard and Mica Hadar Foundation, a Fulbright Fellowship, as well as funding from Wayne State University's College of Fine, Performing, and Communication Arts. I benefited greatly from a Wayne State Humanities Center Residency, which funded the acquisition of secondary resources, and which provided intellectual stimulation in the height of COVID-19 lockdown. I would like to thank Walter Edwards, the outgoing director, as well as my 2020–21 academic cohort. Janine Lanza and Nicole Trujillo-Pagán generously commented on chapter drafts both during and after our residency. I am grateful to my colleagues in Wayne State's Department of Music who have conversed with me on various aspects of this project, in particular Karl Braunschweig, Joshua Duchan, Mary Paquette-Abt, Jeremy Peters, as well as our department chair, Norah Duncan IV. I would also like to acknowledge my Wayne State colleagues outside of music who have listened to my work-in-progress with enthusiasm and encouragement. I look forward to continued collaborations across the West Warren Avenue border.

Parisians love good conversation and a good *terrasse*. This is also true of historians of French music. The *France: Musiques, Cultures* research network is a warm and collegial group of scholars from around the world, and I encourage any young scholar of French music to join. Between the email correspondence, annual conferences, Zoom calls, dinners, drinks, and coffees, the "solitary activity" of writing has had a strong social component for which I am immensely grateful. For their ideas, advice, and camaraderie, whether at AMS, in Paris, or online, I would like to thank Annelies Andries, Francesca Brittan, Matthieu Cailliez, Gabriela Cruz, Katharine Ellis, Mark Everist, Annegret Fauser, Brian Hart, Jens Hesselager, Sarah Hibberd, Jo Hicks, Steven Huebner, Clair Rowden, Tommaso Sabbatini, Megan Sarno, Nicole Vilkner, and Jennifer Walker. Special thanks go to the librarians and archivists at the Archives nationales, the Archives de la Préfecture de Police, the Bibliothèque historique de la ville de Paris, and the Bibliothèque nationale de France.

A version of chapter 5 appeared as "Listening to the Old City: Street Cries and Urbanization in Paris, ca. 1860," in the *Journal of Musicology*. I would like to thank Elaine Kelly and the two anonymous readers for their feedback. At the University of California Press, Raina Polivka has been a supportive and attentive editor, and I thank her for believing in this project from the first pitch through the final revision. Her editorial team, in particular Sam Warren, was responsive and thorough. Rolf Wulfsberg expertly engraved the musical examples. Peer reviewers offered incisive and generous commentary at every stage of the review process, and I thank them for improving this manuscript well beyond its initial submission. Portions of *Fanfare for a City* were presented at the American Historical Association annual meeting, annual and chapter meetings of American Musicological Society, the

Biennial Conference on Nineteenth-Century Music, meetings of the *France: Musiques, Cultures* network, the Modern Language Association, and the Society for French Historical Studies. I am grateful to all who asked questions and offered commentary. Benjamin Downs read portions of the manuscript, and W. Anthony Sheppard offered helpful comments on the book proposal. Aside from being close friends, Gabrielle Cornish and Megan Steigerwald-Ille have been, and will remain (sorry), editors of early drafts and sounding boards for new ideas.

A paragraph makes for a flimsy token of gratitude, but I nonetheless offer one to the friends and family members who have kept me on my feet. Iliya Mirochnik remains a de facto brother, and I thank him in advance for our next enlightening conversation. Much gratitude to Mara and my late father-in-law, Bill, for cheering me on. For daily virtual doses of family while I was completing research in France, I am grateful to Ali, Martin, and Callam. This book and this career would not be possible without the love and encouragement of my mother, Danuta, and my late father, Ryszard. Dziękuję za wszystko. Francis and Archie have offered eight legs' worth of unending joy. Finally, I would like to thank my wife, Liz, for being my partner-in-everything, my editor, my support system, and my favorite person. You have heard about this project more than anyone else, and I hope to have made you proud.

Introduction

THE BOULEVARD DU PRINCE-EUGÈNE was inaugurated in spectacular fashion on December 7, 1862 (figure 1). Named after Emperor Napoléon III's maternal uncle and the stepson of Napoléon Bonaparte, the boulevard connected two central squares on Paris's Right Bank: the place du Trône (now the place de la Nation) and the place du Château d'Eau (now the place de la République). Today, a road completion might involve a mayor, a ribbon cutting, and a photo op for the local newspaper. But in the Paris of Napoléon III's Second Empire (1852–70), a boulevard inauguration was a multimedia spectacle worthy of national attention. During those years, the very act of urbanization—plowing through congested neighborhoods and constructing uniformly designed thoroughfares and buildings—was itself a theatrical performance.

Soldiers, flagbearers, surviving veterans from the First Empire's imperial guard, and band musicians lined the new boulevard early in the morning. The largest crowds assembled around a new *arc de triomphe éphémère*, designed by the famed architect Victor Baltard specifically for the occasion, which framed the head of the boulevard at the place du Trône. Like its more famous, permanent counterpart over the avenue des Champs-Elysées, this triumphal arch functioned at once as a stage, a frame, and a monument. To further define the boulevard intersection as a space of celebration, a semicircular colonnade was erected. At the other end of the boulevard, at the place du Château d'Eau, crowds awaited the imperial procession. On horseback and flanked by state and military officials, Napoléon III rode like a conqueror down the boulevard. Upon arriving at the *arc de triomphe éphémère*, the emperor was greeted by army commander Bernard Pierre Magnan, one of the chief architects of the 1851 *coup d'état* that led to the declaration of empire.

FIGURE 1. The inauguration of the boulevard du Prince-Eugène, 1862. Image: Musée Carnavalet.

But the crowd gathered on the western side of the arch could not yet see the imperial cortège, for in their way was a giant curtain. Adorned with golden bees—an old royalist symbol of immortality and resurrection—the curtain was drawn, revealing the vista to the emperor and the emperor to the crowd. Amid trumpet fanfare and chants of *Vive l'Empereur,* the new boulevard was inducted into the city's imperial landscape.

Waiting for the fanfare to subside was Georges-Eugène "Baron" Haussmann (1809–91), Parisian, barrister, illegitimate baron, and, as Prefect of the Seine, chief overseer of the urbanization of Paris. Despite being well versed in Greco-Roman literature and philosophy, Haussmann was, by all accounts, a mediocre orator. In a speech directed more to the emperor than the crowd, Haussmann detailed how the plans for the new boulevard stemmed from blueprints he had studied in Dieppe in 1853, his first year as Prefect of the Seine. He went on to justify how the newly inaugurated boulevard fit a master urban plan that included previous work on the rue de Rivoli, the Château d'Eau, the rue de Turbigo, the rue Lafayette, the Canal Saint-Martin, and the recently annexed towns of Ménilmontant and Charonne, which now formed part of the twentieth *arrondissement*.[1] Hardly riveting stuff for the bystander Parisian, less so for the non-Francophone tourist in the crowd.

Napoléon III, a seasoned orator, spoke next. Whereas Haussmann saw the new boulevard as a utilitarian node in his urban infrastructure network, Napoléon framed the new thoroughfare in aesthetic terms: "To transform the capital, to make it both more expansive and more beautiful, it is not enough to rebuild more houses than we knock down, nor to provide employment for a host of various industries; rather, it is to reintroduce everywhere the habits of order and the love of the beautiful." The transformed city, Napoléon proclaimed with his characteristic overstated eloquence, was a work of art—and as such, a product of the nineteenth-century urban imagination. The "work" of fashioning a city into a work of art extended beyond demolition and construction. Framing urbanization as a moral imperative, the empire invested in a variety of media campaigns, from boilerplate newspaper announcements and posters to poems, songs, and cantatas. So momentous was this occasion that it disrupted the weekend's concert schedule; even Jules Pasdeloup's famed Concerts populaires series was postponed on account of the boulevard inauguration.[2]

In the months leading up to the inauguration of the boulevard du Prince-Eugène, Parisians were treated to all sorts of celebratory literature hyping the event. Songs, odes, hymns, and choral works flooded the Parisian press, announcing the boulevard not only as a feat of engineering, but also as a monument to the new brand of imperial urbanism brought forth by Napoléon III and executed by Haussmann. The famed street singer Eugène Baumester published lyrics for a "Souvenir du Prince-Eugène," to be sung to the then-popular tune *la Colonne*. Adopting the familiar second-person "tu," Baumester addresses the boulevard directly, as if it were a living organism having just come to life:

> Greetings! Splendid boulevard,
> Who bears such a glorious name;
> An eager crowd has come to see you,
> With a radiant collective grin.[3]

Other songs focused less on the boulevard and more on the family after which it is named. Arthur Halbert d'Angers published a song that praises Prince Eugène's mother (and Napoléon Bonaparte's first wife) the Empress Josephine. Also adopting the informal "tu," Halbert's lyrics ring of more traditional imperial propaganda: "Honor to you, angelic woman,/ No one could deny your virtues."[4] The new boulevard functioned not only as a new public utility, but rather—perhaps more so—as a monument to the imperial family.

One of the longer meditations on boulevard inauguration was by Joseph Desbrières, who published a poem dedicated to Baron Haussmann titled "Paris nouveau: Le boulevard du Prince-Eugène."[5] The twenty-two page ode deploys a plenitude of metaphors for modernity, from the corporeal to the metaphysical; in the opening stanza, Desbrières likens the city to a body, alludes to the inevitable passage of time, and cites Haussmann, the city's "chief magistrate," as the catalyst of progress:

> Another new and marvelous artery
> To shake off the dust of old Paris
> And which alone would secure the celebrity
> Of the great city's chief magistrate.[6]

A common thread linking these celebratory poems and songs is their metacommentary on how the city *should* look and sound. To supporters of the empire, this imagined "old city" needed to be effaced from the urban imagination before real urbanization could take place. In Desbrières's verse letter, demolishing *le vieux Paris*—a fictional, nostalgic version of the city that became something of a literary trope in the 1860s—was akin to sweeping away the dust of the past.

We see this theme of sweeping away the old city in an anonymous cantata text "on the occasion of the inauguration of the boulevard du Prince-Eugène," submitted to censors on November 7, 1862, one month before the inauguration.[7] While I find it hard to imagine an audience of theatergoers being treated to a choral work about a public works project, the French cantata was a musical genre often deployed to such propagandistic purposes, from justifying overseas war to glorifying the mundanities of urban development. So it was the case that this anonymous cantata, which was slated for performance at the Théâtre Lyrique, monumentalized individual acts of urban renewal. The cantata doubled down on evoking "Old Paris" by referencing "Lutèce," the ancient Roman city upon which the medieval city of Paris was built. In an era of space-time annihilation, such works served the purpose of placing urban projects onto a historical continuum:

> Upon the debris of old Lutèce
> Every day, new Paris
> Valiantly flattens the creases
> Of its coat, full of wealth.
> In one of those creases, one discovers
> A splendid and grand boulevard
> That already accommodates the flag
> That we see flying atop the Louvre.
> Let all grateful hearts
> Make a joyful noise
> That resounds in the azure vault
> Of the regenerated city.[8]

There is some striking imagery in this rather opaque stanza, which I have tried to capture in as figurative a translation as possible. The expression "azure vault," a metaphor for heaven, appears in political and religious cantata texts throughout the nineteenth century. These cerulean pathways are lined with trumpet-bearing angels performing a heavenly fanfare; the text thus brings the celestial world into contact with boulevard life. This joyful noisemaking is mirrored in the last two lines of the cantata, likely intended to depict the cheering crowds and military musicians lining the new boulevard. "Debris" appears again, here representing not only the pre-Haussmannian city—the city of Balzac and the 1789, 1830, and 1848 revolutions—but also the old Roman city that stood in the way. Debris, of course, is a byproduct of urban development, a pollutant and a nuisance that temporarily made everyday life unbearable for citizens. Lutèce had long been an obstacle to Parisian urban planners. Its Latin name *Lutetia* ("city of mud"), signified an era before urbanization, when city administrators had little control over infrastructure, and therefore little control over how citizens used urban space. Lutèce did not disappear from Parisian cultural memory, however; in the 1840s, Nouvelle Lutèce was a district that stretched from the Pont Neuf to Notre-Dame.[9] A few decades later in 1869, the archaeologist Théodore Vacquer uncovered a small Roman arena on the city's Left Bank, which turned out to date from circa 200 AD. Haussmann rejected Vacquer's plea to preserve the site, and he designated it for a new omnibus depot; in the early 1880s, following a bitter feud between municipal administration and preservationists, the arena was spared.[10] It is known today as the Arènes de Lutèce, one of the few remnants of the old city predating *le vieux Paris*.

Boulevards welcomed, districts sanitized, arenas excised. Haussmann the urbanist and bureaucrat fashioned himself as Haussmann the surgeon and psychologist. As he wrote in his recollections of the urbanization of Second Empire Paris, "The free circulation of air and water and the access to light serve to combat the effects of crowding, of the concentration of foul air, of the exhalation of miasmas and of evil odors. The straight line therefore reconciles the needs of beauty, the needs of hygiene and the needs of commerce."[11] Marxist readings of Haussmannization have framed it as a strategy of geographic and financial redistribution of capital, enforced through tactics that attempted to curate sensory experience of the city: in short, an urban aesthetics. Paris, then, was not merely the space where human bodies lived; it was perceived *as* a body, sentient and mortal, able to see, hear, and smell. Not only was Haussmann plowing a hole through the metaphorical body of *le vieux Paris* but in doing so, he was altering the perception of urban time and the sensation of urban space.

Maps and urban plans reveal much about how planners hoped their cities would function in the abstract, rational sense. They do not necessarily articulate how cities were actually *used*, nor how different urban communities would have experienced the city. Nineteenth-century press illustrations, pamphlets, posters, guidebooks, poems, and, indeed, musical compositions, all helped to envision idealized, homogenized uses of city space. These documents reveal an infrastructure network of sights, sounds, texts, and spaces that defined the modernizing city for its inhabitants and visitors. But no infrastructure network is devoid of power structures that curate the urban experience on behalf of others. Urban soundscapes, like maps and plans, offer one part of the story. The case of the inauguration of the boulevard du Prince-

Eugène, and the media apparatus around it, hints at a central claim of this book: that the musical activity directly emerging from Haussmannization—from fanfare and cantatas to café and street music—shaped, in no small way, the empire's ability to narrate its own urban history.

FANFARE FOR A CITY

Fanfare for a City examines the intersections between musical and urban history in the Second Empire. By exploring the sonic and spatial worlds of World's Fairs, cafés, and city streets and markets, it shows how popular and ceremonial music in the city became an integral theme in modernist narratives about *le nouveau Paris:* a metropolis at a crossroads between its treasured medieval past and its cosmopolitan imperial future. This interface between urban policy and music resulted in the flourishing of new popular musical institutions, such as the café-concert and operetta. Yet urbanism was also central in debates about civic heritage, censorship, and theatrical deregulation. Musicians played a significant role in these debates, as laws and infrastructure necessitated new ways of thinking about music. In their capacity to erase liminal cultural memory, the boulevards functioned similarly to emerging musical canons and their effect on musical consumption. Just as canons constitute far more than repertory lists, boulevards signified much more than urban mobility: their vastness and straightness represented uncompromising, linear progress that, like canons, drew clear-cut lines between history and the future. In Second Empire Paris, urban planning decisions shaped, and were shaped by, the musical spaces, institutions, and communities discussed in this book.

Readers of this book may be familiar with some of the musical genres most associated with the Paris of the 1850s and 60s: *opérette* (with Hervé and Offenbach leading the charge), *vaudeville,* late-stage *grand opéra,* the Orphéon choral concerts, the revival of older repertories (especially Gluck), the *opéras-comiques* of Auber, Bizet, Gounod, and Meyerbeer, and the influence of Italian and German opera, namely those by Donizetti, Verdi, and Wagner. The December highlights of the 1862 opera season provide a microcosm of what awaited Parisian operagoers as they traversed the new boulevards: at the Opéra, Donizetti's *La Favorite* and *Lucie de Lammermoor* (in French translation); at the Opéra-Comique, Adam's *Le Postillon de Lonjumeau,* Auber's *Le Domino noir* and *Fra diavolo,* Boieldieu's *La Dame blanche* (its thousandth performance) and *Jean de Paris,* David's *Lalla-*

Roukh, and Massé's *Les Noces de Jeannette;* at the Théâtre-Italien, Donizetti's *Lucia* (in the original Italian) and Rossini's *Il barbiere di Siviglia* (with star Adelina Patti singing the role of Rosina). The city's other major opera house, the Théâtre Lyrique, had a new home near the centrally located place du Châtelet, where the company had moved following Haussmann's demolition of the boulevard du Temple earlier in 1862. The occasion was marked with a revival of Gounod's *Faust*.

Resonating deep within the walls of the *grands théâtres,* Paris's operatic spectacles are a litmus of bourgeois tastes, but they do not give the full spectrum of what it meant to listen to urban life. Indeed, the study of operatic modernity, or what Anselm Gerhard calls the "urbanization of opera," says little about the political and aesthetic impact of music *on* urbanization.[12] Moving away from the politics and poetics of the city's theater industry frees ample space to listen to musics *of* the city, and not only in the highly curated edifices located *in* it. Yet *Fanfare for a City* is not a book about "popular music," at least not overtly so. While extant studies of "popular" music in nineteenth-century France tend to frame the years 1852–70 as a sort of "prequel" to the popular music "revolution" of the Belle Époque, *Fanfare for a City* homes in on those middle years of the century to argue that imperial urban planning cannot be separated from the spatial and artistic fields of cultural production.[13] My intention in this book is not to revisit the historiographical frictions between "popular" and "art" music, nor is it to give "voice to the voiceless" (which, as recent scholars of sound studies have shown, is more a neoliberal project of carving out newness than one of unpacking power structures).[14] *Fanfare for a City* looks for music in diverse socioeconomic spaces: train cars, boulevard corners, cafés, salons, exhibition halls, on walls, in police records. My aim is to show music's prevalence in the planning of Paris: how the city was designed, policed, mythologized, and ultimately homogenized as a modern metropolis.

THE POETICS OF URBANIZATION

Second Empire politics and culture permeated every aspect of urbanization. The city map morphed from a serpentine web of alleys into a streamlined graph of intersecting boulevards and avenues. This symbolic metamorphosis occurred both above and below ground. An intricate and organized sewer and aqueduct system modernized the city's water supply. The sewers immediately became a tourist attraction: a visual, acoustic, and (one can imagine) olfactory spectacle. Bourgeois gawkers crowded into the underground tunnels, which were marked with street signs corresponding to the city plan above. In the sewers, trumpet fanfare helped tour carriages navigate the darkness. The photographer Nadar, who famously captured the city's sewers, detailed how these repetitive sounds curated his experience of this underground urban space: "No sooner had we taken our place in the carriage when a long horn call resounded like a marching signal under the archways, to be repeated regularly by other horn signalers in their positions, as we proceeded."[15] Nadar's sonorous description suggests that even to those for whom capturing sight was a profession, sound dictated how the city was to be represented and experienced.

Building on Napoléon's own ambitious sketches, Haussmann laid out a systematic map of demolition that would be divided into three *réseaux*, or networks. The first network, carried out between 1854 and 1858, created a *grande croisée*: the rue de Rivoli and the boulevards Sébastopol and Saint-Michel were elongated to create a perpendicular axis. The second network involved, among other projects, the expansion of the boulevards stemming from the place du Château d'Eau, broadening four key arteries: the avenues Magenta and Richard Lenoir (which paved over the Canal Saint-Martin), the boulevard du Prince-Eugène, and the rue Turbigo. The third network, which continued after the collapse of the Second Empire, called for the elongation of the rue Lafayette and the boulevard Saint-Germain, and also saw the completion of the Palais Garnier, the opulent new home of the Opéra. Paris's circumference also expanded. In 1860, the city annexed the ring of suburban villages that included the villages of Montmartre, Ménilmontant, Charonne, and Belleville, augmenting the number of *arrondissements* from twelve to twenty. Long before they became enclaves for artists and musicians, these villages were pastoral refuges for weary city-dwellers, as well as the new home of displaced workers whose inner-city tenements were demolished to make room for the boulevards.

Despite becoming the face of Napoleonic urbanization, Haussmann did not go it alone. His colleagues and allies, including Jean-Charles Adolphe Alphand, Eugène Belgrand, and Jean-Antoine-Gabriel Davioud, were power players in the city, tasked with redesigning Paris's greenspace, water works, and other urban amenities. Although Haussmann largely took a back seat in planning the 1855 and 1867 Expositions universelles (ad hoc committees did most of the arranging), the infrastructure was thoroughly Haussmannian in style and scope, and the Fairs' grounds, palaces, and pavilions were necessarily plugged into the broader urban infrastructures planned by Haussmann.

If all of this seems disproportionately significant to a musicologist, that is because Haussmannization was more than an urban plan. It was an aesthetic program. Political power spoke outwardly through Paris's elite cultural institutions like the Opéra, as well as through the quotidian business of planning and policing the urban landscape. Second Empire politics and aesthetics were inextricably linked, becoming increasingly legible and audible as Haussmann renovated the city. Recent histories of the period have also defined Haussmann's politics in aesthetic terms. The insistence on "straightness" of individual boulevards betrayed the same "insouciant authoritarianism" that the Prefect displayed in his writings on politics.[16] Rectilinear urban space symbolized for Haussmann the restoration of order to a city map rendered inchoate by the tides of revolution and romanticism.[17] Even in more local and superficial matters, such as the design of streetlamps, benches, and urinals, Haussmann imposed a degree of detail "excruciating" in its obsession with the symmetrical line. This obsession was not pathology; rather it can be credited to Haussmann's conviction that Paris was destined to be the "modern-day imperial Rome."[18] Haussmann's urban reforms thus touched all aspects of the visual, aural, olfactory, and haptic experiences of Parisian life. Although many of his public works built on those from previous regimes, the scale, rapidity, and homogeneity of Second Empire urbanization amounted to an aesthetic regime unprecedented in the city's history.

Outward expansion precipitated a retreat indoors; modernization inspired nostalgic and aesthetic conceptions of the city. Walter Benjamin, building on Karl Marx, diagnosed Second Empire politics in precisely such dialectical terms; Haussmann's grand plans were as forceful as they were brittle. With every new building project came massive displacement on one end of the socioeconomic spectrum, and massive financial gain on the other. The curtains that veiled the new boulevards were no less superficial than were the boulevards themselves. Urbanism extended well beyond the realm of public works and into the world of art: Haussmann's urban aesthetics "corresponded to the tendency which was noticeable again and again during the nineteenth century, to ennoble technical exigencies with artistic aims."[19] Inauguration and demolition were part of the same dialectical process of urban transformation. For every new boulevard, older thoroughfares, buildings, even whole blocks were razed. Such was the irony of the newly inaugurated boulevard du Prince-Eugène; that same year, Haussmann ordered the demolition of the adjacent, theater-lined boulevard du Temple (also known as the "boulevard du Crime" for its many murder plays and melodramas), an act that would irrevocably alter the city's entertainment industry. The visual phenomena associated with Paris during these years—demolition, illumination, veiling, perspective, phantasmagoria—have defined the cultural representation of Second Empire urbanization and its brand of creative-destructive modernity.

Since Second Empire politics and culture were so tied to the policies of urbanization, it is unsurprising that the visual spectacle of urban renewal captured the imagination of writers, and that it continues to inspire scholars. The city's *grands boulevards*, like the boulevard du Prince-Eugène, transformed the way Parisians saw their city, and in consequence, how they viewed themselves. In his 1938 essay on Paris as the "capital of the nineteenth century," Benjamin relied heavily on firsthand testimony of the poet Charles Baudelaire, who mused on everyday visual phenomena like window shopping and for whom the elusive concept of *flânerie* transcended "strolling" in the city. Indeed, the literature on Parisian visual culture is vast, so much so that there exists a *Cambridge Companion to the Literature of Paris*—recommended reading for whomever is holding the present book.[20] While music historians have explored aspects of this visual culture within (mostly operatic) case studies, this book offers a broader investigation into how musical communities shaped—and were shaped by—the city's new public spaces. The ways that Parisians *used* urban space, whether for idle pleasure, for celebration, for revolution, or for work, depended on how planners conceived those boulevards for use. The interconnectedness of musical practice and urban policy invites the opportunity for a sociospatial history of music in the City of Light—or, better for our purposes, the City of Fanfare.

FANFARE

In nineteenth-century French usage, *fanfare* (including the verb *fanfaronner*, to "boast") had multiple meanings. Military or civilian brass and wind ensembles were called fanfares. Stylistically speaking, a fanfare is a musical gesture, signal, or flourish featuring trumpets or bugles, often with percussion; within the realm of musical "topic theory," fanfare is closely related to pastoral, hunting call, and military topoi. A fanfare can also be a whole tune, recognizable by repeated notes, open fifths, and a major key. Honoré de Balzac invokes this stylistic definition of fanfare in a passage from his 1831 novel *La Peau du chagrin:* "Cursy grabbed a horn and began to sound a fanfare."[21] In a figurative sense, the French noun *fanfare* and the verb *fanfaronner* connote a noisy demonstration or outpouring. While this "noise" can be understood in the sonic sense—overstimulation from high volume and pitch—fanfare was also a discursive style that announced authority and favored praise over critique. Charles Augustin Saint-Beuve used it to comment on an essay by the philosopher Victor Cousin: "Cousin's preface [to an unedited essay by Pascal] was unsuccessful; it lacked seriousness, and one detected too much fanfare."[22] Baudelaire deployed the term to render a visual phenomenon (the color red, as used in Romantic painting) in sonic terms. In his "Salon of 1846" he experienced in the work of Eugène Delacroix "fanfares of red" surging from all sides of the canvas, a "harmony of blood" flaring up over the horizon."[23] Baudelaire fixated on the blood-red noisiness of Delacroix's painting, returning to his synesthetic motif in the poem "Les Phares" (The beacons) from *Les Fleurs du mal:* "Under a gloomy sky, strange fanfares/Pass, like one of Weber's stifled sighs."[24] The reference to Weber's supernatural opera *Der Freischütz,* in vogue in Paris at the time, suggests that fanfare lingers in the ear long after it is blared. Its stridency is so piercing that it penetrates the lines between sight and sound. The same concept that denoted brass bands, florid writing, and crimson paint could also connote imperial legacy and the canonization of intellectual and creative works. A few consistencies emerge from these stylistic and figurative uses of the word in nineteenth-century France: that fanfare requires an audience, and that fanfare has the capacity to engulf the senses and trigger the memory.

In *Fanfare for a City,* I take "fanfare" to mean any sonic event or text that outwardly signals power, from literal trumpet fanfare to speeches to songs, cantatas, and hymns, printed in newspapers and placarded on walls. "Power" here is used broadly. Within the context of the urban soundscape, fanfare announced imperial parades and inaugurations, and it featured a diverse collection of genres and performing forces: instrumental military music, eighteenth-century repertory, solo songs, cantatas and hymns, and even speeches. We might think of fanfare as a signal or even a discourse, a projection of a point of view from a source of influence onto a passive public. Michel Foucault used the word "fanfare" to describe a permanent shift in discourse fueled by constant and repeated utterance. Writing about the emerging discourse of sexuality in Europe, Foucault describes the increasing literary interest in masturbation as a shift from silence to noise: "Suddenly, in the midst of this great silencing, in the midst of this transfer of the task of controlling souls, bodies, and desires to things and space, a loud *fanfare* blares out and a sudden and noisy chattering starts up that does not stop for more than a century (that is, until the end of the nineteenth century) and which continues, in a modified form no doubt, down to the present."[25] Fanfare is a sound that is heard, a text that is read. Song and hymn texts were published and distributed widely throughout the city to announce or celebrate achievements in urban modernity, be they the universal exhibitions (explored in chapter 2) or the completion of buildings and boulevards. This wide distribution of "sound documents" was part of the empire's effort to flood the discourse, representing a panoptic sensory campaign far broader than any ideological messages conveyed in the city's large opera houses and theaters.[26]

It is difficult to discuss nineteenth-century Parisian modernity without examining its dramatic overhauls in visual culture, both in art and in everyday life. T. J. Clark's book on Édouard Manet's Paris is a classic in the field of art history, and readers may detect its influence on the present text. Focusing predominantly on the elite artistic and literary class, Clark draws parallels between, on the one hand, the emergence of Impressionism and on the other, the emergence of a mythical "new Paris" identified in part with increasingly numerous and visible institutions of commerce and leisure.[27] Painters thus attempted to give representational form to the spaces and people associated with the concept of "modernity"—a concept which, as the present book will explain, does not paint a full picture of what it meant to be a *Parisien* during the years of the Second Empire. Studies by Patricia Mainardi, Priscilla Parkhurst Ferguson, and Christopher Prendergast examine how the "city" became "written" through urban novels, guidebooks, visual exhibitions. More recently, Aimée Boutin investigates how poets and novelists "made sense" of the disappearing sights and sounds, namely the shifting tonalities of noise among the Paris's laboring classes.[28]

Building on these studies but focusing more directly on urban musical communities, *Fanfare for a City* explores how sound—ambient, intentional, intrusive, melodious, or conceptual—informed the urban policies and histories of musicmaking in the city. Second Empire bureaucrats were heavily invested in constructing homogenized soundscapes. If the *fête impériale*—that permanent state of "imperial spectacle"—was most legible through theatrical offerings, exhibitions, balls, and other bourgeois gatherings, its sounding counterpart was what can be called *fanfare impérial*—the permanent noise of construction and demolition, the parades, the exploding street-song industry, and the increased police presence to enforce that this noise was produced by the empire, and not via dissent from below. As a sonic phenomenon, fanfare is thus inextricably linked with power, in the sense that it saturates the urban sensorium, making it impossible to ignore.²⁹ And if *fin de siècle* republicanism and colonial capitalism turned "peasants into Frenchmen," to quote the historian Eugen Weber, then midcentury *fanfares impérials,* such as the curious practice of boulevard inaugurations, transformed users of urban space into auditors of urbanization.³⁰

HISTORICAL SOUNDSCAPES AND URBAN HISTORICAL MUSICOLOGY

The musical histories told this book necessarily rely on the reconstruction of sound worlds from silent archival sources. In the absence of recorded sound, the written archive functions like a gatekeeper into the sonic worlds—the soundscapes—of the past. When I refer to "the soundscape" in this book, I am thinking of a fictionalized, heavily mediated concept, one imagined by an individual or a collective, and one meant to aggregate disparate voices, technologies, and environments. A historical soundscape—a category we can only theorize and "textualize" via the written archive—forms only a part of a city's broader acoustic culture. Insofar as there cannot be a single urban character or identity, there cannot be a singular urban soundscape, but rather multiple, often competing, acoustic realities that are shaped by different urban spaces. Writing about street music in nineteenth-century Madrid, Samuel Llano views the urban soundscape as a "battle" between musical practices and sounds, "fought" primarily in the realms of policymaking and censorship.³¹ A map, a painting, and a photograph offer very different representations of the urban landscape, but they are just that: representations that reveal as much about the perceiver as they do about the perceived. The soundscape, then, is a mode of scholarly inquiry, a written narrative that offers a set of coordinates for navigating the urban historical imagination. But it is not the final word.

As far as the historian of urban sound is concerned, written archives have much in common with recorded archives. Both are mediated representations of a live sound; they cannot clone the sonic act, but rather process it into another legible form. Moreover, archives do not capture all sounds, but rather reflect what was deemed acoustically significant enough to store for posterity. Scholars working with colonial archives understand this politics of mediation, and they must figure out how to engage with the archive critically, against the grain. "When one listens to the historical archive," writes Ana María Ochoa Gautier of nineteenth-century Colombian archives, "what emerges is a series of practices of listening and sounds that extend beyond our present-day ideas of what counts as a proper genre, music, or language."[32] Any discussion of a historical soundscape exposes a dichotomy of what Annegret Fauser has called "sensual immediacy" on the one hand, and "the silence of historical documents and scholarly discourse" on the other.[33] In other words, archives can open our ears to past sounds, but the resultant scholarly narrative is necessarily a present-day critical engagement with what led those sounds to be "archived" in the first place.[34]

If, as a concept, the archive can be understood as a mediated performance of history, then the notion of a soundscape is likewise a representation, one story among many, as told by a historian. As Lawrence Kramer notes, the "-scape" suffix ties the concept to the rigid two-dimensionality of visual space; the appearance of a landscape may be altered by natural or human intervention, but the "landscape"—the thing captured and studied—does not change.[35] Given that we can never "hear" Second Empire Paris, its historical soundscape (if we call it that) is more a register of the politics of the archive than it is a record of people actually heard. While *Fanfare for a City* builds on the theoretical groundwork laid by subfields like "historical sound studies" and "sensory/auditory history," I believe that another moniker captures its contents more accurately. Insofar as *Fanfare for a City* discusses *ideas* and *policies* around urban sound alongside musical *texts, practices,* and *institutions,* "urban historical musicology" seems more apt. I adapt the term from historians of early modern music, who have engaged in the study of civic musicmaking for far longer than have nineteenth-century historians. Tim Carter has noted how musicology scholars in the 1960s–90s tended to use elite musical spaces as a synecdoche of the whole city: "Renaissance Ferrara" amounted to the Este court of Ferrara, "nineteenth-century Paris" to the Opéra, and so on. Inspired by the work of Reinhard Strohm, Carter instead calls for a more integrative, relational music history that places musical works and institutions "at the interface between individual and the environment."[36] The problem for the self-identifying historical musicologist, then, is how to talk about music *as sound* without performing the reductive work of *soundscaping* an auditory culture into a perceptible, analyzable whole.[37]

A major difference between "historical sound studies" and "urban historical musicology" is the latter's focus on how music is imbricated in urban policymaking, placemaking, and mythmaking. Writers of sonic histories ought to avoid the risk of historicist ad-libbing: siren calls in X city, bellringing in Y town, outdoor festivals in Z countryside. The same goes for analyses of musical institutions, in particular opera houses, within the context of "urbanization," without sustained discussion of how urban policy conditioned musical aesthetics, and vice versa. This conflation of "the city" with a particular institution is not an issue endemic to musicology. In their study of twentieth-century urban infrastructure networks, Stephen Graham and Simon Marvin observe that even architectural and urban historians have concentrated on the design aesthetics and cultural politics within "building envelopes" rather than the networks that symbolically isolate those buildings from the broader urban fabric. Moreover, the enforcers and promoters of infrastructure networks—from nineteenth-century empires to twenty-first century corporations—do so in the name of unification, progress, and some sort of "public interest" or "public utility."[38] The overrepresentation of certain urban repertories and performance spaces over others—the Paris Opéra is one such case—is thus tied to the distribution of information and resources between those spaces and the rest of the city. It is not for nothing that, as Jann Pasler has observed, the very spaces devoted to Third Republic civic enrichment were the most monumental and ornate. Boulevards, buildings, and other nodes in the infrastructure network can efface as easily as they can transmit.[39]

Given the predominance of nationalism in the historiography of nineteenth-century Europe, studies of city culture easily become studies of national identity. This correlation inevitably reduces the city into a single node on the symbolic network of the nation-state. Addressing music scholars directly, Adam Krims has cautioned us to take seriously a city's status as a civic center, and not merely the place where music happened, novels are set, and archives are located. A historical urban musicology ("music geography" is Krims's preferred term) studies the built environment and its relationship to musical production and dissemination and respects a given city's status and structure.[40] Only then can "urban historical musicology" do justice to a city's systems of regulation and policing, its politics of representation and placemaking, and its impact on the experiences of diverse musical communities.

These three categories of analysis—regulating, representing, experiencing—form the crux of my inquiry in *Fanfare for a City* and inform the organization of its chapters. They are loosely modeled after the spatial sociology of the French philosopher Henri Lefebvre. Lefebvre's influential writings on cities have received relatively little musicological attention, and even less in nineteenth-century music studies.[41] Yet his spatial thinking is inherently musical. Music—rhythm in particular—allowed him to think through issues such as urban habit and repetition, shifting collective identities, and the relations between the bodily rhythms of urban denizens and the mechanistic rhythms of industry. Analyzing urban societies in terms of the spaces they occupy, Lefebvre writes, makes one "capable of listening to a house, a street, a town as one listens to a symphony, an opera."[42] To Lefebvre, the rhythmic, embodied experience of city life is but one aspect of thinking about music through space, the ultimate goal of which is to determine who has the "right to the city," and the economic and cultural factors that secure or undermine that right.[43] As Gascia Ouzounian and others have recently demonstrated, sound artists and composers—perhaps most famously, R. Murray Schafer and the World Soundscape Project—tracked the effects of noise pollution on North American cities and towns, while at the same time mining ambient soundscapes for their artistic potential.[44] Sound maps, installations, and experimental works have become bread and butter for scholars of twentieth-century sound. Necessarily, such artistic endeavors were sparse in the pre-recorded era. So how do we trace the social construction of urban space through more traditional media, like musical scores, song texts, or libretti? How do we unmoor elite performance spaces, like exhibition halls and opera houses, from their autonomous (thus hegemonic) status as "monuments" of musical art, and place them as nodes in a broader urban network? How do we rethink musical histories of institutions within an urban framework, without reducing urbanism to the historiographic background of "cultural context?"

Fanfare for a City wrestles with these questions by selecting musical case studies that not only happened *within* urban space but also actively *produced* space. If the Paris Opéra during the Second Empire was an institution intertwined with networks of imperial power, the networked spaces discussed in this book—exhibition halls, boulevard intersections, cafés, taverns, alleys—were defined by the ways ordinary people interacted with them.[45] In the following chapters, I draw connections between governmental conceptions of urbanism, musical renderings of sound in space, and the lived experiences of working musicians and street hawkers. Urbanism shared music history's preoccupation with what Lydia Goehr has called the "regulative concept," or the set of ideological systems that "determine, stabilize, and order the structure of practices."[46] This "regulative concept" did more for historiography than mark an aesthetic watershed between artisanal and artistic work. The so-called "seismic date" of 1800—a round number, privileging not only a Christian sense of calendar time but also Western fixations on symmetry and finality—reveals historical musicology's long proclivity for abstract mapping rather than lived experience, as well as histories of the individual (here, Beethoven), over those of the collective (musical communities and economies).[47]

In spatial terms, the parallel to Goehr's "regulative" work concept would be Lefebvre's "representation of space" (he also calls this *espace conçu* or "conceived space"). This is the space as determined by the "scientists, planners, urbanists, technocratic subdividers and social engineers"—those who regulate and curate physical spaces and subsequently, the sensory experiences within those spaces.[48] Regulation could reflect overt political power—for instance, calling for an ostentatious inauguration of a boulevard while silently passing over the working communities displaced by that boulevard. But the power to "produce" space also lies with those who produce imaginary space through art. Those with power over sensory experience—from imperial bureaucrats to outspoken critics and composers—desired to "notate" the city by hearing it as a unified whole. The famous examples in art and literature—Balzac, Baudelaire, Guys, Cassatt, Manet, Zola, Proust—all shared this desire to be authors of their own urban narratives. By following the ambitions and motivations of a diverse cast of historical actors, from bureaucrats to guidebook writers to street musicians, *Fanfare for a City* is also a musical history of authorship. Urbanization provided these Parisians with opportunities to articulate a collective urban identity. Yet how the city *sounded* as a singular entity—or how it *ought* to sound—depended on who had the power to "produce" urban space.

The first two chapters explore the "bird's eye" perspective: how bureaucrats and state planners conceived the city as a unified work of art and a microcosm of empire. Chapter 1 focuses on Baron Haussmann, the mastermind and namesake of "Haussmannization," and the extent to which Haussmann's career and ideas were shaped by music. Haussmann was a gifted young cellist who studied at the École Royale de Musique et de Déclamation in the 1820s. There, he encountered musical figures like Alexandre-Étienne Choron, Luigi Cherubini, Anton Reicha, and the young Hector Berlioz. Although Haussmann never seriously considered a career in music, he remained an influential patron with a strong preference for the classics. As Prefect of the Seine during the Second Empire, Haussmann hosted and curated weekly soirées at the Hôtel de Ville. Far more than mere gatherings of Parisian elites, these concerts were regarded by the musical press as bastions of the emergent eighteenth-century Austro-German canon. The chapter explains how Haussmann's obsession with urban symmetry, order, and the straight line owe a debt to his lifelong preference for musical practices predating Romanticism. At the same time, the prefect's aesthetic leanings beg comparison with two composers who, like Haussmann, cited the distant past in constructing modernity on a monumental scale: Berlioz and Wagner.

If chapter 1 narrows in on how Haussmann conceived the city, chapter 2 explores broader imperial attempts to curate urban sensory experience. Between the 1848 revolution and the 1851 *coup d'état,* the "Prince-Président" Louis-Napoléon Bonaparte metamorphosed into Napoléon III, Emperor of the French. One his first priorities was to rebuild Paris as a monument to the nascent empire and to showcase this rebuilding to the world. Boulevard inaugurations were a major part of this showcase, but the most ambitious presentations of Paris as a "work of art" were the Expositions universelles of 1855 and 1867. Chapter 2 focuses on the ceremonial music during these exhibitions to show how the imperial commission struggled to balance visual and sonic grandeur. The study of sonic monumentality during the World's Fairs reveals a coordinated effort—a communication network—designed to showcase *le nouveau Paris* as distinct from its republican and monarchical past. The Expositions universelles, particularly the fanfare around them, thus provided an opportunity to deploy the full power of the imperial urban sensorium on its attendants.

The first two chapters explore the utopian and nostalgic ideals of Haussmannization from the regime's perspective—"conceived space," to use Lefebvre's formulation. Yet there was another strand of nostalgia emerging during the Second Empire: fanfare for the "old city" and its social and cultural customs. Chapter 3 explores the urban planning lessons that we can learn from the café-concert, a new form of popular entertainment whose rise was almost simultaneous with the rise of the Second Empire. As Haussmann's public works projects materialized, cafés-concerts began to splinter across socioeconomic and geographic lines. Venues on the outskirts received negative press for their seedy offerings. By contrast, cafés-concerts built along the central boulevards were monumental, gaudy, and accessible from the city's equally monumental train stations. By the late 1860s, cafés-concerts were staging operettas, causing a crisis of identity and ontology among the café-concert's greatest champions and detractors. The unique geographic and temporal natures of the early cafés-concerts, with their loosely defined scheduling, seating, and audience etiquette, offered a refuge from Haussmann's politics of spectacle. Though described in the scholarship as the epitome of Second Empire frivolity—and a prequel to the *fin de siècle* music hall—the chapter argues that the café-concert was not a monolithic institution, nor was it merely a source of distraction. These ubiquitous social spaces, vastly understudied in musicological scholarship, subverted Haussmannization's campaign to control sensory experience in the city by offering patrons a democratic alternative to imperial urbanism: one rooted in spontaneity, fluidity, and community formation.

To imperial planners, Paris was a map, a two-dimensional, abstract puzzle that needed solving. The final two chapters of this book take place in the streets, where the consequences of a straight line drawn through a map's center were felt at a most visceral level. Chapter 4 focuses on the popular song industry and the politics of representing urban life from the street level—what Lefebvre might call "perceived space." Through their lyrics as well as through published memoirs, songwriters offered vivid commentary on economics and politics in Second Empire Paris, often focusing on the detrimental effects of urbanization on everyday musical life. The songs discussed in this chapter offer a resonant account of how citizens and foreigners engaged with transformations to their urban environment. The chapter also profiles the performers of these songs: itinerant street musicians, café singers, and barrel organists. Street musicians were repeatedly represented as an urban subculture in newspaper reviews, cartoons, guidebooks, and memoirs. On the one hand, street musicians were regarded as iconic urban heroes whose lowly stature and haggard appearance undermined the manicured and pretentious habits of Second Empire high society. On the other hand, tourist guidebooks and police decrees cast these musicians as hindrances to the flow of urban life, while literary elites blamed street songs for the overall dumbing-down of Parisian musical culture. These contested attitudes reflect the widespread ambivalence toward Haussmannization and the distinct brand of fast-paced, mass-produced urban aesthetic that it precipitated.

Of all the working-class communities uprooted by Haussmann, Paris's street hawkers were considered to be among the greatest victims of urban demolition. Chapter 5 examines how street cries, endearingly called the "cries of Paris" (*les cris de Paris*), helped to forge a defiantly nostalgic counternarrative to imperial notions of modernity—a "lived space" (to borrow from Lefebvre) distinct from the bourgeois edifices lining the city center. Music sits alongside tourist guidebooks, literary *mémoires,* and newspaper criticism as evidence for the growing nostalgia for the urban past, what eventually became known as "the old city." The case of the *cris de Paris* demonstrates that there were as many versions of "new" or "old" Paris as there were conceptions, representations, and lived experiences of urban life.

ONE

Baron Haussmann's Musical Imagination

WHEN HE WAS NOT TRANSFORMING Paris into a modern-day "imperial Rome," Georges-Eugène Haussmann hosted music parties. In 1854, Haussmann launched a series of weekly Saturday soirées in his private apartments at the Hôtel de Ville, where he welcomed student and professional musicians and entertained domestic and foreign dignitaries. These soirées promised to become one of the city's marquee weekly musical events. J. L. Heugel, editor of *Le Ménestrel,* attended several iterations. From him we learn that Haussmann spared little expense in bringing in the musical *crème de la crème* from Paris and abroad: the opera singers Sophie Cruvelli, Mme Busio, Marc Bonnehée, and Gustave-Hippolyte Roger; the pianist Alexandre Édouard Goria; the organist Alfred Lefébure-Wély; and the Norwegian composer of the 1836 version of *La Sylphide,* Baron Herman Severin Løvenskiold.[1]

Leading these musical soirées from both the piano and the podium was Jules Pasdeloup, who would eventually make his name conducting German repertoire at his Concerts populaires. Pasdeloup and Haussmann's relationship lasted the duration of the Second Empire; Pasdeloup provided Haussmann with his regular audience and musician collaborators, while Haussmann served as Pasdeloup's regular guarantor, subsidizing the Concerts populaires and overseeing Pasdeloup's ownership of the Théâtre Lyrique in 1868.[2] Thus the bureaucrat known for his systematic demolition of old Parisian institutions had a soft spot for music, so much so that by 1860 Haussmann had earned the nickname "Le Baron mélomane."[3]

In addition to his weekly soirées, Haussmann also hosted larger *fêtes* and *spectacles* at the Hôtel de Ville, whose repertories aligned more closely with typical ceremony fare during the Second Empire. For example, on May 6, 1857, Haussmann hosted a large reception for S.A.I. le Grand-Duc

Constantin, for which a fully functional theater was erected in the Hôtel de Ville's Galérie des Fêtes. R. Mme la Grande-Duchesse de Bade and the Princesse Mathilde Bonaparte were other distinguished guests. The mood was celebratory, and the repertoire reflected eclectic musical tastes that would also suit a ceremony for international dignitaries. Pasdeloup's orchestra began with the Russian national anthem, followed by fragments from operatic works: Rossini's *Moïse*, Vaccai's *Roméo et juliette*, Thomas's *Psyché*, Verdi's *Ernani*, and Gluck's *Armide*.

That a Second Empire bureaucrat hosted musical events was not, in and of itself, remarkable. Within Napoléon III's inner circle, Princesse Mathilde Bonaparte hosted musical and poetic salons which, as Nicole Vilkner points out, reproduced the vibrancy of boulevard life through the coordinated circulation of bodies and ideas throughout the salon's interior.[4] Rather, what is noteworthy is the broader context of Haussmann's lifelong encounters with Parisian musical life, as well as his steadfast and outspoken devotion to repertoire classics. Following a July 1854 soirée, Heugel reported on the prominence of semi-staged scenes from the seventeenth century, notably Jean-Baptiste Lully's *tragédies en musique*. Haussmann evidently had a taste for older opera; he hosted Daniel Auber's opéra-comique *Le Concert à la cour* (premiered 1824), put on in honor of the Congrès de Paris ending the Crimean War in 1856, as well as scenes from Mozart's *Così fan tutte* and Rossini's *Moïse* during the Lenten season of 1857.[5] "Haussmann does not disdain great music," Heugel argued. "Here is a good example set for our theaters, and we are yet to comprehend why the Académie impériale has yet to stage a masterpiece from the great old school [of French opera]."[6] Indeed, Heugel saw these soirées not merely as pleasant diversions, but as models for how the city's musical institutions ought to embrace canonic repertoire.

Heugel was not alone in his praise for Haussmann's classical tastes. The *Revue et gazette musicale* was delighted that the prefect had transformed the standard *fête musicale* into "soirées of pure etiquette." Paul Scudo commended Haussmann for his willingness to bring historical prestige to the Parisian soirée scene: "Honor to the music-loving prefect who placed, on such a large and beautiful pedestal, the music of our classic and contemporary masters at official parties in the capital of the empire! Honor to the chief magistrate of our city, who thought to evoke the spirit of Gluck, who to us, degenerate musicians of the nineteenth century, is like our Corneille."[7] This was not the first time that Gluck was likened to Corneille. As Mark Everist explains, to invoke Gluck in the 1850s was to summon the specters of French cultural history: "Gluck was not only one of the emblems of eighteenth-century *tragédie lyrique* in its nineteenth-century guise as *grand opéra* but of French opera, *tout court*."[8] What Haussmann presented was therefore no mere musical entertainment for imperial bureaucrats, but a musical demonstration of the continued importance of history to the empire.

Reading these press reviews of Haussmann's soirées, it seems as if the prefect had hit a nerve. The question of canonicity—as a historical awareness of the musical passage of time—had bubbled away in the musical press for the better part of the nineteenth century. With the Second Empire and its monumental displays of urban modernity came a renewed obsession with the ghosts of classicism, and the degree to which they haunted—or ought to haunt—modern life.

The aim of this chapter is twofold: first, to explain the extent to which Haussmann's lifelong connection to music informed his unique approach to urbanism, and by extension, his embrace of classical forms; and second, to gauge Haussmann's aesthetic leanings alongside those of two contemporary composers who, like Haussmann, relied heavily on the distant past to articulate their own modernity: Berlioz and Wagner. I hope to show how urbanistic and musico-dramatic discourses intersected in a period that was defined by monumental spectacle, the veneration of authoritarianism, and the reevaluation of the distant past. Like Berlioz and Wagner, Haussmann's work and ideas took on lives of their own. As with Wagner and "Wagnerism," "Haussmannization" outlived the man after whom the concept was named. Haussmann's legacy became defined not only by the urban "networks" he stitched across Paris, but also by the very idea that a city could function like a unified work of art, with an urbanist as its artist.

"HAUSSMANNIZATION"

How do we define Haussmannization? As a style? An aesthetic? A policy? More often than not, historians invoke the term casually, either with upper or lowercase, as a stand-in for midcentury urbanization. It is usually but not always limited to Paris, and it can encompass a set of ideals extending beyond the man after which it takes its name. Philip G. Nord defines Haussmannization as "shorthand for a complex of urban transformations largely, although not exclusively, the achievement of the baron Haussmann."[9] Widespread usage of the term suggests that the word functions as an "always-already given," Louis

Althusser's concept of an ideology that determined collective consciousness.[10] As ideology, Haussmannization was not merely a policy, but a process that subjected citizens to itself and affected their lives in significant ways. Read as an "always-already given," Haussmannization signifies cultural power by associating it with an ordinary human, and not a god or even a godlike sovereign, like an emperor. Haussmann did not hide behind the imperial apparatus, nor did he ever claim to be any more than the empire's servant. It is thus striking that a term like "Haussmannization" became so commonplace during the years of the Second Empire, as it suggests the immense trust and confidence the emperor placed in him—not least, trust that the powerful prefect would remain loyal to Bonapartism.

Another way of looking at "Haussmannization" is through its suffix, which suggests a finite operation and not an infinite state of being. Music historians are accustomed to identifying and analyzing "-isms" in their research and teaching: one speaks more of "romanticism" than of "romanticization," "modernism" more than "modernization," and so on. Textbook musical histories of style spend a great deal of time unpacking these "-isms" by trying to locate their emergences and dissolutions. Within the cultural politics of Second Empire France, "-isms" and "-izations" existed in tandem as distinct structures of power. In English usage, the suffix "-ism" connotes era-defining ideology. "Bonapartism" survived the first Bonaparte and became a form of late-century imperialism far beyond what the original Bonaparte could have imagined. "Wagnerism" is perhaps the most commonly used derivational morpheme in Western music history, as it largely connotes the composer's influence on future musicians (especially after Wagner's death), rather than his own compositional style. By contrast, the suffix "ization/isation" is a state of movement, a process of becoming, or a state of putting into place. This concept is perhaps less familiar to musical-historical circles as it mechanizes artistic consciousness: no one today would write that d'Indy or Chabrier underwent "Wagnerization," for example. Nor did Wagner "Wagnernize," but according to nineteenth-century writers, Haussmann did "Haussmannize." In 1868, when the Parisian press began to report on the prefect's exorbitant debt financing, an anonymous author published *Paris désert. Lamentations d'un Jérémie haussmannisé*, a fictional biblical pamphlet in which the prophet Jeremiah complains about socioeconomic segregation in the city.[11] To be *haussmannisé*, according to the pamphlet, was to be made a victim of creative destruction. An unlikely pair of historical actors, Wagner and Haussmann, as we will later see, became synonymous with a polarizing artistic ethos that valued relentless forward motion toward totalization. Their surnames became the roots of modernist progress, even though both rooted their ideologies firmly in the past.

Interestingly, "Haussmannism" came to connote the worst of urbanism's creative-destructive potential. Writing of the destruction caused by the Franco-Prussian War and the subsequent Commune, the British journalist W. M. Torrens argues that Parisians "should have been ready to incur like horrors of civil war, sooner than return to the humiliating and ruinous system of Haussmannism."[12] In the twentieth and twenty-first centuries, historians equate the term with the vulgar commodification of all public and private space. David Turnock, for instance, calls Haussmannism an "abrasive ethos."[13] References to Haussmannism mostly amount to such passing disparagements of reckless urban demolition. Colin Jones evokes both Haussmannization and Haussmannism as a way of distinguishing, respectively, the holistic process of renewal and the namesake ideology that defined the era: "It was not 'Napoléonism' but 'Haussmannism' that was recognized as an influence—a continuing influence—on the remodeling of the capital."[14] If Haussmannization, according to Jones, refers to the process of urban renewal, Haussmannism is the ethos behind it. To speak of urban reform this way, then, is to aestheticize the production of abstract space: an aesthetics grounded in principles of top-down totality.

Musicologists have not clearly articulated how "Haussmannization" is distinct from the broader and more nebulous project of "modernity." This slippage, writes Sharon Marcus, has led historians of different disciplines to presume that Haussmann himself was a modernist through and through.[15] When a name becomes an -ism or an -ization, it transcends the individual and becomes ideology. To understand the emergence of "Haussmannization" is to comprehend how the material realities of urban renovation informed artistic consciousness. It is also to understand the specific role that music played in the life of this influential figure in Parisian urban and cultural politics.

HAUSSMANN, MUSICIAN

Georges-Eugène Haussmann came from a family of government officials. His paternal grandfather, Nicolas Haussmann (1760–1846), served as Député de Seine-et-Oise in the Assemblée législative (1791–92), before serving as Député à la Convention nationale (1792–95). His maternal grandfather, Georges

Frédéric Dentzel (1755–1828), was a Lutheran chaplain in the *régiment Royal-Deux-Ponts,* an infantry battalion established in 1757, before becoming a member of the Convention nationale, the Conseil des Anciens, and finally an officer in Napoléon Bonaparte's army. Dentzel was named "Baron" by Bonaparte, which explains why his grandson Georges-Eugène, though never officially receiving it, adopted the "Baron" moniker for himself. Though shaped by his family's connections to high-ranking government positions, Haussmann's bureaucratic prowess was forged in the disciplined dabbling of his early years. Forays between music and literature, biology and engineering, often saw the young Haussmann running from the laboratory to the practice room. This devotion to education, coupled with his strong family ties, defined Haussmann's later pursuits; as he wrote in his *Mémoires,* "the milieu in which each of us is born, the education we have received, the feelings, ideas, and opinions we share as a result, have an influence on at least the early part of our life."[16]

Here and elsewhere, Haussmann reveals himself to be an individual indebted to past experience. While his later reputation as an *artiste-démolisseur* might suggest otherwise, Haussmann's aesthetic and moral code was in fact predicated on this balance of diversity and discipline, memory and forgetting. Music would not play a direct role in his capacity as Prefect of the Seine, nor can Haussmann be considered a "failed musician" who sold out to the private sector. Instead, music helped Haussmann actualize his professional ambitions and urbanistic aesthetic. As he wrote in his *Mémoires,* "never did I consider music to be, for me, anything but a distraction to lift the spirit, the most agreeable of pastimes."[17] But the lessons, experiences, and artistic tastes of Haussmann's youth informed his later idea of the city as a work of art, with himself as the artist.

From an early age, Haussmann demonstrated an eclectic curiosity as well as an unwillingness to commit to a singular field of study. Haussmann fondly recalled learning Greek and Latin in his boarding school in Bagneaux, a small commune southeast of Paris.[18] Haussmann learned the two languages by reading the same ancient texts in dual-language books in order to compare how grammar and syntax translated across them. His tutor, a retired *oratorien* named (aptly) M. Legal, drilled him on the rules of prosody and sentence structure. Already as a young child, Haussmann found aesthetic pleasure not so much in literature's ability to express, but rather in its comparative and abstract formal structures and procedures. In addition to learning classical languages, the young Haussmann also studied still-life drawing (mostly draftsmanship) and music—both of which, he boasted, came easily to him.

Theory and practice were thus inseparable; indeed, to Haussmann, practice was a means of unlocking theory and not the other way around. Haussmann attributed his success as an administrator to these formative years of voracious education, between the ages of nine and eleven, in the classics and arts. This period of eclectic learning also explains the dilettantism of his adult years, dabbling in many languages, arts, and industries without ever committing to the singular pursuit of one.

Haussmann played music as an eleven-year-old student at the prestigious Lycée Henri IV in Paris: a period in which, in his words, "classics and romantics lived in a constant state of open war."[19] As a teenager, Haussmann played cello in orchestras, but he was also proficient enough to fill in on other "less practiced" instruments as was needed. His musical interests, like his other academic pursuits, focused on coverage and not necessarily specialization. He brought a managerial mindset to his musical activities, one that preferred to have a say on a number of issues rather than join the professional rank and file of this or that specialty. This mindset would serve him well as he later reimagined the entire urban and cultural infrastructure of Paris, here making unilateral decisions, there delegating to specialists. In his teens he made the acquaintance of Alexandre-Étienne Choron (1771–1834), who served as regisseur of the Paris Opéra (1815–17) then, after his ouster, director of the Institution royale de musique classique et religieuse (1817–32). Throughout the Bourbon Restoration (1814–30), Choron eschewed "modern" developments in opera composition in favor of sacred and instrumental music. Modeling his curriculum on London's Academy of Ancient Music, Choron vowed in an unpublished essay to "conserve the masterpieces of all ages"—evidently excluding those of his own.[20] Choron introduced Haussmann to the organ—an appropriate instrument for someone who thrived on control—and likely forged his young pupil's conservative musical palate. Uncompromising in his devotion to classicism, Choron promoted what Katharine Ellis has called a "museum" mentality to musical culture: Choron's "'museum' repertory was, in fact, a model, living repertory that he wished to see adopted nationwide for the good of the French citizenry."[21] Like Choron, Haussmann tied monumentality to morality. His own relentless pursuit of classical unity—in his case, in urban blueprints—was motivated by the belief that moral order would only result from rigid structure.

Given Haussmann's early predilections for classical learning and his later taste for monumental planning, his encounter with the young Hector Berlioz makes for fascinating reading. Indeed, Berlioz is the only composer who

Haussmann writes about at length. Consequently, Haussmann biographers have compared the two men, albeit superficially. It is unknown if Haussmann held Berlioz in personal contempt; this encounter, recorded in Haussmann's *Mémoires*, suggests a disdain not for the composer but for the iconoclastic modernity that he represented. "Berlioz," Haussmann recounts, "belonged to the romantic school, and his music—pompous, rather untidy, noisy rather than sonorous—seemed to conjure a certain poetry that was much admired all the same."[22] Reading these words in connection to his earlier thoughts on artistry, it is clear why romanticism left such a bad taste in Haussmann's mouth. As Georges Laronze has noted, the debates between classicists and romantics taking place at the Conservatory reflected broader intellectual tensions in 1820s Paris—specifically those in the academically vibrant Latin Quarter—which in turn foreshadowed the political tensions of later decades.[23] Romanticism, according to the future prefect, was a dangerous force and anathema to classical beauty.

While completing his law degree, Haussmann filled his free time by shuttling between courses at the Sorbonne, the Collège de France, and the Conservatoire, where he first appears in attendance books in 1827. The courses he audited amount to a Who's Who of French letters: literature with Villemain; philosophy with the founder of "eclecticism," Victor Cousin; physics with Gay-Lussac; chemistry with Thenard and Dulong; minerology with Beudant; calculus with Cauchy; and—returning to his childhood musical interests—counterpoint with Anton Reicha at the Conservatoire. It was in Reicha's eleven-student class that Haussmann met Hector Berlioz, whom he sarcastically refers to in his *Mémoires* as a "student-artist" (*élève-artiste*).[24] The future *artiste-démolisseur* had found his counterpart in the musical world of the late 1820s.

Haussmann approached music like an engineer and not like a poet. His disdain for romanticism was not only a result of his loyalty to traditional structures of authority, but also suggests an artistic philosophy based on dissection and organization, as opposed to free expression. Haussmann seemed particularly perturbed by Berlioz's approach to the Conservatoire curriculum, observing that the French composer was writing opera overtures (Haussmann mentions Berlioz's overture to the unfinished opera *Les Francs-juges*, composed in 1826 and premiered at the Conservatoire in 1828) before learning how to write a proper fugue. Such conservative musical views reveal an analytical mind more interested in the symmetrical inner workings of eighteenth-century forms than in adopting contemporary musical structures—which, on more than one occasion, Haussmann wrote off as "imperfect."

Whether he resented Berlioz the person, the philosophy he represented, or both, Haussmann seemed to relish moments when Berlioz's ego was checked by authority figures. In a colorful anecdote, Haussmann recounts a Conservatoire composition exam during which the director, Luigi Cherubini, confronted Berlioz about two measures of rest in the student's submitted score. "What is this?" Cherubini grumpily asked. "*Monsieur le Directeur*, I tried to create a special effect with this pause," replied Berlioz. "Ah! You think that the suppression of these two measures would be effective on listeners?" retorted Cherubini. "*Mais oui, Monsieur.*" To this Cherubini suggested, "suppress the rest, then: it would be more effective still!"[25]

Why did Haussmann cite this anecdote in his *Mémoires*, talkbacks and retorts intact? Was he in the room, or was it hearsay? Berlioz does not recount this episode in his own *Mémoires*, but he does describe a similarly biting exchange when he mistakenly entered through the "females only" door to the Conservatoire. He was stopped and lambasted by an enraged Cherubini, who was as furious at the trespass as he was that Berlioz was en route to the library to study, of all things, Gluck. But Haussmann does not recount the squabble between Berlioz and Cherubini to dwell on the young composer's character, but rather to diagnose what he believed was a sign of the times. Haussmann uses the Berlioz episode to reflect on the broader imposition of romanticism, as he understood it, on art and society in Paris. If *Les Francs-juges* was the problematic work, then it is possible that he conflated all forms of musical rule-breaking with "romantic" impulse—whether or not those works could be deemed stylistically "romantic." As David Cairns has suggested, the orchestration of *Les Francs-juges* bears a closer resemblance to Gluck than to Weber, which led the Berlioz biographer to conclude that in this youthful work, "there is no Romantic Orchestra."[26] Be that as it may, Haussmann offers his own definition of "romantic" music in his *Mémoires*, in which he repeats—nearly verbatim—his characterization of Berlioz: "Pompous, rather incorrect, noisy rather than sonorous, aspiring to a certain kind of poetry, and too much admired."[27] Understandably, Haussmann scholars have taken these words as a sign of Haussmann's conventionality and resistance to the contemporary tides of idealistic romanticism. Given the young Haussmann's Enlightenment-rooted pedagogical values, Berlioz was to Haussmann, in biographer Georges Valance's words, "a colleague, not a companion."[28] Of Haussmann's artistic spontaneity, Laronze writes that "he worked at music, like all things, with more method than personality, without spirit, yet driven by a rare will."[29] Musically speaking, Haussmann was good but not great, thorough but not obsessed, informed but not avant-garde. Haussmann's dilettantish, conservative approach to the musical arts reflected his general antagonism toward romanticism and the social and aesthetic norms associated with it.

Yet this anti-romanticism should not be bracketed off as personal prejudice and thus irrelevant to his professional activities. To separate the future prefect's artistic tastes from his aesthetic approach toward urbanism is to ignore the dependence of one on the other. Despite his negative comments about romanticism, Haussmann saw in Berlioz's status as *élève-artiste* his own future stature as *artiste-démolisseur*. After all, both had studied the hard sciences as students and would draw on their experiences at various points in their respective careers. Both were—at least by proximity—"classmates" at the Conservatoire. Finally, both relied, to various extents, on the favor of the empire. These parallels have led the famed Berliozian Jacques Barzun to draw an artistic parallel between the two men: "The Baron [Haussmann] ... had ideas on the grand scale like Berlioz but working as he did in the tangible medium of cobblestones, his plans met more easily with official favor."[30] Barzun's reference to an urbanistic "medium" is consistent with Haussmann's own self-fashioning as an artist. Yet "grand scale" thinking could, in the nineteenth century, result in aesthetic decisions as disparate as those between the beautiful and the sublime. Writing decades later, Haussmann could not forget Berlioz's attempts to demolish tradition during that Conservatoire exam. It was not chaos, noisiness, bombast, or formlessness in Berlioz's score that upset Haussmann. In Haussmann's retelling, it was those two measures of profound silence that cut like a bulldozer through institutional norms. By turning his ambitions away from the classical ideals of symmetry, order, and perfection, Berlioz turned his back on institutional tradition—epitomized by the grumpy Cherubini—and embraced a sound world intent on moving the masses. So, too, did Haussmann turn his back on the medieval layout of Paris, cutting through its center with monumental effect as the aesthetic goal.

After their encounter at the Conservatoire, Haussmann and Berlioz lived parallel but separate lives until the 1850s, when the two would both become codependents of the politics and aesthetics of Second Empire Paris. Haussmann, plucked from the relative obscurity of his post in Bordeaux as Prefect of the Gironde, had quickly become a household name, speaking publicly at many boulevard inaugurations, such as the 1862 festivities described in this book's introduction. The ascent of Napoléon III, then, meant the ascent of Haussmann. Berlioz's personal and professional journey during the Second Empire was rockier. In 1854, during the first full year of Haussmann's tenure as Prefect of the Seine, Berlioz laid to rest Harriet Smithson; although they had been separated for years, he nonetheless felt connected to her until her death. It was at this time that Berlioz began seriously considering his legacy and broader questions of existence and permanence, and he made substantial progress on his *Mémoires* in the following months. As he lamented Harriet, Berlioz asked "how meaningless are all these questions of fate, free will, the existence of God, and the rest of it; an endless maze in which man's baffled understanding wanders helplessly lost."[31] Such sentiments seem to contradict the assertive hot-headedness that Haussmann ascribed to Berlioz during their student years.

As for Berlioz's opinions of Second Empire urbanization, they remain a topic of debate. What is clear is that Berlioz believed his own grand, "architectural" musical style was in alignment with the empire's aesthetics of urban monumentality. To that end, he repeatedly sought opportunities for career advancement within the empire, particularly in opera. In 1860, having failed to secure a contract with the Opéra for *Les Troyens,* Berlioz saw an opportunity in the soon-to-be-rebuilt Théâtre Lyrique—to be rebuilt, that is, on account of Haussmann's imminent demolition of the theater-lined boulevard du Temple, where the old Théâtre Lyrique had stood since 1847. After signing a contract with the director of the Théâtre Lyrique, Léon Carvalho, Berlioz appealed to his bureaucratic contacts to hasten the construction of the venue. It is in this context that on February 2, 1860, Berlioz penned his only known letter to Baron Haussmann—a letter that only exists in the redacted form presented below. The location of the original autograph is (at the time of writing) missing:

To the Prefect of the Seine:
    (...) I wish for the honor of discussing with you an issue that concerns me directly, but which involves the construction of the new théâtre lyrique. Permit me to solicit from your benevolence a few moments of an audience (...)

Hector Berlioz
Membre de l'Institut[32]

Between the unsentimental, formal greeting and Berlioz's signature as an elected member of the Académie des Beaux-Arts of the Institut de France, there is no sense that the two men knew each other intimately, despite their earlier acquaintance as music students. Moreover, there was a clear power dynamic motivating this letter: Berlioz needed Haussmann to navigate his precarious situation. He wrote of his intent to solicit the prefect in his more personal correspondence. To Pauline Viardot, Berlioz disclosed that he intended to visit the Prefect of the Seine to "talk Carvalho," and to his sister Adèle, Berlioz vented his frustration at needing to schmooze with those in power: "At present, I must solicit the Prefect of the Seine so that he would grant Carvalho a little more space for his new théâtre lyrique, so that my opera could be performed there. Always soliciting!"[33] From his correspondence, we can deduce that the adult Berlioz regarded Haussmann like he did the rest of the imperial apparatus: perhaps "necessary evil" would be too strong a phrase, but Berlioz's success with securing imperial patronage never seemed to materialize to the extent that the composer had envisioned.

If Berlioz and Haussmann maintained a formal relationship akin to that of patron and artist, both men independently regarded authoritarianism with an artistic sensibility. In 1851, Berlioz described Louis-Napoléon Bonaparte's *coup d'état* in artistic terms as "a stroke of genius, an utter masterpiece."[34] In his 1844 short story *Euphonia, ou la ville musicale*, Berlioz imagines a musical town of the future whose urban rhythms are literally dictated by a central organ that leads citizens in daily performances of musical works. Euphonia is a militarized, industrial, fundamentalist enclave, and it indoctrinates all who live there in Greco-Roman aesthetics, tonal supremacy, and a taste for collective monumentality. Needless to say, authoritarian overtones resonate loudly; Katherine Kolb has also posited that Berlioz channeled his lingering rage over Marie Moke—who decided to marry Camille Pleyel and not him—to write a "ferocious revenge story."[35] Berlioz thus not only betrayed authoritarian sympathies, but also vividly imagined them as manifest through the production of urban space. As for the prefect and his urban reforms, Berlioz never discussed Haussmannization directly, and his comments on urban life could be contradictory. Berlioz separated Paris's infrastructure from its culture. When it was convenient, Berlioz would urge on urban demolition and construction, as evidenced by his desire to appeal to Haussmann regarding the new Théâtre Lyrique. When discussing Paris as an abstract form, what Henri Lefebvre would call "conceived space," Berlioz seemed favorable to Haussmannization. In an 1864 letter to the composer Auguste Morel, Berlioz wrote that "Paris becomes more beautiful from day to day. It is a pleasure to see it flourish so rapidly."[36]

Berlioz's view of *le nouveau Paris* became more morbid when he connected the city to artistic culture or his own personal experience. In these embodied modes of urban experience, what Lefebvre would call "perceived" or "lived" space, Paris no longer glistened, but festered. This sense of morbidity is palpable in an 1859 letter to Princess Carolyne Sayn-Wittgenstein: "Paris is for me like a cemetery, to me its paving stones are funeral slabs. I only live in the past. Everywhere I find memories of friends or of enemies who are no more."[37] Morbid nostalgia was not the only fuel for Berlioz's occasional antipathy toward the imperial city. If the changing urban layout pleased him objectively but disorientated him personally, then the changing institutional and bureaucratic norms decentered his identity as a musician. As Berlioz wrote to a young American composer named Jerome Hopkins in 1863, "if to you New York is the Purgatory of musicians, then to me, who knows it well, Paris is their Hell."[38] Notwithstanding his stature in Second Empire musical life, Berlioz envisioned success as supplying a steady stream of imperial fanfare. Between conducting massive ensembles in massive spaces, serving on juries for the Expositions universelles, and composing the so-called "architectural" works for festive occasions like his *L'Impériale,* discussed in the next chapter, Berlioz's career and output became tethered to the monumental aesthetics of empire—tethered, in other words, to the planning decisions that Haussmann made in the offices of the Hôtel de Ville.

Living in the same city yet worlds apart, Berlioz and Haussmann are seldom discussed in tandem. However, both individuals saw themselves as a multifaceted artists fascinated with science, engineering, literature, architecture, and acoustics, and with how all of these could be deployed to sway large audiences. For Berlioz, survival as an artist meant balancing lives as a critic, composer, Conservatoire librarian, and conductor. This balancing act made Berlioz the most famous exemplar of what Emmanuel Reibel has called a "crossed career" (*carrière croisée*), or a more-or-less full-time pursuit of music criticism en route to more prestigious opportunities as a composer or librettist.[39] Haussmann likewise saw the role of Prefect of the Seine as an artistic balancing act. His thoughts, replete with some arresting musical imagery, are worth quoting at length:

> Indeed, the Imperial Prefect of the Seine was an administrator doubling as an artist; loving all of the finer things; easily seduced by the harmony of vast ensembles; enchanted by the poetry of order and of equilibrium, which amazed us through the celestial spectacle of architecture; impassioned by the Beautiful, that excellent and artistic form of the Good; while considering

everything else as secondary; but knowing, through experience, and these secondary things are not to be neglected.[40]

Haussmann here paints a vivid image of a prefect's life, one that no doubt romanticized the everyday goings-on of an imperial bureaucrat. His decision-making was evidently motivated in no small part by aesthetic considerations, such as the balance between sensory pleasure and abstract notions of order, and the prioritization of monumental public works over more mundane projects.

Key to Haussmann's thought process is the balance of the aesthetic categories of the Beautiful and the Good. These terms undoubtedly emerge from Haussmann's earlier philosophical education when he audited the lectures of Victor Cousin. Famous for his oft-applied theory of "eclecticism," Cousin built a career as a proponent of truth, unity, and a *juste milieu*, a popular catchall term for philosophical centrism. While never committing to a singular school of thought, Cousin overall rejected a totalizing objectivity, opting instead for an embrace of multiple perspectives, albeit from a rigidly organized perspective. Some of his public lectures were consolidated into his most famous text, *On the True, the Beautiful, and the Good* (*Du vrai, du beau, et du bien*), which was published in 1836. In an often-quoted passage originally delivered during his Sorbonne lectures of 1818, Cousin builds on Kant's notion of Beauty as "purposiveness without purpose" and applies it to social systems like organized religion and politics: "We must have religion for religion's sake, morality for morality's sake, as with art for art's sake.... The beautiful cannot be the way to what is useful, or to what is good, or to what is holy; it leads only to itself."[41] It is likely that Haussmann not only read this passage in Cousin's book, but also heard a version of it during Cousin's lectures. This primacy of form over function was a tempting proposition to a generation of artists, writers, and bureaucrats for whom the slogan "art for art's sake" could mean a temporary relinquishing of social duty for the sake of an imagined ideal.

That Haussmann framed his urbanistic philosophy around the aesthetic philosophy of Cousin is, of course, no secret. Walter Benjamin leads off the Haussmann section of his essay "Paris, Capital of the Nineteenth Century" with a quote from the prefect: "I worship the Beautiful, the Good, great things, beautiful nature inspiring great art, whether it enchants the ear or charms the eye."[42] While Benjamin spends the rest of the essay pulling threads between urban monumentality and finance capital, we again witness

Haussmann evoking both the aural and the ocular in his definition of art. Haussmann's conception of rational, classical Beauty, modeled on Cousin, informed his approach to the production and policing of urban space. Thus Haussmann's later renown as an *artiste-démolisseur* was a small part in the larger role that he fashioned for himself: that of an artist-bureaucrat, who marshaled his power in an attempt to bring imperial politics into harmony with the multisensory experience of urban form.

HAUSSMANN'S TOTAL ART

When invoking totalizing artistic forms, multisensory manipulation, and outspoken views on aesthetics, there is another individual to whom Haussmann ought to be compared: Richard Wagner. The German composer's turbulent relationship to the French capital continues to inspire scholarly reflection. Annegret Fauser interprets the infamous 1861 *Tannhäuser* premiere—or at least Wagner's telling of it—as a modernist master narrative told from the composer's own perspective.[43] More recently, Jeremy Coleman raises the point that the "Wagner in Paris" scholarship exposes the limits of reception history, as it "essentially produces a lack in the historical object in order to supplement it with discursive play, typically that of identity politics."[44] While I do not fully agree that reception history relies simply on identifying a historiographic pairing of person/work and place/community, I do believe that the temptation to analyze Wagner's Paris through Wagner's own perspective on Paris is strong. It is much harder to position an outspoken, outsized figure like Wagner as yet another actor in a broader network of musical communities and spaces. Reception history can be reconfigured in an infinite number of ways; as it portends that musical meaning is largely contingent on context, the unlimited number of contexts—from city to city, continent to continent, year to year—would potentially yield an infinite number of histories. Coleman instead argues that an alternative to the "Wagner in Paris" tale may be "to demythologize the 'master narrative' by brushing it against the grain (to adopt Benjamin's phrase) in order to unearth some of the contradictions that lie at its basis."[45]

My contribution to this ever-expanding Wagner discourse is not to ask Wagner any more questions, nor to consider the city through his eyes. Rather, I want to imagine an intellectual relationship between Wagner and Haussmann—to posit a Wagnerian urban aesthetics.[46] This is not to say that

Haussmann shared Wagner's modernist views on art. As established earlier in this chapter, it is myopic to equate "Haussmann" and "Haussmannization" with "modernity," and the same goes for "Wagner" and "Wagnerism." I am interested instead in the author-oriented, classically motivated facets of Haussmann's artistic tastes, which point me in the direction of Wagnerian thought. Some of the historiographical myths of Wagner and Wagnerism in Paris do find conspicuous parallels in the equally mythical narrative of Haussmann and Haussmannization, as both feature stories of creation, destruction, and totalizing views of artistic form.

There does not seem to have been any eventful encounter between Wagner and Haussmann in Paris, and I am confident that they would have disagreed on most political matters. Yet despite no on-record encounter, contemporary critics did not hesitate to draw connections between the two. In particular, the metaphorical notion of "demolishing" existing structures in the name of artistry inspired comparisons between composer and bureaucrat. On January 3, 1869, *Le Ménestrel* published a translation of an 1868 essay by Richard Wagner on Gioachino Rossini's musical influence. While the German praised the Italian's contributions to musical life in Paris, he also took the opportunity to respond to a critique that Rossini had made of him. In his opening paragraph, Wagner quoted an alleged dinner conversation between Rossini and Saverio Mercadante that was reprinted throughout the European press. When Mercadante asked Rossini what he thought of Wagner's *unendliche melodie,* the gourmand composer allegedly replied, "granted, a plate of sauce without fish would suffice for a man who contents himself with music without melody."[47] In a brief response to Wagner's essay, the paper's editor, Heugel, took issue with Wagner's ventriloquized conversation between the two Italian composers. Heugel's commentary not only summarizes some of the broader ambivalence toward Wagner's persistent presence in French musical discourse, but it also namedrops another larger-than-life figure whose professional activities were inseparable from his self-image: "We have battled against [Wagner's] writings, because a musician who complains so bitterly about the slightest of pleasantries with a fellow composer should abstain from vain theories and proclamations against consecrated masterworks. If everyone were to add their own stone to the edifice, all the better; but let us keep from demolishing, as this will benefit art less than do Haussmann's demolitions in new Paris."[48]

Heugel's Haussmannian analysis of Wagner is a rare instance of the composer and prefect being placed on the same aesthetic plane. Presciently, Heugel suggests that artists of a certain persuasion feel that creation must follow from destruction. Urbanization is a dialectical act. To demolish urban space, or to have it demolished, suggests ownership over the production of that space. Whether acquired forcibly, through a land grant, or through the commodification and sale of land as property, demolition is a uniquely capitalistic conception. Furthermore, demolition is an aesthetic position. What is already there is no longer useful or profitable; at worst, demolition is disgust put into action, a privileged form of contempt for the current state of things. Demolition, Heugel seems to suggest, is a form of being in the world, insofar as one has control over the physical shape of that world. In English as in French, wording is crucial. The poor or enslaved or colonized do not demolish; they "loot," "raid," "occupy," or some other form of guerrilla-style act of collective uprising. As an aesthetic category, then, demolition implies the subsequent creation of something in its place, whether directly over the rubble, like a palimpsest, or relocated elsewhere. As the composer Gustave Nadaud put it in an 1868 chansonnette, Haussmann "demolished in order to build,/ And he built in order to demolish." (I return to Nadaud's song in chapter 4). With Wagner we have a different form of dialectical creative destruction, not one of building/destroying physical space but of appropriating/rejecting tradition. Paris, to Wagner, was the land of grand opera, the genre he attempted to emulate and would eventually renovate. When success at the Paris Opéra did not materialize, Wagner abandoned the site—so to speak—to build and dwell elsewhere. Bayreuth, then, mapped Wagnerian aesthetics onto urban space. Wagner's Festspielhaus was the production of space *par excellence,* an invented locale that soon became synonymous with the Bavarian town.

To Wagner, Bayreuth was the anti-Paris. Wagner's meticulous planning of the Festspielhaus resulted from his general disdain for midcentury urban modernity and his idealization of pastoral antiquity. Marvin Carlson has detected a "Rousseauesque hostility toward urban centers" in the composer's correspondence; in an 1852 letter to Franz Liszt, Wagner wishes his work were produced not in capitals, but rather "in some beautiful retreat, far from the smoke and industrial odors of city civilization."[49] While other midcentury "modernists," like Baudelaire, confronted the contradictions of industrial modernity from the inside, Wagner opted for an older model of patronage. Having gained prestige as Dresden's *Hofkapellmeister,* he found a lucrative patron in Ludwig II, who invited him to oversee a metaphorical operatic "court" in provincial Bavaria.[50] This decision to build the Festspielhaus in Bayreuth—or any urban planning decision, for that matter—was motivated not only by geography, but by demography. Wagner's Germanic nationalism was predicated on an anti-urban sentiment, which was fundamentally linked to his anti-Semitism. Wagner believed that the modern metropolis was fundamentally "un-German" as it promoted industrial (and in his mind, Jewish) values, and that German cities were at best poor attempts at urbanistic conformity.[51] Provincialism was, to Wagner, an escape from the mass industry of theater, and by extension, a refuge from Jewish influence. Wagner routinely took things personally (as evidenced by his passive-aggressive Rossini essay), and he read the success of his Jewish colleagues in Paris—namely Giacomo Meyerbeer and Jacques Offenbach—not as a failing on his part, but as an institutional preference for urban Jews over provincial Germans.

Readers might be familiar with Wagner's thoughts on the French capital through his prose writings, but he recorded some of his most forceful anti-Parisian sentiment in, of all things, an operetta libretto. In his 1870 satirical comedy *Eine Kapitulation, Lustspiel in antiker Manier* (Capitulation: Comedy in the antique style)—which Thomas S. Grey notes is a sort of "companion piece" to the composer's earlier essay "Judaism in Music"—Wagner relished the downfall of Napoléon III, the Second Empire, and the theatrical culture of the Parisian boulevards. Wagner even cast Offenbach as the character epitomizing a bankrupt imperial regime.[52] Wagner's libretto (he never wrote a note of music for it), replete with offensive sketches of Offenbach, Victor Hugo, and Léon Gambetta, featured absurdities like a chorus of rats dancing a mock cancan in the finale. Wagner attempted to drape this outpouring of unhinged rage over the skeleton of an Aristophanic comedic structure, with its gestures toward know-it-all Choruses and a Dionysian ensemble finale. But, as Grey notes, *Eine Kapitulation* betrays Wagner's confluence of ancient Greek comedic practice and the modern *opéra bouffe* model pioneered by Offenbach—a conflation that suggests Wagner's condescending fascination with the quintessentially Parisian comedic genre.[53] Despite his anti-urban German provincialism, Wagner toyed with urban popular theater only once it was disarmed of its potency. Content with seeing the French capital crumble, Wagner picked through the rubble and attempted to fashion an Offenbach-style operetta into a Wagnerian display of total artistic control. Francophobic, anti-Semitic, and aligned with antiquity, *Eine Kapitulation* demonstrated Wagner's proclivity to attack while retreating.[54] Leaving Second Empire Paris in its wake, Wagner's would-be operetta clues us into the composer's all-encompassing anti-urbanism.

How might we frame Haussmann's urbanism as Wagnerian, or Wagner's *Gesamtkunstwerk* as Haussmannian? Wagner's notion of the "total artwork" has spawned a monumental number of musicological takes, and so it is perhaps unsurprising that this notion also permeates historiographies of the nineteenth-century city. The common denominator is, again, Walter Benjamin, for whom art, technology, and spectacle were inseparable in nineteenth-century Parisian life. From the *Offenbachiades* to the World's Fairs to the inaugurations of boulevards, Benjamin saw urbanism not only as a material embodiment of capitalist logic, but as lived aesthetic experience. Howard Caygill proposes that Benjamin saw in the flames of the Paris Commune "a fittingly destructive end to 'Haussmann's work of destruction' and its reshaping of the city as an alienated *Gesamtkunstwerk*."[55] In Benjamin's Marxian imagination, "destruction" was anticipated in the form and content of "Haussmann's work." Like Brünnhilde burning down Valhalla, the fiery ending of Napoléon III's bourgeois dictatorship was adumbrated from its radical conception via a *coup d'état*. This watershed was followed by other acts of creative destruction: rapid urbanization, military expansion, colonization, and monumental celebration of all of these during the Expositions universelles, the subject of the next chapter.

Thus, when comparing Wagner and Haussmann, "Old Paris" serves as an appropriate barometer, for, as we shall see in the final chapter of this book, fantasies of nostalgia counterbalanced the phantasmagoria of the modern, consumerist metropolis. Haussmann's and Wagner's personal attitudes toward "Old" Paris amount to respective fight/flight responses. In the 1840s, Wagner tried to conquer the city musically, both its performance and intellectual spaces. When he couldn't, he left. Haussmann, within his own discipline, tried—and succeeded—to bend the city to his aesthetic leanings. Wagner, looking for an urban home for his total artwork, failed to find it in the French capital. Haussmann's self-imposed mission was to transform the city into a unified work of art. Perhaps Haussmann was thinking of Wagner when he wrote of "this grand and difficult work (*oeuvre*): the Transformation of Paris, for which I was the devoted instrument between 1853 and 1870, and of which I remain the main editor, in a country where one personifies all things."[56] For Haussmann, urbanism was a continuous process of creation and revision in the name of moral order and artistic wholeness.

Of course, not all Parisians saw Haussmann's city as an artwork. "Monotony" and "opacity" were common complaints, as was the overreliance on abstract geometric forms, largely at the expense of organic, intuitive placemaking.[57] Writing in 1872, the architect Daniel Ramée reflected that "during the eighteen years from 1852 to 1870, Paris and many other towns in France have completely changed their aspect. The venerable monuments which recall the national traditions and memories and glories of the past have been gravely marred and mutilated, cut down ... to make way for edifices of no intrinsic artistic merit."[58] Such was Haussmann's complicated relationship with Paris's history. If he believed in his mandate to transform Paris by breaking with the past (a myth that David Harvey has thoroughly dissected), his detractors saw the prefect as manipulating space "to influence the processes of societal reproduction."[59] The genius of Haussmannization, then, was how it veiled this stratification of social space through urban spectacle and monumentality. In this sense, Haussmann's Paris, his own "Artwork of the Future," was a projection of power through the guise of art.

This chapter has sketched a portrait of Baron Haussmann as a man of the arts, whose developing relationship to Paris's musical scene paralleled his rise in social standing. It would be too facile to claim that Haussmann's musical exposure "made" him, or that his musical amateurism dictated his subsequent work as a state figure. Yet his musical tastes and his urban aesthetics align in their devotion to abstraction, rationality, disciplined order, geometric beauty, and committed separation of mapping and analysis from lived experience. As a loyalist and an apologist for colonialism, Haussmann thus crafted a complex public persona. He adored the past but hated nostalgia. His social views made him at once a prototypical nineteenth-century conservative and an *ancien régime* holdover resistant to the tidal waves of liberalism and romanticism. These contradictions made Haussmann a quintessential midcentury modernist.

I have also argued that Haussmann's lifelong engagement with the arts helped him manufacture the notion that urbanism could be a sole-authored enterprise. As we have seen, his relationships to musical literati provided him with reference points from which to construct an *auteur* urban philosophy the likes of which Europe had not yet seen. Art provided Haussmann with a totalizing worldview from which his persona as *artiste-démolisseur* was crafted. It is indeed ironic that it is Haussmann, not the emperor, who takes up the oxygen in discourses about Second Empire urbanization. This arrangement seemed to benefit both men: Haussmann was granted relative autonomy for designing and financing his public works, which allowed him to "express" himself and his organicist views on form through urban development. Napoléon could witness the city transform into a monument to his legacy, but the figurehead of Haussmann guaranteed that if things went awry, it would be he, not the emperor, who absorbed public criticism. By

1869, this would turn out to be true. The very relationship between Haussmann and Napoléon, then, was that of a transaction between patron and artist. It recalls that of Wagner and Ludwig II of Bavaria; the latter provided the means and received the glory, while the former executed the work and received the attention. Haussmann was ultimately a civil servant rooted in eighteenth-century notions of order and progress, which marked him as distinct from Wagner and his classical-liberal views on art as freedom. Ultimately, the namesake of Haussmannization was a card-carrying imperialist who understood his task: to redirect all physical, sensory, and social aspects of the urban experience into fanfare for the empire.

TWO

Fanfare City

THE EXPOSITIONS UNIVERSELLES

THE EXPOSITIONS UNIVERSELLES of 1855 and 1867 were two of the most widely attended and heavily advertised events during the two decades of the Second Empire. Between May 15 and November 15, 1855, over five million people visited the French capital to either attend or participate in the Exposition. Twenty-seven countries sent exhibits including industrial machinery, new agricultural technologies, and musical instruments, as well as paintings, sculptures, and other works of art.[1] The 1867 Exposition attracted over eight million visitors and exhibits from sixty nations as well as colonies. In addition to showcasing inventions and artworks, the Paris Expositions introduced massive new structures to the city's landscape. Intended as a rival to London's Crystal Palace, which was built for the Great Exhibition of 1851, the iron-and-glass Palais de l'Industrie was the main exhibition space of the 1855 World's Fair, as well as the site of numerous ceremonies and performances during the Second Empire. Beyond the exhibition grounds, visitors marveled at Paris's new public works projects, such as the widened boulevards and the well-lit and nearly odor-free sewers open for public tours beginning in 1867.[2] Together, these two Expositions universelles—which nearly flank the respective declaration and dissolution of the Second Empire—generated immense amounts of publicity in the form of guidebooks, magazine and newspaper coverage, illustrated and photographic images, and paraphernalia, as well as musical compositions such as cantatas, café songs, piano quadrilles, and band marches.

This chapter begins by exploring what it means to "read" the Expositions universelles musically. Apart from their ostensible function to bring together the worlds of art and industry, the Expositions universelles showcased France's imperial achievements while feting Paris's urban reforms. The chapter then discusses how planners attempted to transfer visual ceremonial aesthetics into the realm of sound, specifically during the extravagant awards ceremonies. These events promised to celebrate the union of art and industry in spectacular fashion, and the visual preparations were by all accounts stupendous. However, various disagreements and miscommunications suggest that imperial planners did not have a full grasp of what exhibition fanfare ought to sound like. By reconstructing the dysfunctional performance circumstances of three cantatas written specifically for the closing ceremonies—*L'Impériale* by Hector Berlioz (1855), *Les Noces de Prométhée* by Camille Saint-Saëns, and *Hymne à Napoléon III et à son vaillant peuple* by Gioachino Rossini (both 1867)—I show how a monumental aesthetic was deployed, to varying degrees of success, to amplify imperial identity. In doing so, the chapter also reveals the incongruent relationship between visual and sonic fanfare in Second Empire Paris.[3]

READING THE EXPOSITIONS UNIVERSELLES

As their names suggest, Expositions universelles, also known as "World Exhibitions" or "World's Fairs," celebrated the material achievements of Western Europe, North America, and Europe's colonies, and served as vast playgrounds for both host citizens and international visitors. In doing so, these massive events reinforced a host-guest relationship, which served to underscore Paris's dominance over its provinces, France's dominance over its colonies, and the empire's standing amid its geopolitical rivals. While the café-concert was a porous space of sociability, the exhibition was an incubator of distraction, a space of passive spectacle. Walter Benjamin's aphoristic writing succinctly captures this phenomenon: "World exhibitions propagate the universe of commodities."[4] Scholars of French music continue to riff on Benjaminian motifs of microcosms, illusions, dream images, and veils, translating his poetic readings of visual culture into the realm of exhibition sound. For example, Annegret Fauser has extensively detailed how the sounds of the 1889 Exposition universelle—during which the Eiffel Tower became a metonym for modernity—offered not only technological tourism but also "the illusion of 'authentic' encounters with other cultures, both historical and geographical."[5] The power and prestige of the Second Empire World's Fairs relied in no small part on such sensory manipulation, thus anticipating the modernist fantasies of 1889.

Symbols of empire were not restricted to large, curated spectacles like the World's Fairs. They also informed Paris's everyday urban rhythms. Workers' schedules punctuated the transformative spectacle of Haussmannian demolition and construction. Train timetables not only accented the flow of mobility, but also determined the start and end times of operatic works.[6] Horse-drawn omnibuses connected the new city plan with the fairgrounds. In addition to the staccato rumble of wheels and hooves against macadam pavement, omnibuses blared fanfare through mechanical horns, often using opera tunes to announce stops and itineraries.[7] Even the annual rhythms of national holidays shifted during the Second Empire. Soon after his self-inauguration, Napoléon III replaced July 14—Bastille Day—with August 15, his uncle's birthday, as the new French national holiday. Every August 15 during the nearly two decades of the Second Empire, Paris's theaters were ordered to stage sycophantic cantatas and allegorical stage works glorifying the holiday known as the Saint-Napoléon.[8] Ceremonial fanfare was key to the imperial aesthetic of what Benjamin would lambaste as the *fête impériale,* or the perpetual sensory distraction and overload in the city. Karl Marx himself noted his disdain for Napoléon "le petit," famously observing that the theater of French imperialism, from Napoléon Act 1 to Napoléon Act 3, presented itself "first as tragedy, then as farce."[9]

Despite France's prominence in the arena of staging exhibitions, it was London's Great Exposition of 1851 that introduced the world to the conceited notion of a "World's" Fair. The event, officially titled "The Great Exhibition of Works of Industry of All Nations," had for the first time an international agenda: not only to showcase British achievements in commerce, technology, and fine arts (painting was excluded), but also to host a competition featuring exhibits from other nations. The exhibition took place in the Crystal Palace, a lavish glass-and-iron edifice conceived by the architect Joseph Paxton. The palace was to be both awe-inspiring and easy to construct, as it was conceived as a temporary structure that could be disassembled and transported. Perhaps because of his experience as a gardener, Paxton designed the palace as a massive greenhouse, 1851 feet long by 454 feet wide. The construction utilized the latest industrial machinery—later displayed within the exhibition hall itself—to support four thousand tons of iron beams and sixteen ribs of the transept arch on a thousand columns also made of iron. By the exhibition's closing ceremony on October 11, over six million people had paid a modest daily admission fee to tour the palace. It earned the Victorian government a profit of over 180,000 pounds and international renown for its achievement in urban efficiency and technological ingenuity.[10]

The French fared well at the Great Exhibition, winning 1,051 out of 5,187 prizes.[11] Yet following Louis-Napoléon's conversion of Paris into an imperial capital, bureaucrats and critics alike began to propagate the myth that Paris and London were in competition over which city was the capital of the industrialized world. Léon de Laborde, who served as French Commissioner to the London Fair, complained that "England, shameless imitator, has stolen from us the initiative of a Universal Exhibition."[12] A major critique of the London Exhibition was its irreverent juxtaposition of industrial products with the fine arts. The critic Jules Janin sarcastically attacked the insensitive presentation of certain exhibits: "How inept! Go on then, seat the *Venus de Milo* on an anvil; hitch up the *Apollo Belvedere* to a bale of merchandise, make a beer advertisement out of Phidias's *Jupiter!*"[13] As Janin saw it, the British exhibition committee highlighted neither art nor industry. This perceived failure, coupled with the opportunity to stage a grand debut for the nascent Second Empire, provided the impetus for Napoléon III to host the first "universal" Exposition—"universal" not only in terms of international participation, but also in terms of presenting the widest possible coverage of human achievement in industry and the fine arts.

Yet this spirit of "universality" did not extend to planning and oversight; Napoléon III's regime weighed in on virtually all executive decisions. This included hand-picking insiders for leadership roles, not least the emperor's younger cousin, Prince Napoléon-Jérôme "Plon-Plon" Bonaparte, who became the 1855 exhibition's chief administrator. "Plon-Plon" (a childhood nickname that stuck) took his job seriously, visiting construction sites and offering enlightened musings on art and industry to planners and builders. Indeed, as he enumerated in his retroactive report to the emperor, the tasks of the *commission impériale* were considerable: develop, renovate, and build all exhibition infrastructure; facilitate the submission process for all entrants; negotiate any issues with legislators; draft official rules and regulations for the exhibition's judging process; organize all public services from transport to toilets; appoint members to committees who share the values of the empire; vet all jury decisions; organize the awards ceremony in a way that minimizes allegations of favoritism and corruption; and last but not least, "celebrate France with all the people of the globe, who would be hosted for six months in Paris."[14]

Haussmann did not have an official role on the *commission impériale* that planned the exhibitions. But given that much of its work directly involved his "turf"—namely, the development of Parisian urban space—it is not far-fetched to imagine that he offered input, even if informally. As spokesmen of the empire, both Haussmann and Plon-Plon were charged with producing urban space in the empire's image. But where Plon-Plon's liberal, anticlerical leanings often created friction in the Tuileries Palace, Haussmann and Napoléon were remarkably synchronized on matters of politics and aesthetics; it is said that their only disagreement concerned Haussmann's ouster in 1870.

As Matthew Truesdell writes, the 1855 and 1867 exhibitions "created organized and ordered worlds that bore a striking resemblance to an idealized and perfected liberal capitalism."[15] The many individual galleries—and promenades that connected them—can be read as microcosms of Haussmannian urban planning. Like the boulevards, the exhibits played with perspective. To the passerby, there was diversity, variety, and overstimulation. Viewed from above, absolute unity reigned. Thus in addition to being feasts for the senses, the World's Fairs were also virtuoso displays of micromanagement.

Haussmann's most direct involvement in official musical proceedings came, unsurprisingly, in the form of a house party. On August 23, 1855, Haussmann organized an extravagant ball at the Hôtel de Ville honoring the arrival of Queen Victoria and Prince Albert to the Exposition universelle. Unlike the weekly soirées discussed in the previous chapter, Haussmann's exhibition ball was a symbolic ceremony, a diplomatic welcoming of the British sovereign. The daily newspapers all quoted the same "official" report sent to them by the state newspaper, *Le Moniteur,* focusing more on the décor and the guests (allegedly six thousand attended) than on the music. The *Journal des débats,* among other newspapers, reprinted the details of which dignitary danced quadrilles with whom: Queen Victoria with Emperor Napoléon, Prince Albert with Princesse Mathilde Bonaparte (famed salonnière and Napoléon III's cousin), Prince Adalbert of Bavaria with Octavie de Laharpe Haussmann (the prefect's wife).[16] In addition to organizing and hosting this *fête impériale,* Haussmann attended to diplomatic matters. At his request, Queen Victoria agreed to give her name to the recently opened avenue linking the place de l'Hôtel de Ville and the place du Châtelet; it remains the avenue Victoria to this day. Naturally, the queen also understood the symbolic and transactional nature of this honor. Before her departure from Paris, she communicated her praise of Haussmann to Napoléon III. The following year, Haussmann was named Grand Officer of the Légion d'honneur.[17]

Haussmann's official capacity as Prefect of the Seine thus encapsulated much more than the construction and demolition of streets; his was not merely a municipal job but a diplomatic, geopolitical one. By the late 1860s, critics of the empire spoke out against the unprecedented power of the Prefecture of the Seine. Lambasting the exorbitant costs of the boulevard du Prince-Eugène, Adolphe Thiers (future president of the French Third Republic) observed in an 1868 speech that "if the title of vice-emperor belongs to anyone it is not to M. the minister of State. It belongs to M. the prefect of the Seine."[18] As critics like Thiers warned, Haussmann's influence transcended his title. For his part, Haussmann understood that attention to detail—be it a boulevard inauguration or an exhibition—symbolized the economic and political progress of the empire.

Haussmannian aesthetics permeated the sonic landscape of the World's Fairs, from the careful staging of pair dancing at his *bal de l'Hôtel de ville* to the imperial fanfare and orchestral classics that blared during the opening and closing ceremonies. The tried and true works selected for the opening and closing ceremonies—by Gluck, Weber, Beethoven, and Meyerbeer—balanced prestige, viability, and pragmatism. As Mark Everist explains, Gluck's neoclassical aesthetic theories and evocative orchestrations were celebrated in Parisian subscription concerts throughout the 1850s, which set the stage for the Théâtre Lyrique revival of *Orphée* in 1859.[19] But Gluck's orchestral music was also scalable to massive performing forces, as were the Meyerbeer opera excerpts expressly scored for the Opéra. The challenge, then, was to weave unproven new work into this carefully curated sonic tapestry.

MONUMENTAL CONTINGENCY

Two concepts that guide my analysis of this balance are *monumentality* and *contingency*. The term monumentality connects "bigness"—the giant exhibition spaces, the massive industrial machinery, the crowds, the large orchestral and choral ensembles—as projections of the union of art and industry. In his book-length study of musical monumentality Alexander Rehding notes that monumentality is more a contingent concept than a fixed aesthetic category: "Monumentality is not just about big musical effects per se but also about what they stand for and how they are used."[20] The term is also distinct from sublimity. The latter, at least in the Kantian sense, is a moment of retrospection and awe at the limits of human perception. If sublimity is ultimately an individual experience of awe, monumentality is a manipulation of collective experience. Monumentality is a unidirectional force stemming from authority figures and aimed at a mass public. Rehding sees musical monumentality as resembling, but ultimately falling short, of the Kantian aesthetic categories that continued to dictate notions of art in the nineteenth century. "Monumental music," he writes, "should rather be understood as *non*-purposive *with* a purpose; it therefore doubly falls short of the Kantian categories for beautiful art."[21] Within the world of exhibitions, monumentality was thus an ideology, deployed in a variety of forms—giant halls, large choirs, orchestras, military processions—to showcase the splendor of *le nouveau Paris,* a modern, urbanized city distinct from its republican and monarchical past. These midcentury Expositions universelles, particularly the fanfare around them, thus provided an opportunity to deploy the full power of the imperial urban sensorium on its attendees.

Monumentality does not necessarily mean permanence. To pull off two World's Fairs in the midst of substantial urbanization required flexibility and efficiency on the part of planners. To that end, the perception of monumentality was tied to what Christopher Mead calls "urban contingency," or a patchwork set of planning decisions aimed at financial pragmatism and a degree of indeterminacy. Within the context of Second Empire urban spectacle, monumentality and contingency are interlinked, the sensory efficacy of one relying on the malleability of the other. As Mead notes, Haussmann's supposedly absolute master plan, rooted in classicism and inspired by ideas of artistic canonicity, "was as historically contingent as were the more modest planning programs of his predecessors."[22] In other words, one should not be fooled by the grandness of the exhibition halls, as grandness does not necessarily mean premeditation. Some of the largest buildings constructed in *le nouveau Paris* were never intended for longevity, even if their design superficially mimicked the canonic permanence of a Panthéon. Cases in point were nineteenth-century exhibition halls, which were inhabited only temporarily, and either stood vacant after the exhibition closed, or were used for one-off occasions like musical events, civic ceremonies, or museum exhibits.[23]

World's Fairs manufactured a distinct form of seeing and hearing. Participants in the Expositions universelles were not cultural delegates but rather competitors for modest prizes handed out by the emperor. As such, exhibits were less about education and enrichment and more about enticement and entertainment. We can thus think of an exhibition gaze, or a collective mode of spectatorship that fabricated hierarchies along class and ethnic lines. Just as travelogues ought to be read as subjective reactions rather than objective accounts, so too do exhibition guidebooks offered a curated catalogue of the sights and sounds a visitor might encounter.[24] Writing about the representation of Arab communities in nineteenth-century British imperial fairs, Timothy Mitchell has noted the deleterious effects of exhibitions on the Western perception of non-Western cultures. In a society whose members were perpetual spectators, Mitchell argues, it became tempting to view the world as if one were viewing an exhibition: "This reality-effect was a world rendered up to the individual, according to the way in which, and to the extent to which, it could be set up before him or her as an exhibit: as mere objects recalling a meaning or reality beyond."[25] The exhibition gaze emerges when reading primary sources like guidebooks and official reports, especially when such reports were compiled under the watchful eye of the imperial host city. These documents also help to parse the differences between what Alexander Geppert calls the "exhibition city"—the curated space of performance and ritual, represented in countless idealized images on postcards, posters, even scarves—and the "exhibiting city"—the physical urban space where actual people dwell and interact.[26] Planners worked hard to translate these idealized, two-dimensional images of exhibitiongoers to the "lived," three-dimensional space of the architecture. The paper trail of these real and imagined exhibition spaces begins well before the opening of the 1855 Fair, with the planning and construction of the Palais de l'Industrie.

SPATIAL MONUMENTALITY AND THE PALAIS DE L'INDUSTRIE (1855)

Shortly after declaring empire, Napoléon III launched a competition to design and build his own version of a Crystal Palace, a "Palace of Industry" on an open space between the Seine and the Champs-Élysées. The competition was won by architects Jean-Marie-Victor Viel and the engineer Alexis Barrault. In August 1852 a statement by the administrative council granted the building contract to a private holding company, Ardoin et Compagnie. The company invested thirteen million francs into the project, on the conditions that the state guaranteed a 4 percent return on investment and that Ardoin had autonomy over production costs, including ticket prices.[27] As a result, the 1855 Exposition was the first French event of its sort to charge an admission fee to the exhibits and performances. Many members of the press reacted negatively, noting that admission fees undermined the inclusivity purportedly at the heart of the Exposition's mission; *L'Illustration* charged that "the presence of tariffs, in a place such as this, stands in contradiction to the noble hospitality that France is accustomed to show."[28] This public /private partnership between Ardoin and the state was in fact the continuation of what would be a long relationship: Haussmann's first major achievement, the boulevard de Strasbourg, was the result of a partnership between Ardoin and the City of Paris.[29]

Ticketed entry was but one step toward engineering a modern (read: capitalist) exhibition city. From the onset, the construction of the Palais de l'Industrie was motivated by competition with London. An 1855 poster promoting the upcoming fair, which featured a bird's-eye lithograph of the Palais, printed details about contractual conditions and precise architectural dimensions, as evidently this information was intended for public consumption. Flaunting the Palais's unprecedented scale, the poster boasts that "while Hyde Park's Crystal Palace was nothing but a sort of provisional tent, the Palais de l'Industrie is a lasting monument that will survive the Exposition universelle." The poster projects confidence that Paris will attract more visitors than London thanks to its thriving industries and temperate climate: "Paris, metropolis of art, good taste, and pleasure, offers its visitors a clearer and more pleasant sky and a friendlier and more jovial environment—things that the city of London, with its eternal fog, does not offer."[30]

On numbers alone, Paris produced the bigger exposition. The Palais de l'Industrie was monumental: 850 feet long, 350 feet wide, and boasting 408 windows. Its semicircular trusses bridged an 80-foot span to create a giant exhibition room. The crown jewel, however, was the façade (figure 2). Napoléonic "N" crests were juxtaposed with relief portraits of *ancien-régime* men of letters, neoclassical sculptors, and Greco-Roman architects, their printed names (rendered in French) clearly visible from afar. The emperor, it was made clear, was channeling the ghosts of the classical past. The entrance portal, itself a giant *arc de triomphe,* was adorned with a twenty-one-foot-tall limestone sculpture by Élias Robert called "France Crowning Art and Industry" (some years later, Frédéric Auguste Bartholdi would revisit the motif of the robed, crowned woman in his New York-bound magnum opus "Liberty Enlightening the World"). Robert's sculpture rendered visible the most basic premise behind organizing the exhibition: namely, that the allegorical female figure of *La France* welcomed art and industry in her embrace. The Palais de l'Industrie thus set the precedent for the Eiffel Tower of 1889, as both structures ultimately functioned as monuments that tied political ideology (imperial and republican, respectively), national heritage, and capitalism into a single, profitable bundle. Both were also intended as contingent

FIGURE 2. The Palais de l'Industrie. Photograph by Édouard Baldus, ca. 1860. Image: Metropolitan Museum of Art.

attractions for the cosmopolitan crowds of the fairs. But whereas the Palais outgrew its utilitarian function as a performance space and was eventually replaced by the Grand and Petit Palais in 1900, the hollow, iron, webby Eiffel Tower—in all its architectural uselessness—remains an immortal visual symbol of the city.

Ironically, the very design of the Palais undermined the emperor's call for a "union" between industry and art. Despite its massive size, the Palais was too small to house all the exhibits and still be convertible into a festival space for the closing ceremonies. Thus two extra buildings were added to the exhibition grounds. The first was the Galerie des machines, which was originally built as an annex to the Palais and ultimately housed the overflow of industrial machinery. The second was Palais des Beaux-Arts, a temporary structure that stood adjacent to the Galerie des machines. Designed by the architect Hector-Martin Lefuel, the horseshoe-shaped structure housed a floor-to-ceiling exhibit of European painting, as well as exhibits of engravings, sculpture, lithography, architectural plans, and medallions.[31] Divided between three buildings, the 1855 Exposition still betrayed the decades-long tradition of separating the fine arts from machinery exhibits. The name of the flagship building, moreover, suggested in no subtle way the Second Empire regime's preference for the latter. Yet while the imperial commission was able to mask its contingent urban planning in the name of "industry," the closing ceremony resulted in a logistical misfire that exposed the rift between monumentality in theory, and monumentality in practice.

MISFIRE 1: BERLIOZ'S *L'IMPÉRIALE* (1855)

The 1855 Exposition universelle closed to the public in early November. Preparations immediately began for the November 15 closing ceremony, during which the emperor would distribute medals to exhibitors and bring the exhibition to an official end. The nave of the Palais was cleared of all exhibits, and an amphitheater seating thirty thousand people was installed in the nave. Since the ceremony was open only to dignitaries, award winners, journalists, and performing musicians, each entrance and seat was strategically predetermined along geographic lines. Seating charts for the closing ceremonies suggest that the committee sought to represent the ceremonial space as a truly worldly gathering, in which guests now took the place of exhibits. This transformation of the Palais de l'Industrie from free-flowing promenade to fixed theater, writes Matthew Truesdell, "provided an opportunity to link politics and culture by integrating images of [Napoléon's] regime into powerful representations of the world of production."[32] Despite its contingent construction, the Palais was fashioned into a monument made to reflect a Napoléonic version of historical progress.

Although the organizing committee planned every visual detail of the event from décor to seating arrangements, several oversights in acoustics and timing caused the November 15 awards ceremony to be something of a sonic misfire. The task of preparing the 1200-member orchestra and chorus, consisting largely of students from the Conservatoire, fell to Berlioz. Although his experience conducting large-scale concerts likely made him the obvious choice, Berlioz was summoned only one month before the closing ceremony to select and rehearse the concert program. As he wrote to his sister Adèle on October 21: "I am taking advantage of a moment of freedom to write to you; I will not have much of it shortly. Prince Napoléon summoned me yesterday and suggested that I direct a concert of Babylonian proportions."³³ In addition to providing music for the closing ceremony on November 15, Berlioz was to give two full-length concerts on November 16 and 24, also at the Palais de l'Industrie.

Berlioz would conduct an orchestra and chorus positioned in the gallery behind the throne, so the musical program necessarily involved works that would suit the large ensemble in the enormous, resonant space. Although he had never led an ensemble of such a size, Berlioz had conducted a group of nearly a thousand as part of the Festival of Industry held in Paris in 1844. This "monster concert," as the London *Times* put it, featured works by Gluck, Spontini, Weber, Beethoven, Meyerbeer, Rossini, Halévy, and Berlioz's own *Hymne à la France*, a patriotic cantata with text by Henri Auguste Barbier, written specifically for the occasion.³⁴ The organizing committee had celebrated the size of the concert, noting the number of performers—863 in total—in bold typeface on the program, dwarfing the names of the composers and performers. In the context of French festivities, the size of the ensemble dictated the repertoire, not the other way around. Berlioz's 1855 program was therefore not unusual, nor was it tailor-made for the specific occasion. Rather, Berlioz drew on his earlier experiences as well as on the anticipated tastes of the imperial public, who by 1855 had grown accustomed to repeated hearings of orchestral works played by oversized performing forces.

Despite two regime changes separating the 1844 and 1855 ceremonies, Berlioz's Exposition universelle program closely resembled the July Monarchy's Festival of Industry program, with the same works by Gluck, Weber, Beethoven, and Meyerbeer appearing on both bills. But rather than repurpose his *Hymne à la France*, Berlioz programmed a new *pièce d'occasion*: a nine-minute cantata for chorus, soloists, and orchestra titled *L'Impériale*. David Charlton has recounted the confusing position that the work holds in Berlioz's output. In 1854, an army captain named Achille-Louis Lafon had composed a patriotic poem in honor of Napoléon III and somehow managed to read it in the emperor's presence.³⁵ It is unknown whether Lafon approached Berlioz with his text, or whether it was the composer who asked the army captain to set it to music (the latter is unlikely, given Berlioz's well-known taste in literature and the conventional patriotism of Lafon's poem). Hugh Macdonald's biting judgment of both Lafon's text and of the emperor is worth quoting: "The text ... is a grossly fawning encomium of the emperor, as obsequious as anything ever offered to Louis XIV, in praise of a man whose personal qualities Berlioz knew full well to be imperfect, especially as regards his nation's culture."³⁶ In any case, Berlioz interrupted his work on *L'Enfance*

EXAMPLE 1. Hector Berlioz, *L'Impériale*. Brass and percussion sections, measures 1–7.

du Christ to compose a *cantate impériale* based on Lafon's text, with the intention of having the work premiered as part of the Saint-Napoléon festivities of August 15. But in a letter to Liszt dated July 1, 1854, Berlioz expressed concern that the roof of the nearly constructed Palais de l'Industrie would not be completed in time (it was not).[37] On December 29 of that year, Berlioz wrote to the Ministre d'état asking to program a concert at the Théâtre-Italien that would feature two new works: his recently completed *L'Enfance du Christ*, and a "cantate à deux chœurs."[38] Berlioz attached Lafon's complete text in the letter, and made his case regarding the timeliness of such a work: "The cantata, for which I am attaching the words, has no direct relation to the event, it is true. But the sentiment that it expresses still has currency in France, and so no matter how much pomp and solemnity a performance would give, it would not be too much."[39]

Yet Berlioz saw greater potential in the work beyond the political relevance of the text; in a letter penned to his sister Adèle that same day, Berlioz boasted that *L'Impériale* was a "work of *grandissimo* effect that one has not yet known."⁴⁰ *L'Impériale* is a late example of the composer's proclivity toward sonic vastness, or what Julian Rushton has called a "spatial" element in the composer's output.⁴¹ Space here is both literal and metaphorical: in many of his works for large orchestra (especially the sacred works), Berlioz fostered a sense of depth through manipulation of silence, pitch span, placement of offstage instruments, the use of antiphonal or double choirs, as well as a technique that Berlioz dubbed the "law of *crescendo*," which he had discovered in studying dynamics in Beethoven's symphonies.⁴²

We hear this effect in the opening fanfare of *L'Impériale* (example 1). Following a bombastic introduction that Julian Rushton calls eight "till-ready" bars, a melody for choral basses in the "heroic" key of E-flat major is accompanied by pulsing strings, with wind instruments gradually filling out the texture.⁴³ The visual and sonic symbolism of the male chorus's syllabic chanting of "du peuple entier, les âmes triomphantes" (for all the people, triumphant souls) is almost too obvious to be noted. Less than one minute into the work, the tune has already been heard twice, the first time in the brass and then immediately echoed by the tenors and basses. Such sonic repetition was consistent with the visual symbolism of the fair. The countless identical flags, the innumerable adorned Napoléonic crests, as well as the sheer spectacle of mammoth orchestra and chorus seemed to mirror the monumental aesthetic of Napoléon's entry into the hall, in the presence of an endless parade of distinguished guests. So far so good.

Berlioz fashioned the opening moments of *L'Impériale* as a sonic mirror of the Palais de l'Industrie. Robust, resonant, and triumphant, the work's opening section seemed to set the appropriate pace for the closing ceremonies. To clear the air of celebratory noise, Berlioz notates a *tutti* half-note rest following the E-flat cadence at measure 92 (example 2). Here Berlioz overplayed his hand. When the music resumes, the strings play a hushed tremolo C diminished chord, while the chorus chants the text in unison, a passage that Hugh Macdonald has dubbed "abject recitative."⁴⁴ The mood changes from militaristic chest-beating to death and religious transcendence: "Out of the sepulchre emerged/like a Messiah/the imperial dynasty." This subdued choral passage requires attentive listening, not only because of the gravity of the text and the musical setting, but also because the *piano* strings and the chorus's low-register voices would have been difficult to hear in a cavernous space. The intent was to recontextualize the word *impériale* from adjective to noun, from mode of spectacular fanfare to a rite of religious institution. This tremolo moment is relatively short, and the work's final pages are filled with a cacophonous, sevenfold choral repetition of *Vive l'Empereur!* But the imperial commission was clearly unfamiliar with the sudden pause at the end of the exposition, and Berlioz would not reach this triumphant recapitulation. At 12:35 p.m. on the day of the closing ceremony, military drummers in the Palais de l'Industrie announced the approach of the emperor. Berlioz took this as his cue to begin the program. The state procession commenced ten minutes later, when Berlioz had already begun conducting. Spontaneous cheering immediately drowned out the orchestra, which was positioned in such a way that it could not cut through the noise of the crowd. Moreover, the Prince Napoléon had already taken his place by the time the fateful E-flat cadence approached, and he took the half measure of rest as his cue to begin his opening speech. The premiere was halted a third of the way through. Berlioz's paranoia about conducting in an unfinished hall came, in a roundabout way, to fruition. Berlioz recounted this dysfunctional episode in his *Mémoires*:

> I had twelve hundred performers, accommodated in a gallery behind the throne. In this position they made little effect; but in any case music was so unimportant on the day of the ceremony that in the middle of the opening piece (the cantata, *L'Impériale*, which I had written for the occasion) I was interrupted and obliged to stop the orchestra at the most interesting point, because the Prince had to make his speech and the music was going on too long.[45]

The daily press failed to mention the interrupted premiere of Berlioz's *L'Impériale*, and focused instead on the enthusiasm that greeted the arrival of the emperor and his cortège.[46] In a full-page description of the hour preceding the prince's speech, *La Presse* devoted a scant sentence to Berlioz's efforts: "The orchestra played a prelude, and a choir of 500 performers intoned an occasional cantata, Berlioz's *Impériale*."[47] The *Journal des débats* described the music in slightly more favorable terms, but dared not present the afternoon's events as anything less than perfect: "Immediately following the arrival of the imperial party, the orchestra, directed by M. Berlioz, played several pieces of the program that had been made known, and which produced the grandest effect."[48] The "official report" of the ceremony, reprinted verbatim in numerous newspapers and guidebooks, went as far as to provide an alternate reason why Berlioz's cantata was cut short, taking the blame off the Prince Napoléon's premature speech and shifting it to the spectators, who overwhelmed the orchestra with their enthusiasm for the imperial entry.

EXAMPLE 2. Hector Berlioz, *L'Impériale*. "Sudden" choral recitative, measures 94–98.

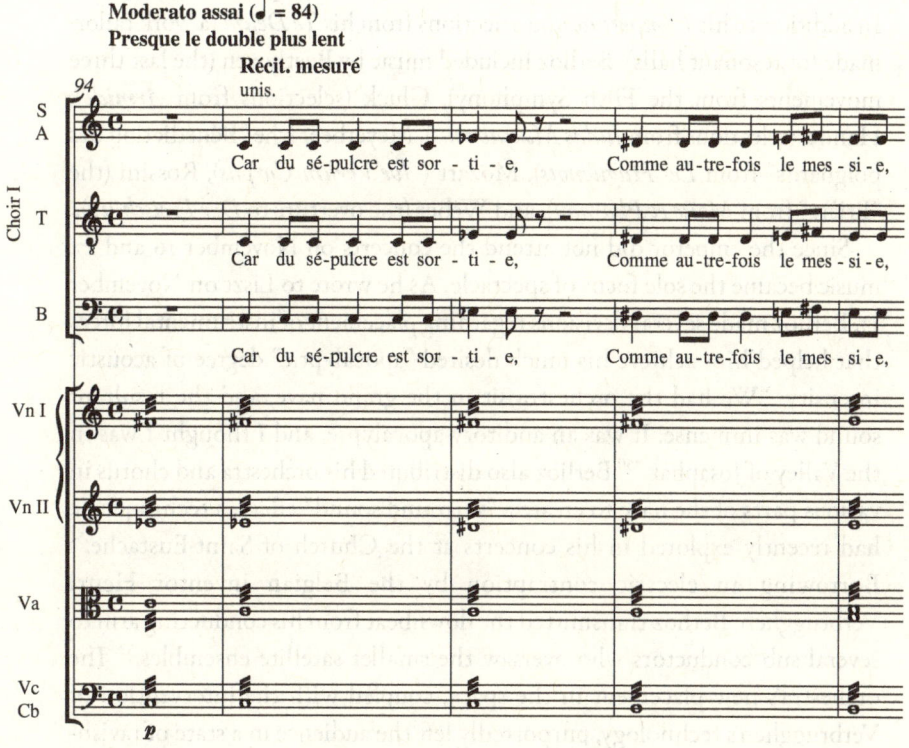

"Upon the entrance of Their Majesties, everyone stood up in one motion," reads the report. "The orchestra played a cantata written for the occasion but the cries of *Long Live the Emperor! Long Live the Empress!* completely covered up the formidable group of musicians, of whom there were at least twelve hundred."[49] This version of the story rather unsubtly downplays the agency of the musicians—neither Berlioz's name nor work is mentioned—and instead depicts the crowd as a unified mass of loyalists. Of course, we cannot reenact the order of events to see who was indeed responsible for disrupting the musical performance. The imperial government, through its control of print media (namely the official newspaper, *Le Moniteur*) presented the "official" timeline to the public, one full of fanfare and devoid of any misfires.

Whether it was interrupted by the prince's voice or drowned out by the crowd's roar, *L'Impériale* had its full premiere at the Palais the following day, when no processions, speeches, or proclamations of imperial allegiance would distract attention. The expanded concert program included stalwart orchestral and choral works that withstood large ensembles and vast performance spaces. In addition to his *L'Impériale* and selections from his *Te Deum* (a work tailor-made for resonant halls), Berlioz included music by Beethoven (the last three movements from the Fifth Symphony), Gluck (selections from *Armide*), Handel (selections from *Judas Maccabaeus*), Meyerbeer (the "Bénédiction des poignards" from *Les Huguenots*), Mozart (*Ave Verum Corpus*), Rossini (the "Prière" from *Moïse et Pharaon*), and Weber (the overture to *Der Freischütz*).

Since the emperor did not attend the concerts on November 16 and 17, music became the sole focus of spectacle. As he wrote to Liszt on November 17, Berlioz made several decisions regarding placement of instrumental forces that helped him achieve his much desired "apocalyptic" degree of acoustic intensity: "We had the orchestra sit in the grand nave, and the resultant sound was immense. It was an auditory apocalypse, and I thought I was in the Valley of Josaphat."[50] Berlioz also distributed his orchestra and chorus in various parts of the nave to create a "surround sound" effect, a technique he had recently explored in his concerts at the Church of Saint-Eustache.[51] Borrowing an electric contraption by the Belgian inventor Henri Verbrugghen, Berlioz transmitted the downbeat from his conducting arm to several sub-conductors who oversaw the smaller satellite ensembles.[52] The orchestra's new placement in the space, coupled with the intervention of Verbrugghen's technology, purportedly left the audience in a state of ravishment; as the *Revue et gazette musicale* reported on November 18, Berlioz's orchestra generated such an imposing effect upon the auditor that it rivaled even the emperor's sublime aura. The music "took its seat like a sovereign, surrounded by the marvels of all the arts and industries, all of which seemed to be there to honor its arrival and triumph."[53] Such futuristic caricatures of the electric metronome exemplified the "industrialization of time and space" that was experienced by Berlioz's contemporaries.[54] When transplanted to a different performance context, *L'Impériale* became immediately legible as a manifestation of industrial modernity.

Had Berlioz truly achieved this level of "sovereignty" with what was otherwise a concert of well-worn, familiar works? Or was this performance just one of many large-scale orchestral and choral concerts whose purpose was to close out the exhibition year in a grand form? The philosopher Umberto Eco wrote that "the basic ideology of an exposition is that the packaging is more important than the product, meaning that the building and the objects in it should communicate the value of a culture, the image of a civilization."[55] Exhibitions, in other words, were designed to display the greatest possible number and diversity of objects, and not to create a space for aesthetic or intellectual contemplation. Despondent, Berlioz indicated a similar sentiment when his work was cut short during an event that uncomfortably blended the attentive listening required of a concert with the noisiness of an imperial cortège.

We can extend the scope of the exhibition gaze beyond the tangible and the visible to include the aural. Canonic musical works, as well as ceremonial cantatas, served primarily to signify a clear, relatable, and unified message of imperial grandeur. Ever critical of Haussmannization, Joseph d'Ortigue questioned the Palais de l'Industrie as a viable performance space, as its massive size could never inspire deep contemplation of musical sound. "It would be difficult to persuade me," he wrote, "that a group of forty, fifty, sixty thousand, or however many the transept of the Palais de l'Industrie could hold, constitutes a real musical audience. It is not as much an audience as it is an assembly of curious spectators."[56] To d'Ortigue, these exhibition concerts were sonic embodiments of the exhibits that lined the walls just weeks before; the music was no match for the fleeting attention span of the Exposition-goers. But the underlying political message of these oversized musical festivals was clear: the largest buildings, the biggest crowds, and the loudest music will always be dwarfed by the monumental presence of the emperor. Berlioz's derailed performance, an ostensibly trivial moment of musical reception history, reveals how the microcosmic world of the Exposition universelle was constructed around a delicate balance of monumentality and contingency, a balance that intended to maintain the exhibition gaze on the emperor. Although, as we shall see, the planning committee of the 1867 Exposition universelle decided to include musical works more directly in the form of an open competition, the call for compositions made it evident that the aim of the contest was to generate pomp and not to produce works to be savored by an audience for their aesthetic merits. Such ceremonial music ultimately assumed a similar role to the one it had assumed in 1855: as an inventory of objects whose purpose was to amplify—but not overshadow—the manufactured spirit of the Second Empire *fête impériale*.

THE IMPERIAL CANTATA COMPETITION (1867)

Although hymns, cantatas, chansons, and musical ephemera populated Paris's streets, cafés, and theaters in 1855, this music appeared independently of the exhibition's ceremonial musical activities. Due to the many French and foreign composers who penned appeals for more representation at the Exposition universelle in 1867, the imperial commission, led by "Plon-Plon" Bonaparte, finally decided to include musical composition along with visual arts as a part of the exhibition of "artisanal work."[57] Special committees oversaw the various musical activities taking place that year. The names of the Comité de la composition musicale, a parade of the French musical elite, were published in newspapers across the country: Gioachino Rossini (honorary president); Daniel François Esprit Auber (president); Hector Berlioz; Michele Carafa; Félicien David; Jean-Georges Kastner; Émile Henry Mellinet; Auguste Mermet; Prince Józef Michał Poniatowski; Napoléon Henri Reber; Ambroise Thomas; Giuseppe Verdi (secretary, and also in town to oversee the Paris premiere of *Don Carlos*); Charles Gounod (secretary); Ernest Lépine (assistant secretary); and Émile Norblin (assistant secretary).[58]

The Comité de la composition musicale decided that there would be a competition for two relatively short compositions for orchestra and voices—a "Hymne de la paix" and a "Cantate de l'exposition," respectively. The winners would have their works performed at the closing ceremonies and would receive an exhibitor's medal and a monetary award. The first step was to solicit texts for these two compositions, which also took the form of two open calls for texts. The *Revue et gazette musicale de Paris* published the announcement on March 17, 1867, with a submission deadline of April 10: "The Exposition cantata will be written for soloists and choirs. The Hymn of Peace will only contain four strophes of at most eight verses each, all rhythmic in the same manner and ending with a masculine rhyme."[59] Newspapers published the results on May 10. The gold medal prize for the "Hymne" text was awarded to two poets: François Coppée, a proponent of the Parnassian school of poetry who wrote about the toils of the working class, and Gustave Chouquet, a music journalist who contributed to *La France musicale, L'Art musical,* and the *Revue et gazette musicale de Paris*. The winning entry for the "Cantate de l'exposition" was "Les Noces de Prométhée" by Romain Cornut *fils*, who was at the time a nineteen-year-old pupil at the Lycée Bonaparte. The title "Hymne de la paix" alludes to the popular imperial motto "The Empire Means Peace," a slogan that Napoléon III repeated during his 1852 victory tour and maintained throughout his reign. As a result, the submissions for "Hymne" texts emphasized ceremony and patriotism. The announcement for a "Cantate de l'Exposition" left no indication as to the type of subject matter sought by the committee, likely because it was intended as the more substantial of the two competition works.

Romain Cornut's poem "Les Noces de Prométhée" struck a balance between Greek mythology and glorification of the regime: the text intersperses moments from the myth of Prometheus, the Greek titan who stole fire from Mount Olympus and gave it to humanity, with direct references to the exhibition, its venues, as well as the country and regime that sponsored it. In a preface to the 1867 published edition, Cornut explains in florid prose how he repurposed the Prometheus myth to match the perceived monumentality of the World's Fair: "But it was not enough to create an infinitesimal reduction of the subject. It needed to be reattached to fit the circumstances of the contest, to fit the splendid and colossal Exposition universelle of 1867, which will remain, despite everything, the most profound celebration that Humanity has ever given itself on this earth, as a most solemn pledge of peace and fraternity of humankind."[60]

Cornut based his retelling of the Prometheus myth on *Prometheus Bound*, the Greek tragedy long attributed to Aeschylus. In it, Prometheus not only steals fire, but also presents humanity with the so-called Catalogue of the Arts, a mystical text that contained information on a variety of subjects such as writing, medicine, mathematics, astronomy, architecture, and agriculture. The part about Zeus punishing Prometheus by having his liver eaten by a vulture is conveniently left out of Cornut's poem. Instead, Cornut connected the 1867 Exposition—and by extension, the emperor—to Prometheus's sacrifice. The "noces" or "marriage" in the poem's title refers to the union of humankind and divinity, with the exhibition hall serving as the chapel.[61] The sixty-four-line poem alternates between abstract meditation and direct allusion to the fair. In the opening lines, Cornut evokes the twin pillars of the World's Fair—art and industry—as byproducts of Prometheus's famous gift to humanity:

> Fire, which made Art and which made Industry,
> Which produced Genius and which produced Love,
> And which, in order to regenerate our withered race,
> Astonished mortals used to make gods in turn.[62]

Fire, of course, signified not only human ability to create materials of art and industry—paper, glass, iron—but also implied that the exhibition was a "gift" to the world:

> The hour of deliverance,
> Dear lover, has sounded.
> Under France's beautiful sky,
> See our union delivered.
> See this palace that stands,
> And the immense riches
> That my love has offered you;
> See all the people gathering
> In their royal pomp,
> For the nuptial celebration.[63]

Although Cornut's "Les Noces de Prométhée" draws on more literary and philosophical subject matter than do the more overtly patriotic "Hymnes de la paix" by Coppée and Chouquet, the language of the poem nonetheless glorifies the nation ["le beau ciel de la France"], the exhibition space ["ce palais"], the exhibition inventory ["cette immense richesse"], as well as the emperor's crown ["pompe royale"]. Cornut thus cast Napoléon III not as a vengeful Zeus but as a Promethean hero, who had not only orchestrated an exhibit on a global scale, but also helped create the economic conditions for Paris to host the event.

MISFIRE 2: SAINT-SAËNS'S *LES NOCES DE PROMÉTHÉE* (1867)

With the competition texts selected and published throughout French newspapers, the Comité de la composition musicale issued the official call for composers, both French and foreign, to submit their entries by June 7. Composers wishing to submit a "Hymne" setting could choose between Chouquet's and Coppée's texts. Entrants were also permitted to submit both a "Hymne" and a "Cantate" setting. Yet it soon became clear that the "Cantate de l'Exposition" was to be the main musical prize. Composers were asked to submit full scores for orchestra, soloists, and chorus. The committee granted artistic freedom by guaranteeing that "every resource necessary for the performance of this important work will be at the disposition of the winner" (as we will see shortly, the committee would rescind this promise).[64] Composers submitting a *Hymne de la paix* were asked to supply a single vocal line of melody. The *Hymne,* the committee made clear, was intended for the massive Orphéon concerts, which emphasized unity, fraternity, and homogeneity; the melody ought to be "rhythmic, bringing together as much as possible qualities that would make the work popular." To remain anonymous, composers identified their scores with epigraphs in the form of a motto or a quote. These epigraphs, along with the full name and address of the competitor, were attached in sealed envelopes.[65]

The competition attracted a diverse pool of applicants, which must have pleased the imperial commission with their calls for universality and inclusion at the 1867 Fair. Entries were submitted from all over France, as well as from cities throughout Europe, including Berlin, Brussels, Bucharest, Florence, Frankfurt, Geneva, Leipzig, Lisbon, London, Madrid, Mannheim, Milan, Naples, Riga, and Warsaw.[66] The male and female entrants spanned a variety of professions outside music: the nonprofessional musicians included teachers, students, bureaucrats, lawyers, retirees, aristocracy, and garrisoned military personnel. Many applicants wrote their epigraphs in languages other than French, and even translated the competition poems into foreign languages. This multilingual strategy was perhaps intended to appease the international exposition committee (although it likely annoyed them). The most commonly used foreign languages were Greek (especially for the epigraph), Latin, English, German, and Dutch. Jules Massenet, for instance, chose a biblical slogan—"Domine salvum fac scriptum!" ("Let it be written!")—as his epigraph for his setting of Chouquet's poem. This diverse range of applicant nationalities, professions, and languages reinforced the pervasive ideology governing the exposition: that the world gathered in Paris to share common achievements in art and industry.

The results of the "Hymne de la paix" competition created a stir. Despite receiving over eight hundred entries, split evenly between settings of Chouquet's and Coppée's texts, the committee did not select a winning composition. No one knew why, as the entire judging process was kept a secret from the press as well as from contestants. Georges Bizet, who submitted an entry using the pseudonym "Gaston de Betsi," wrote to his friend Edmond Galabert about the perplexing and anticlimactic turn of events: "The hymn contest. 823 submissions of the first order. An absent jury. Three members adjudicated, declared that [all entries] are the same. Impossible to discern a prizewinner. Contest canceled!"[67]

The committee did, however, select a winner of the "Cantate" competition: thirty-one-year-old Camille Saint-Saëns. The press was aware of the nationalist stakes; if the jury selected a winner who was not French, then it would be perceived as an embarrassment to the hosts. In a report whose veracity should be taken lightly, Ange-Henri Blaze de Bury reenacted the drama of opening the winning envelope: "Who will be the author? Here emotion overtook the members of the jury; it was not merely curiosity, but a matter of patriotism. After scientific scrutiny, M. Auber smells a German, and his sense of national pride is perturbed. They break the seal, and what a surprise! The work is signed 'Camille Saint-Saëns' and everyone is delighted and astounded."[68] Bizet, who also submitted to the "Cantate" competition, laughed to Galabert about the method that Saint-Saëns may have used to disguise his musical footprint: "Saint-Saëns had written his cantata on *English paper* to disguise his copy, and the gentlemen believed that they awarded the prize to a *foreigner!!!!!!*"[69]

Although the winning cantata was scheduled to premiere during the July 1 prize ceremony, the committee suddenly decided to pull Saint-Saëns's work from the program. In its place, they programmed another work, not by a Frenchman but by an Italian: Rossini's recently completed *Hymne à Napoléon III et à son vaillant peuple* (more on this work shortly). The press reacted to the decision to withdraw the work strongly in the composer's favor.[70] Hippolyte Prévost petitioned on the composer's behalf in *La France,* but Paul Ramond published a heated response in *L'Opinion nationale* that the length of Saint-Saëns's work—an estimated twenty-five minutes—would be too long for the awards ceremony. He added that the many recitatives would be inaudible given the Palais de l'Industrie's cavernous acoustics. In short, Ramond implied that Saint-Saëns's cantata would be ill-suited for the "colossal" dimensions of the Palais, and that it did not conform to the musical characteristics of a work that would thrive in such a large space.

Other journalists blamed the withdrawal of "Les Noces de Prométhée" entirely on the committee's oversight and organizational incompetence. Charles d'Amblie railed against the vague wording of the competition announcement: an "imperial commission" named the jury, but while the identities of the jury were made public, those of this "commission" remained anonymous. Moreover, the announcement mentioned "concerts" in the plural, with no specifics as to the date, venue, or length.[71] J. L. Heugel, writing in *Le Ménestrel,* was suspicious of the jury's decision to rescind their promise to fund the performance of the cantata. As Heugel argued, the committee should have been transparent in their decision-making and Saint-Saëns was justified in protesting the change of agreement. Turning his guns on the committee's chair Auber, Heugel added: "Should we continue to boast that it is a French musician who must suffer in his own homeland because of such inexplicable negligence? If it were a German musician, for example, would all of Germany be unjustified in protesting in front of the entire European musical community?"[72] Saint-Saëns did protest, appealing directly to Pierre Guillaume Frédéric Le Play, the *commisaire générale* of the 1867 Exposition. Le Play corroborated the committee's decision, adding that no additional funds were available to mount a concert at which *Les Noces de Prométhée* could be performed as part of the Exposition's festivities. Saint-Saëns walked away with a consolation check for 2,500 francs and no premiere date.[73]

Was this haphazard, contingent treatment of ceremonial music an echo of 1855? Did the abandonment of the competition's initial aims—to provide new music for the awards ceremony—reflect the imperial commission's indifference toward music and musicians? We may never know the complete reasons why no *Hymne* was chosen despite awarding two prizes for a text. Nor can we conclude why the musical committee ultimately abandoned Saint-Saëns's *Les Noces de Prométhée* —which they allegedly deemed the only "perfect" submission—and replaced the work with one by a committee member and non-Frenchman, Rossini. Reports cited length and acoustics as two reasons. Yet a contradiction arises: on one hand, Saint-Saëns's cantata was too long, too expensive, and too musically complex. On the other hand, certain moments of the work, especially the recitatives, were too intimate for the giant and resonant ceremonial space.

Within this contradiction lies the superficiality of monumentality as an imperial aesthetic. The same mode of urban contingency that governed Haussmann's replanning of the city was also present in how ceremonial sound was manufactured and curated during the 1867 Exposition universelle. Although they differ greatly in their symphonic structure, Berlioz's *L'Impériale* and Saint-Saëns's *Les Noces de Prométhée* both belong to a rather strange subgenre of failed monumental works. But this failure had little to do with the compositional integrity of these works. Rather, the aesthetic categories by which they were judged and received shifted in real time, in a contingent fashion. While the established Berlioz had the privilege of a premiere—albeit an interrupted one—the up-and-coming Saint-Saëns saw his opportunity to shine on the exhibition stage denied for reasons outside of his control. As we will see, *Les Noces de Prométhée* tried to double as a throwaway *pièce d'occasion* and as an attempt at a symphonic representation of sublimity. Musical monumentality—at least of the imperial variety—requires a delicate balance of content and context. The artist must emit enough subjectivity to merit notice but must also serve as a subject to the hegemonic structure that commissions such a display of monumentality. The work's premature cancellation thus presents a case of politics out of balance with aesthetics, a monumentality misunderstood.

Unlike Berlioz's imperial fanfare, the opening of *Les Noces de Prométhée* is contemplative: harps, winds, and brass utter a unison D across four octaves. Prometheus's theme emerges from this delicate orchestral fabric as a unison melody played by the tenor trombones and alto saxophones.[74] The modal flavor of the melody, enforced by the C natural, adds a religious solemnity to the opening moments of the cantata. In this extended opening recitative, Prometheus rejects any notion that his is a voice of fanfare. Alone, he laments his crime and subsequent imprisonment. Yet when he extols the virtues of "divine fire" as originator of art and industry, the key changes from D minor to E flat and the high winds and strings animate the text with arpeggios. The remainder of the opening recitative section—the first five pages of the full score—unfold in a similar fashion to the first page, with the stoic modal theme reappearing in the trombones and saxophones and with Prometheus bemoaning his fate in a low baritone register.

A key shift to D major initiates the second part of Cornut's narrative, in which the allegorical character of Humanity receives Prometheus's gift of fire and unchains him using the trifecta of art, industry, and human love. After the character of Humanity extols France's "beautiful skies," she sings an expansive, arioso-like melody and even elongates the phrase "immense richesse," as if the soloist were praising the exhibits in the Palais through text painting. An eight-part chorus echoes Humanity's arioso with a homophonic ode to peace and liberty, but then shifts into a quasi-fugal passage sung a capella: perhaps a dubious choice of texture given the Palais de l'Industrie's infamously poor acoustics. The most direct evocation of the Palais de l'Industrie occurs during the "Chant de Prométhée," the moment when Prometheus is unshackled by Humanity and witnesses the fruits of his sacrifice (example 3). This is a moment of transfiguration. Prometheus asks where he is being carried off and subsequently finds himself awestruck by the architecture and by the treasures surrounding him: indeed, a moment of sublime aesthetic experience.

> Superb porticos,
> Your magical splendors
> Enchant my eyes;
> All is a surprise
> Charm, desire, For my joyous senses.[75]

EXAMPLE 3. Camille Saint-Saëns, *Les Noces de Prométhée*. Prometheus's arrival to the Palace, rehearsal N.

Saint-Saëns approaches this moment of transport via a change in tonality from D-flat major—functioning as a Neapolitan chord within the C-major key—to B-flat. Shimmering arpeggios from the *divisi* harps create a sense of cosmic travel; indeed, this is the first sense of musical momentum in the cantata. Two measures of low Fs in the tympani mark an end to the journey: as Prometheus arrives in the palace, the harps strum a rigid, march-like tune, a stark contrast to the heavenly passage heard moments ago. High in the baritone register, he expresses his surprise at the "magical" effect of his surroundings on his senses. Having spent the first part of the cantata in a state of contemplation, Prometheus finally turns his gaze to the exhibition.

It is not until the last section of the work—approximately fifteen minutes in—that the chorus sings an extended musical passage. The chorus recapitulates the rising sixth "redemption" melody heard earlier in the orchestra and, in a painfully slow tempo, concludes the work with praise of human glory, peace, and liberty. But was this final choral explosion too little, too late? According to the committee's spokesperson Ramond, the work's opening lacked the bombast that was expected of festive *pièces d'occasion*. The bulk of the text, a philosophical story of enslavement and redemption, seemed to lack the anticipated energetic, patriotic, repetitive message typical of such works. Moreover, the work rejected the communicative functionality of monumental fanfare, drawing instead on an introverted aesthetics of program music. Instead of a "musical offering," Saint-Saëns penned a solemn, poetic opening to a work that reframed the commodities of the Exposition universelle as products of sacrifice and hardship: themes hardly appropriate for lavish festivities. The extended recitative, the contrapuntal writing, and the sudden modulations were perceived as incongruent with the monumental dimensions of the Palais. After all, as we have seen, the space was not designed with contemplative musical performances in mind, but rather with the intention of easily being converted from an exhibition space to a site of imperial ceremony and pomp.

Saint-Saëns would have to wait until September 1, 1867, to conduct the premiere of *Les Noces de Prométhée,* during an impromptu concert of the composer's works at the Cirque Olympique. The concert, funded independently by Saint-Saëns, featured an ambitious program of the composer's own works, including the famous *Introduction et rondo capriccioso* op. 28 (with Pablo de Sarasate as soloist) and a now-obscure youthful work, an unpublished and unnumbered "Symphony in D," which by all accounts remained incomplete but was nonetheless praised. But even within the context of a composer's concert, where the artist himself was the main attraction, the most sympathetic critics seemed to agree that the work, through brilliant, did not fit the template of a monumental *pièce d'occasion* compatible with what was needed at the fair. Heugel blamed not the work but rather the intended performance space: the giant dimensions of the Palais de l'Industrie dwarfed many orchestral and choral works that would otherwise sound imposing in smaller venues. Indeed, Heugel noted that Saint-Saëns "doubled" and even "tripled" the effect of the cantata when it was finally premiered at the Cirque.[76]

Perhaps the most convincing reason why Rossini's *Hymne* eventually replaced *Les Noces de Prométhée* had to do with the political context of the ceremony. Critics present at the eventual premiere of Saint-Saëns's cantata remarked on the transformative experience the work had on its audience; as Hippolyte Prévost recalled in *La France,* "The public, transported by those luminous harmonies, entered directly into the composer's heart."[77] Yet this characterization of sublimity was a primary reason why it was pulled from the ceremony program. As I have argued in this chapter, a successful nineteenth-century exhibition cantata was functional, and as such, it had to amplify the grandeur of a ceremony, not overshadow it. In other words, *Les Noces de Prométhée* failed as fanfare precisely because it tried too hard to evoke a sublime experience in its listeners. In doing so, it would have refracted attention from the ceremonial figurehead—the emperor—and amplified the image of the young composer as transfigurative, romantic artist.

ITALIANATE *FÊTE IMPÉRIALE*

The work that replaced Saint-Saëns's cantata presents a notably different interpretation of sonic monumentality. There is nothing subtle about Rossini's *Hymne à Napoléon III et à son vaillant peuple,* scored for solo baritone, mixed chorus, orchestra, military band, and a percussion battery that includes cannon and bells. Lasting about eight and a half minutes, it sets a straightforward patriotic text by the Franco-Italian librettist Émilien Pacini.[78] His forty-five-line poem, which Comettant described as "overly bellicose," consists of a series of appeals to God for strength on the battlefield on behalf of the people of France. Written entirely in the second person, the *Hymne* is more a *prière* that calls for the emperor to act as interlocutor between heaven and the French soil. Rossini's work, like the unawarded "Hymne de la paix" prize, amplified Napoléon III's slogan "The Empire Means Peace," which implied that celebrations of world peace necessarily involve celebrations of imperial war. The optimistic lines that conclude the poem suggest that the purpose of the *Hymne à Napoléon III* was not to inspire contemplation, but to invoke patriotism: "Holy Father,/Arts, industry,/ To your genius/ All give honor./ Long Live the Emperor!"[79]

In stark contrast to the slow development of *Les Noces de Prométhée,* Rossini's *Hymne à Napoléon III* is episodic fanfare, consisting of brisk, militaristic passages alternating with a more subdued hymn-like setting.[80] At the onset, an offstage military band introduces two recurring musical ideas: the first, a dotted eighth-note rhythmic motive, and the second, a bouncy

EXAMPLE 4. Gioachino Rossini, *Hymne à Napoléon III et à son vaillant peuple*. "Buffo" theme played by offstage military band, measures 13–24.

"Rossinian" wind melody (example 4). Following this military band introduction, a baritone soloist and supporting chorus proclaim the sanctity of the French state. Mirroring Pacini's terse, staccato prosody, Rossini composes the melody as a series of three-measure phrases. Comettant showered the music and its composer with praise: "Never has a melody more simple, more sincere, more natural, more characteristic, and more original fallen out of the pen that wrote *Moïse, Semiramis, Le Siège de Corinthe,* and *Guillaume Tell.*"[81] The *alternatim* presentation of this melody produces a call-and-response effect, as if the seated audience should join the chorus in echoing the soloist's line. Moreover, the baritone's music is built around an insistent repetition of the aforementioned dotted rhythm. This rhythmic sameness, along with the easily digestible F major melody, suggests an aesthetic diametrically opposed to that employed by Saint-Saëns: a total lack of pretention on the part of the composer, and a careful simplification of musical material that would permit any layperson to sing along. Paraphrasing Comettant, Rossini managed to pen a melody that was at once honest and grandiose, the sonic equivalent of a dignitary blending in with the crowd.

With the benedictions and supplications out of the way, Rossini returns to the military band music that opened the *Hymne à Napoléon III*, as Pacini's text changes tone from religious prayer to military ode. A chorus of *vivandières* (military women who distributed canteens) is soon joined by the male chorus members who are named *soldats* and *grands prêtres* in the score.

As Comettant noted, this section seemed tailor-made to the acoustics of the Palais de l'Industrie and complemented the expansive grandeur of the avenue des Champs-Élysées, where the Palais stood: "This movement may seem vulgar if performed in a hall of ordinary dimensions by a small number of musicians. But it seemed perfectly appropriate in the immense Palais des Champs-Élysées, and it was even made to sound noble by the large mass of performers."[82] One month later, the *Hymne à Napoléon III* would be performed at the Opéra during the August 15 Saint-Napoléon festivities—presumably yielding the same effect.

Rossini's score takes no more harmonic risks beyond this double chorus. In a strikingly direct communicative gesture, the baritone adumbrates the bombastic finale through an emphatic appeal to "stand up!" (*Relevez-vous!*) The proclamation directs the soldiers' chorus to take up the main *buffo* tune in a rousing recapitulation, a gesture that one could easily see on an opera stage. The *Hymne*'s coda bears a not-so-subtle resemblance to the finale of Berlioz's *L'Impériale*. The chorus sings *Vive l'Empereur* five times, yet another performative gesture that invited the now-electrified Palais audience to join in the chant. Yet Rossini does Berlioz one better, concluding the *Hymne* with a cacophonous blast of bells and cannons, a bombastic orchestral finale that anticipates Tchaikovsky's *1812 Overture* by thirteen years. Rossini biographers have (perhaps rightly) not taken Rossini's imperial ode too seriously; Rossini himself joked that he conceived the work not for Paris but for Passy, his suburban home, where it was to be premiered among friends before its "official" debut in the Palais. Indeed, Richard Osborne observes that the work seems to parody its own grandiose effects.[83] But inside the Palais, those effects were sensational. The *Journal des débats* remarked that "the cannon fire and the bells, which concluded the work in truly original fashion," were greeted "with the liveliest applause."[84] The most successful aspect of the *Hymne à Napoléon III* was its militant "noisiness": the cannons, the bells, and not least, the roar of applause that blurred the line between the double bar and the rest of the festivities.

Rossini knew his intended audience. As Pierre Véron observed in *Le Monde illustré*, "By attributing to himself words he had never before uttered, the master wanted to make them sound authentic. He showed spirit, of that there is no doubt, but the spirit was his own; so, he tried to *parisianize* it."[85] Rossini's and Saint-Saëns's exhibition pieces could not have been more disparate in style, duration, and attitude. Whereas Saint-Saëns composed a work whose text and setting required attentive listening, Rossini offered a showpiece that drew attention to its effects on the audience, and not to itself.

FIGURE 3. Closing ceremonies of the 1867 Exposition universelle. Lithograph by Cosson, Smeeton, & Best. Image: Musée Carnavalet.

As was the case in 1855, the 1867 awards ceremony was ultimately an exercise in imperial spectacle that valued size and scope over content.[86] The twenty-five thousand spectators who crowded into the Palais de l'Industrie on July 1, observed Comettant in *Le Ménestrel,* represented the highest caliber of lavish couture: "Nothing but flowers, ribbons, silk, lace, gold, and diamonds from the impoverished to the most affluent of our species!"[87] E. Bauer of *La Presse* portrayed Paris's inhabitants and visitors as a mob of spectators eager to catch a glimpse of the imperial cortège and who, in the process, emitted an overwhelming collective noise: "Whichever way you look, on the rue de Rivoli, on the rue de Faubourg Saint-Honoré, on the place de la Concorde, on the docks, on the bridges, in the Jardin des Tuileries, on the avenue des Champs-Elysées, all the way to the Arc de Triomphe, you see the rolling waves of a human sea, from which arose an immense noise."[88]

Whereas Bauer focused on how the *fête impériale* pervaded the city's landmarks and liminal spaces as well as its outdoor soundscape, other journalists reported on the "human sea" within the exhibition grounds. Press illustrations captured this sense of the monumental; in numerous lithographs, spectators, military, musicians, and awardees fill the Palais to its seams, dwarfed only by the emperor's throne (figure 3). This immensely detailed illustration demonstrates how the exhibition gaze rendered the individual anonymous. No single human body is distinguishable from the other, and yet the near-uniform direction of their bodies draws the eye to a point just off the page, presumably where the emperor would make his grand entrance. Of the three works discussed in this chapter, only Rossini's succeeded in rendering this type of imagery through sound. His score did not impose individuality, but rather gestured to it, supported by the contextual fact that he, through Italian, was an elder statesman of French music in 1867. Berlioz, having had his attempt at generating exhibition fanfare in 1855, was now a delegate and a commentator and remained conspicuously silent. The daily newspapers covering the ceremonies left little room to deify the artists who created the conditions for celebratory pomp. Instead, they focused on the emperor.

THE EMPEROR'S SPEECH

Napoléon's closing speech made several front pages, including *Le Constitutional* and *Le Figaro*. The emperor opened with the expected rhetorical fanfare, announcing 1867 as the sequel to 1855 and drawing ties between empire, industry, and moral uprightness: "After an interval of twelve years, I come before you for a second time to distribute awards to those who most distinguished themselves in their respective craft, and whose work enriches nations, improves our lives, and softens our spirits."[89] Napoléon's rhetoric soon shifted to historical context. Despite his investment in modernizing the city, Napoléon had eyes for the past, whether it was expanding the architectural monumentality of his uncle's city projects or promoting a distinctive "Second Empire" architectural style that blended neoclassical and Italianate elements. In promoting the exhibition, however, Napoléon went further back in time, drawing on Greek antiquity and its competitive spirit in showcasing artisan work: "The poets of antiquity brilliantly celebrated those solemn games where the different peoples of Greece came to compete for prizes. What would they say today if they attended these modern global Olympic games, where the world's people, fighting with their intelligence, pursue an infinite path of progress, toward a distant ideal, without ever being able to reach it?"

Historians have explored the connections between musical culture, Third Republic politics, and an increased fascination with Greco-Roman society at the *fin de siècle*. French archaeologists in Delphi discovered an ancient Greek "Hymn to Apollo" in 1893, which advanced the prevalent notion that Third Republic France was the product of assimilation between Greco-Roman and Gallic traditions.[90] A year later, the Baron Pierre de Coubertin founded the Comité international olympique, leading to the first modern Olympic Games in Athens in 1896. Napoléon's statements show how the Second Empire was fixated on the imagined aesthetic and economic majesties of Greco-Roman antiquity, and how notions of classical beauty informed not only cultural politics of the Belle Époque but also the *fête impériale* that predated it. In his closing speech, Napoléon not only evoked Greece to promote the type of meritocratic modernity that enriched his confidants while driving the poor from the city center, but he also foreshadowed the massive-budget ceremonies that would define the Olympic Games for the next century. It is thus doubly surprising that the emperor himself would not have intervened on Saint-Saëns's behalf to see and hear himself staged as a metaphorical Prometheus gifting the treasures of the ancient world to a modern imperial economy.

Reporters who commented on the emperor's speech did so with unbridled praise, not so much of what he said but of how he said it. With the entire transcription of the speech readily available for readers, the press focused instead on recounting the sensory experience of the ceremony. Far from obscuring the emperor's voice, the Palais's cavernous acoustics cooperated with it, amplifying it and rendering his diction faultless. The Bonapartist daily *Le Constitutionnel* was particularly sycophantic; Paulin Limayrac gushed that "the entire audience was under the spell of his eloquence," and that the emperor touched on a range of topical tonalities, from facts about the exhibition to "the highest regions of politics and philosophy."[91] Boniface Demaret echoed these sentiments, suggesting that non-Francophones would still understand the message thanks to the emperor's command of tone and timbre: "The emperor enunciated his speech with a full and sonorous voice, which allowed him to be heard in every part of the edifice."[92] *Le Figaro* added that every line of Napoléon's speech was greeted with thunderous applause, but reinforced the fact that the emperor's "crisp, clear, and powerful voice" allowed the speech to be heard throughout the Palais.[93]

By praising form, content, and delivery, the press equated the empire's rhetorical power with its classicist vocal grain. Vocal clarity denoted comprehension and confidence, but it also connoted order and longevity. As we have seen, the acoustics of the Palais de l'Industrie had been a problem since 1855. The care with which Haussmann and the exhibition commission presented

Paris as a visual signifier of modernity and classical order seemed missing in the realm of sound. Thus the desire for sensory control—through not only curating the musical fanfare but also controlling the narrative of the event—manifested itself to varying degrees of success during the closing ceremonies of the 1867 Exhibition. The apparent disconnect between pulling Saint-Saëns's *Les Noces de Prométhée* on the grounds of acoustics—as compared to the apparent sonic effectiveness of Rossini's *Hymne à Napoléon III* and the emperor's own speech—reveals the extent of the Second Empire's desire to control sensory experience in the city, even if it meant bending their own rules. Framed as a microcosm of Paris—and, thus, the world—the Palais de l'Industrie was the echo chamber of imperial fanfare. Inside the Palais, as elsewhere in the city, an imagined, curated utopia—the one presented in newspapers and subsequent reports—was layered atop a lived reality of contingent policymaking and a misunderstanding of exactly what type of incidental music was necessary. Imperial monumentality was thus a balancing act between superficial displays of sublimity and improvised efforts to maintain the gaze and ear on the center of power.

"World's Fairs," writes the anthropologist Burton Benedict, "presented a sanitizing view of the world with no poverty, no war, no social problems and very little nature."[94] Put another way, those problems were concealed behind symbols, both physical and bureaucratic, seen and heard. The celebratory cantata, promoted as the main event, functioned as a sonic curtain, a fanfare that announced the empire's monumentality without giving up control over the sensory experience of the moment. Artists like Berlioz in 1855 and Saint-Saëns in 1867 faced embarrassment because they misread those symbols, or because their vision did not conform to the closed-door plans of imperial commissions. This contingent approach to visual and aural symbolism governed not only the ceremonies around the 1855 and 1867 exhibitions, but also informed the broader approach to urban planning between those pivotal years of the empire. Whereas the boulevard and the Haussmannian apartment building were symbols of a utopian vision of urban design—clean, expansive, homogenous, redolent of classical, formal beauty—the Expositions universelles represented the extent to which ceremonial sound formed a part of that master plan. Within the halls of the Palais de l'Industrie, the empire thus staged a utopian vision of the cosmopolitan city, in which military fanfare, cannon fire, and chants of *Vive l'Empereur* developed into a soundtrack for the empire.

As we will see in the next chapter, the influx of international crowds to Paris presented opportunities for those outside the empire's circle to forge new leisure spaces free of the contingent, and at times haphazard, rules of imperial fanfare. If the Expositions universelles were Haussmannian utopian master plans in miniature, and if operetta provided what Walter Benjamin called "the ironic utopia of the enduring reign of capital," then another dominant Second Empire institution—the café-concert—provided lessons for an alternate mode of urbanism: one that privileged a culture of participation over a society of spectacle.[95]

THREE

Urban Planning Lessons from the Café-Concert

IN EARLY 1867, PARIS was preparing to become, once again, an exhibition city. In a matter of months, crowds would swarm the monumental Champ de Mars and enjoy the latest innovations in technology, agriculture, and fine art. As we have seen in the previous chapter, the Expositions universelles also showcased the latest in Haussmannian urban planning, both in what was new and what was destroyed. Projects that had been construction zones in 1855 were now a regular part of the Parisian landscape. In 1862, the old theatrical district along the boulevard du Temple was razed to expand the boulevard Prince-Eugène. While some of the smaller theaters along the so-called "boulevard du Crime" never reemerged, others, like the prestigious Théâtre Lyrique, were rebuilt closer to the center of the Right Bank.

Having been moved off the demolished boulevard du Temple in the east and closer to the Châtelet, the Théâtre Lyrique could now charge a premium as a centrally located venue. The increasing cultural rift between center and periphery marked a shift in theater demographics from a more modest audience base to a more affluent one willing to pay higher ticket prices.[1] A byproduct of this urban geopolitics was a geopolitics of genre. Performance spaces in the city's refurbished Right Bank catered to an audience who expected performances on a par with the grandiosity of the Opéra, the Comédie-Française, and the Expositions universelles—and by extension, on a par with the monumentality of the city plan.

One emergent institution resisted some of the compartmentalization taking hold in the theater industry: the café-concert. Part tavern, part theater, the café-concert (also known as *café-chantant* or abbreviated as the familial caf-conç) quickly became a year-round staple of the entertainment sector over the course of the Second Empire. Cafés-concerts were the epicenter of

Parisian popular culture, bringing together song, drink, and unpretentious socialization. These establishments were everywhere: between 1860 and 1890, 37 percent (approximately 121) of cafés-concerts were situated in the ninth, tenth, and eleventh arrondissements; about a quarter were in the third, fourth, fifth, and eighteenth; and the remaining 38 percent were scattered throughout Paris.[2] Proposals to open cafés-concerts flooded the theater division of the Ministère de la Maison de l'Empereur et des Beaux-Arts, suggesting that there were far more café-concert concepts rejected than approved.[3] One reason for this burgeoning interest in opening cafés-concerts was the relatively modest resources needed; venues were by and large renovated rather than erected, and all that was needed inside was a bar, movable tables and chairs, and a modest stage. This type of performance setup was extraordinarily mobile: one proposal offered to open a café-concert *beneath* the famed Pont Neuf.

Another reason was the uniqueness of the concept, which flanked the worlds of the theater and the tavern. Admission was free, but customers were required to buy a drink and refill it regularly. Patrons were also free to roam about during song sets, talk openly, sneak backstage to flirt with performers, and enter and exit as they pleased. The thin film between street and venue not only created pedestrian congestion but also upended the perceived sociospatial divide between the public proletarian and the private bourgeois. In response to the urbanization of the Château d'Eau quarter (present-day tenth arrondissement), an 1855 petition blamed the café-concert for this sociospatial transgression: "... [A] *café-concert* with a sordid strip of canvas for a door and where there is a side-show of giants, a public dance hall of the lowest type with broken-down walls which looks unbelievably dreadful and about to collapse on all sides.... This state of affairs, which has been disgracing the quarter for more than seven years, *encourages immorality and endangers security.*"[4] This model of porous socialization—in which patrons move in and out of performance spaces—was a stark contrast to the regulated theaters, which required spectators to navigate a series of vestibules, staircases, and boxes in order to ensure complete separation between the stage and the street. In the 1850s, private investors dumped large sums of money into larger café-concert venues on the Right Bank, like the Alcazar lyrique, Bataclan, and Cheval Blanc, thereby creating a disparity in quality between lavish establishments located in the center of Haussmann's Paris and shabbier ones modeled after drinking establishments known as *guinguettes* located in the peripheries, like Belleville's Grand Café-concert de Calliope. Here, terminology matters. Placemaking words like *faubourg, quartier, banlieue,* and indeed, *goguette* and *guinguette,* had long been used in nineteenth-century literature to reinforce distinctions of wealthy/poor, native/foreigner, and center/periphery. These binaries, however, were often intertwined; a poor *guinguette* in the *banlieue* could be a second home to foreign-born or provincial workers who were priced out of the wealthier Parisian center. The catchall "café," then, was a purposeful word choice, as critics could lump all of Paris's lowbrow or "foreign" cultural activities into a single concept. "What does Paris have more of than cafés?" asked the 1861 guidebook *Paris et sa splendeur.* "Nothing, except the pavement of the streets. In popular neighborhoods, it is difficult to take twenty steps without encountering one."[5]

This chapter argues that the monumental aesthetics of Haussmannization did not entirely agree with the porous aesthetics of the café-concert. The latter's spontaneity and democratized openness ran counter to Haussmann's efforts to compartmentalize, taxonomize, and sanitize the city plan. If the city's government-sanctioned *grands théâtres* were defined by the ancient Greek notion of *logos,* the curated delivery of the written word, then the café-concert offered *pathos,* a more direct, embodied experience of the spoken, improvised word. Even operetta, an institution synonymous with Second Empire pleasure, was in no small part tethered to the tradition of French dramatic comedy dating back to the eighteenth century, in which the audience, though bent over in laughter, did so from their seats.[6] Born out of a republican-inspired "democratic egalitarianism," the café-concert celebrated visceral pleasures, and it was this body-over-mind sensibility that led many critics to judge its offerings inferior to those of the state-subsidized theaters.[7] While cafés-concerts did flourish amid Haussmannization, they by no means embodied Haussmann's urban aesthetics (as explained in chapter 1). Just as debates about Haussmannization reveal tensions between modern and classical forms of urbanism, so too did the café-concert industry betray an uncertainty about how old modes of theatrical fanfare could coexist with the new.

The Parisian café-concert was ubiquitous, but it was not homogeneous. While most were small, smoky taverns that sat dozens, some were built to rival the city's *grands théâtres.* One such café-concert, and one of the most prestigious popular venues in Second Empire Paris, was the Eldorado, located at 4, boulevard de Strasbourg, a twenty-minute walk from the Châtelet. In the late 1850s the architect Charles Duval marshalled a total budget of almost 600,000 francs to design a gilded edifice to suit its name. Dwarfing the typical intimate café-concert, the Eldorado stood on a 23- by 35-meter rectangular parcel facing the recently refurbished boulevard de Strasbourg.[8] A portico lined with double columns framed the entrance to a large vestibule with chandeliers, statues, bas-reliefs, and fountains, which would serve as the main lobby and dining area. Beyond the vestibule was the main performance area: an auditorium of marble tables and café chairs that could seat fifteen hundred, a staggering number for a "café." Balconies, galleries, and an orchestra pit that housed twenty-five staff musicians rounded out the hall.[9] Using language redolent of the Expositions universelles, journalists commented on the "monumentality" of the venue, both in terms of its size and in terms of its lavish, neoclassical décor. One writer noted that the Eldorado building had "veritable importance, like a work of art."[10] Yet despite its prime geographic location at the heart of the Right Bank, its vast dimensions, and its opulent décor, "L'Eldo" fell on hard times soon after opening in 1858. Patrons, accustomed to the intimate spaces and relative anonymity of the city's cafés-concerts, turned elsewhere. The venue's fortunes turned when Charles Joseph Éleazar Lorge, a financial impresario, purchased the Eldorado in 1861 from its previous proprietors, Lecharpentier and Dubos, and improved the venue's furniture and beverage offerings. According to published records of the sale, Lorge was to uphold the strict ontological stipulation that a café-concert was in no way a *théâtre*. As a journalist reflected in 1860, "considering that if the café-concert presents certain similarities and analogies to actual theater, and if the law has assimilated them in certain respects (concerning police measures and collection of royalties), it is incontestable that these are two distinct industries and that they cannot be confused."[11] While the Eldorado is remembered today alongside the Alcazar as the café-concert *par excellence*, its identity was unclear from the outset. If it was a café, then why was it built like a theater? And if it was a theater, then why did it offer café-style entertainment?

A night at a café-concert was more a boisterous gathering than a curated spectacle. Nightly shows blended singing, joking, and crowd interaction. Although advertisements specified hours—typically from seven to eleven in the evening—shows did not begin and end with clocklike rigidity, but rather extended through the afternoon and evening in a quasi-cyclical fashion, with singers taking turns doing sets and patrons coming and going as they pleased. Sound—we can only imagine—was omnidirectional and unpredictable. Broken glass, clanging silverware, ambient street noise, songs both sung and spoken, cheers, whistles, a pit orchestra (or pit pianist) executing a revolving door of repertoire: the caf-conç did not so much blare a unified fanfare for a city as much as it presented it *à la carte.*

The ambient sound worlds of cafés-concerts call into question the extent to which Haussmannization touched every aspect of Parisian social life. There was a conspicuous parallel between the geographic and generic rules omnipresent in the city performance spaces, and how the city itself was being designed as both a space of movement and as an art object. Haussmann designed what Richard Sennett would call a "closed city" plan—sharp edges, defined boundaries, and with an emphasis on mass mobility. To illustrate the inefficacy of closed planning to level the playing field for all, Sennett compares Haussmannization to the crinoline skirt popular at the time: "The economic ecology of [Haussmann's] new city resembled soiled underwear beneath a ball gown."[12] One way to interpret Sennett's colorful analogy is to equate "soiled underwear" with "spoiled revolutionary sentiment." Haussmann's obsession with cleaning up the city was part of the urbanistic campaign to prevent easy barricading in the street, and therefore to transform Paris into a panopticon, albeit an aesthetically pleasing one. The grid pattern of crinoline, a symbol of both uncompromising gender standards and bourgeois pleasure, saw its parallel in the symmetrical lace of the refurbished boulevards.

Whereas crinoline and the *grands boulevards* presented model of geometric and social rigidity, the café-concert espoused openness—open doors, no tickets, mobile tables and chairs, and an open flow between musical and gastronomic spaces. Singers and patrons were not rooted to their respective designated positions, the stage and the seat. Instead, they interacted with one another, shuttling between the stage, house, and sidewalk (in café-concert slang, the stage was known as a *tremplin,* or "diving board"). The musical offerings were open-ended, as well; a typical café-concert evening circa 1860 would feature *chansonnettes* (songs for one voice), romances (songs for one to two voices), dancing, the occasional opera aria, a *saynète* (a long-form duet interspersed with spoken dialogue), as well as non-musical acts like patriotic poems, acrobatics, and juggling. The diverse programming matched the diverse ways that patrons could engage with the performance space. An 1866 description of a typical evening, vividly written in the second person, helps brings this sense of audience freedom to life: "You toss and turn in your seat, you relax, you sit with your face, profile, or back to the stage, you chat, you drink, you smoke, you read, you are attentive or distracted, happy or sad, without anyone saying anything to you."[13] Café directors sketched the evening's setlists on placards and placed them to the side of the stage, a stark contrast to the fixed, publicized repertoire of opera and operetta theaters. The frequent changes in repertoire and personnel added to the identity of the café-concert as a cultural palimpsest, where every visit would yield a different audiovisual experience. (I will say more about the song repertoire in the following chapter). Cafés-concerts did not need hired *claqueurs* to generate the illusion of an ovation; audience members engaged directly with the singers, speaking to them, catcalling them, even whistling at them; members of the Jockey-Club, the group infamous for disrupting the 1861 premiere of Wagner's *Tannhäuser*, were regulars at the Eldorado. Singers spoke back from the stage, regularly breaking the fourth wall. Borrowing heavily from the traditions of the *goguette* and *comédie-vaudeville*, the café-concert offered a front-row seat to the ebb and flow of republican and imperial ideologies in the city, reflecting the musical and cultural preoccupations of a half-century's worth of Parisian society.

HISTORICIZING THE CAFÉ-CONCERT

Despite its prevalence in mid-nineteenth-century urban life, the café-concert remains vastly underrepresented in contemporary music histories of the period. It is often folded into blanket histories of Second Empire leisure, without even a clear distinction between the cultures of café-concert and those of operetta.[14] As William Weber writes, one area of nineteenth-century musical practice that has received little attention is "the fabric of casual social life, the daily come-and-go in parks, cafés, home gatherings, and the various entertainment worlds."[15] Where Weber sees social life as a "fabric," Derek Scott sees in the café-concert "new and expanding networks of stage managers, lighting experts, venue managers, poster designers, and so forth," a list that would also include ushers, waiters, cooks, cleaners, and of course, the musicians. These social "fabrics" and "networks" present teaching moments for those who wish to decenter the musico-historical narrative from the rhetoric of greatness, exceptionalism, and privilege. Yet Anglophone textbook histories spend little to no time on the café-concert, even as music history's pedagogical ambitions increasingly emphasize the cultural and aesthetic importance of popular music that predates recording technology. Norton's *History of Western Music* featured Edgar Degas's 1877 *Le Café-concert aux Ambassadeurs* on the cover of its eighth edition (figure 4). Degas's pastel image depicts a busy night by striating three social communities across

FIGURE 4. Edgar Degas, *Le Café-concert aux Ambassadeurs*, 1876–77. Image: Musée des Beaux-Arts de Lyon.

a colorful, almost two-dimensional plane: a bourgeois audience, outfitted with gaudy eveningwear and hats; the pit orchestra, crowded between the stage and the hall; and the onstage bodies, who include the red-dressed soloist but also a coterie of audience members who are both spectators and spectacle. Degas plays with perspective by blurring the space between audience and orchestra. Is a musician wearing the top hat in the center-left, or a stray audience member? Who exactly is playing the trumpet in the bottom center? Is the woman's blue bonnet also the contrabass player's sleeve? Greenery frames the canvas, suggesting that the performance is partially out of doors. The illuminated soloist suggests the abundance of street lighting in the city. In short, Degas's *Le Café-concert aux Ambassadeurs*—though composed shortly after the café-concert heyday that is the focus of this chapter—reveals much about how popular culture was consumed in the French capital.

Despite the painting's colorful musicality, the Norton *History* devotes a mere sentence to the café-concert, mentioning it in a paragraph with operetta, cabaret and the *revue*—omitting the generic and architectural differences between the three institutions.[16] Carl Dahlhaus does not mention the café-concert at all in his influential *Nineteenth-Century Music*. Nor does Richard Taruskin in his *Oxford History of Western Music*. Nor does Walter Frisch in his *Music of the Nineteenth Century*. I cite these omissions not to criticize the authors and editors—any comprehensive history must omit more than it includes—but rather to highlight the opportunity to pursue multivalent research into nineteenth-century popular music industries, especially in connection with urban policy. As will become clear, the café-concert faced bureaucratic and aesthetic pressures that theaters devoted to operetta did not have to deal with. Whereas operetta fit snugly into the existing laws and regulations surrounding theatrical production and performance, cafés-concerts, with their diverse programming, rotating rosters, and hybrid architecture, resisted the "master plan" of Haussmannization. As a consequence of Western music history's emphasis on the serious and the victorious, the café-concert slid into historiographical anonymity and from there, into oblivion.

The lived realities of cities often contradict their master plans. So too do a city's leisure spaces resist homogenization. One reason for this, as this book shows, is the relative inaccessibility to those lived experiences from a historiographical perspective, as opposed to the wealth of source material detailing urban social life from a bird's eye view. In his influential work on sound and political economy, Jacques Attali frames the caf-conç phenomenon in pernicious terms, attributing the institution to the bourgeois "confinement" to for-profit spaces and the consequential disappearance of the street music tradition. This claim is overstated; as we will see in chapters 4 and 5, street music was pervasive in Paris through the end of the century, although various bureaucratic measures, such as licensing, zoning, and policing, tempered the ability of its practitioners to move freely in the city. Of course, one of Attali's ambitions in *Noise: A Political Economy of Music* was to trace the preconditions of nineteenth-century popular music's "entry into the commodity market and competition."[17] While this entry did eventually happen, Attali pins the commodification of musical experience to the institution of the café-concert, rather than on the systemic efforts of Napoleonic/Haussmannian policy in the 1860s to engineer an ordered metropolis that balanced imperial authoritarianism and classical liberalism. Indeed, Attali's specific discussion of the café-concert jumps from 1850, when "the caf-conç seemed to multiply," to 1870, when the multitude of cafés-concerts in the city closed the "trap of commercial selection ... tightly on popular music."[18] What is missing is the acknowledgment that cafés-concerts did not spontaneously sprout *because* of Haussmannization, but rather that they persisted *in spite* of it. Nor were all cafés-concerts created equal. Lorge's efforts to transform the vast Eldorado into a space of canonic listening and spectacle were in no small part due to pressures from a surveillance regime and a liberalized theater market, supported by a poetic yet hegemonic discourse that framed the café-concert as an unruly social space, and though new, a cultural remnant of *le vieux Paris*.

This naturistic and classist narrative is not uncommon in café-concert historiography, which has treated the feral practices of Second Empire everyday life as the precursors of Third Republic mass culture. Situating the café-concert in context of Third Republic liberalism, Jann Pasler defines cafés-concerts as "theaters of the poor."[19] In fact, Second Empire contemporaries did not consider the café-concert to be a theater at all. Moreover, its success was not moored to that of popular song. In an essay on theater deregulation published in 1867, Hippolyte Hostein posited that an intangible atmosphere kept these venues at capacity: "Whether it is because of the very genre of song, or because of the casualness (*sans-gêne*) of these establishments—a *sans-gêne* that corresponds to the particular mores of the present generation—does not matter. The result is that the cafés-concerts are never empty."[20] The main product was not liquor or a meal or even a performance, but rather a *sans-gêne* mode of sociability that blended the love for imperial spectacle with the republican desire to commune through song. Later in his book, Attali writes that by the early twentieth century, "the drugstore jukebox wins out over the singers of the caf-conç."[21] With recording technology, the early twentieth-century middle class no longer needed the café-concert for musical consumption. Indeed, Derek Scott has traced a proto-mechanistic aesthetic present in the café-concert, present in the form of a ruthlessly repetitive genre of song known as the *scie* (more on this in the next chapter).[22] But to think of the caf-conç as a mere auditory vessel for musical reproducibility is to miss an important point: despite being a center for a nascent musical mass market, the Second Empire caf-conç also functioned as a free space for sociability. Drinks and songs, even political ideas, could be packaged and sold, but the *sans-gêne* atmosphere promised by cafés-concerts could not be as easily reproduced.

It is in this light that we can read famously nasty testimonies of the café-concert that contributed to its reputation as a pleasure palace. In their account of an 1865 outing to the Eldorado, the Goncourt brothers reveal less about the period's hedonistic tendencies than they do about conservative paranoia toward open, democratized spaces: "The house," they write of the Eldorado, "was enthusiastic, delirious . . . it appears to me that we are nearing revolution."[23] Simply put, the café-concert did not distract from the city: it *was* the city, with air, liquid, and personal space shared between classes and professions. The Goncourts pinpointed exactly what they thought was at stake: the interior, bourgeois life, one operated and maintained specifically by women. The café-concert was oblivious to the gendered norms of salon life, and this openness terrified them: "I see women, children, households, families [in the Eldorado]. The [bourgeois] interior is passing away. Life threatens to become a public affair. The club for those on high, the café for those below, that is what society and people will come to."[24]

Second Empire modernity—if we are to diagnose it as a collective mentality or *epistème*—was thus caught between the past and the future, and never in the present, and this tension was on full display inside the café-concert. Defenders of the café-concert's theatrical autonomy wanted to preserve a democratized sociability that seemed condemned to demolition. The critic Edmond Texier did not mince words when he juxtaposed the "democratic" spatial practices of the café-concert with the dungeon-like "bourgeois" enclosure of a *grand théâtre:* "A box where one suffocates, where one is crowded as if one were aboard a slave ship, where one cannot stretch one's legs or move one's arms, and from where one leaves sore and stiff."[25] Conservatives like the Goncourts, on the other hand, saw the café-concert as the death of refined bourgeois interiority. Critics on both sides of the café-concert bandwagon did not separate perceived aesthetic value of the musical offerings from the physical experience of being within, and around, the city's entertainment venues. This synergy between aesthetic judgment and embodied urban experience is, in fact, a key to understanding the politics of spectacle under Haussmannization. Although much musicological commentary on the café-concert stems from studies of the Third Republic, I want to emphasize that Second Empire-era discourse around cafés-concerts was uniquely polarized over precisely *which* version of modern life was on display.

CLASSICISM AND THE CAFÉ-CONCERT

By the 1860s, tensions between classicism and vernacular modernity boiled over into a reckoning with which theatrical and musical genres should be presented in the cafés-concerts. This reckoning was particularly apparent in the bigger-budget establishments, which by then were as well known to foreigners as the city's *grands théâtres*. One fascinating case study is the Eldorado's 1867 season, which brings into relief these conflicting discourses over what a café-concert *should* be, as opposed to what it *could* be. Taking advantage of the café-concert's inherent flexibility with programming, Lorge hired Cornélie, a celebrated, classically-trained actress formerly on the Comédie-Française roster, to perform verses from seventeenth-century playwrights Corneille and Racine in period costume (figure 5). The run was widely publicized and attracted both café regulars as well as Europe's artistic elite. Verdi and Rossini attended. So did Paris's most celebrated critics, particularly of *Le Figaro*. Georges Mailliard captured the sense of wonder when Cornélie took the stage, commenting on the stark contrast between her performance and the frivolous *chansonnettes* that came before: "Here is the tragic muse embodied, the grand and august muse, ascending this long-disdained stage, sweeping the boards with her lofty tunic, diadem on her head and a classic dagger in hand. Where popular refrains once resounded, the majestic hemistiches of Camille, Hermione, and Phaedra will now resound."[26]

The day after this rapturous review, Jules Valentin noted the drastic shift in audience behavior when Cornélie took the stage. The usually boisterous Eldorado house listened in silence, as if they were taking part in a ceremony: "They listened religiously. Racine's verses landed one after another, sonorous and superb, onto profound silence."[27] The critic Alphonse Duchesne was likewise supportive of hearing classical drama in a space not designated for

FIGURE 5. Gédéon, "La Tragédie au café-concert," 1867. The verse at the bottom of the caricature is from the 1853 vaudeville *Les Folies dramatiques:* "C'est Rome à chaque vers, toujours Rome qu'on nomme! J'aime, après mon dîner, tous les grands vers de Rome..." (Rome in every verse, everything is about Rome! I love hearing these verses about Rome after eating my dinner...") Image: BnF.

it. "One could not sustain the argument," he writes in *Le Figaro,* "that what is deemed moral on one street is immoral on the next street; that dramatic literature changes its character and scope according to the arrondissement in which it was presented."[28] Engrossed, sophisticated listening seemed profoundly out of place in a singing café, even for those who were in favor. Whether it was Racine or Cornélie's own presence, the Eldorado audience adopted a mode of spectatorship that larger institutions, such as the

Comédie-Française and the Opéra, had engineered for decades. Noting the power that the *tragédienne* held over her audiences, the famed critic Francisque Sarcey dubbed Cornélie the "Thérésa de la Tragédie."[29] A comparison to Thérésa, the star of café-concert culture (and to whom we will return later), was telling. Lorge was transgressing the norms of classical theater by staging it—in costume, no less—at the Eldorado, a theater that had no prior business with the likes of Racine and Corneille.

While some forward-thinking critics lauded the unexpected presence of Baroque drama within a café-concert setting, many were unimpressed, even shocked. As some critics complained, performing classical tragedy alongside popular song was not just unusual. It was illegal. Paris was very strict about its theaters long before Napoléon III declared the Second Empire on December 2, 1852. In 1807, in an effort to control the messaging in theatrical spectacle—what today would be called a consolidation of state media—Napoléon III's famous uncle, Napoléon Bonaparte, had issued a series of decrees that reduced the number of licensed theaters to eight (four *grands théâtres* and four *théâtres secondaires*) and assigned each a specific repertory.[30] These genre regulations were strictly enforced until 1864, when Napoléon III issued a decree known to historians as *la liberté des théâtres,* which essentially amounted to a financial and generic deregulation of the theater industry. The decree stated, among other things, that theaters could henceforth stage any genre they wished. This "liberté," in fact, thwarted the insurgence of cafés-concerts—which were thought to steal audiences from the *grands théâtres*—and dealt considerable damage to Paris's popular theater industry.[31] At first, the abolition of the licensing system did not apply to cafés-concerts or any café that hosted singing. According to Article VI of the 1864 decree, "curiosity shows, marionettes, so-called singing cafés, cafés-concerts, and other similar establishments remain subject to the regulations currently enforced."[32] What also remained was censorship. Despite its popularity, the café-concert was legally deemed a "curiosity," offering the same sort of fringe entertainment as did the city's puppet shows and circus acts. Cornélie's costumed performance of seventeenth-century verse was thus in violation of French law and an affront to theatrical mores in place since the early nineteenth century.

Lorge's decision to stage Racine in costume was the culmination of pressure he put on Camille Doucet, the state's Manager of Theater Administration, to lift the remaining restrictions and allow for costuming and staging in cafés-concerts. Doucet signed away these restrictions on March 31, and Cornélie's costumed recitations made history as the first legal appearance of costuming on a café-concert stage. But Doucet did nothing to change the regulations around censorship or genre. Out of ignorance or out of sheer ambition, Lorge appointed the operetta singer and composer Florimond Ronger—better known by his stage name, Hervé—as the Eldorado's new music director. In the midst of Cornélie's sensational run, Hervé prepared the Eldorado house orchestra for a fully costumed staging of his 1862 operetta *Le Retour d'Ulysse*. Set to a libretto by Édouard Montagne, *Le Retour d'Ulysse* is a one-act, four-character farce that tells the story of how Pénélope, left alone by her husband, fends off a chain of suitors with increasing impatience. This fully-staged production, on the heels of Cornélie's orations of classical tragedy, thus prompts the question of why Lorge became so interested in staging such repertoire in a venue accustomed to short, catchy songs. Critics both for and against cafés-concerts complained that such excursions into costumed spectacle would be the death knell of the café-concert. Some did not believe that Doucet had actually *legalized* costuming, but rather merely tolerated it. Abuse of such tolerance, warned P. Schaff in *Le Foyer*, could very well lead to the demise of the café-concert as an institution. "Believe me, since you are *tolerated*, be satisfied; the day when *prohibition* arrives, you will do what you did before. But remain a CAFÉ-CONCERT, as it is not in your present interest to become anything else. If you cease to be one, the day will arrive when you will be ordered to revert, and you will be RUINED."[33]

The introduction of new genres and repertoires into the café-concert signaled a crisis of identity for the institution. Did it extend the French tradition of bardic song, from the troubadours to the singing societies (the *caveaux*) to the famed Pierre-Jean de Béranger, nodding to France's glorious songwriting past along the way? Did it offer a break from tradition, in the form of a thoroughly modern, hedonistic respite from the pressures of bourgeois modernity? This chapter is hardly the place for an overview history of the café-concert; such chronologies are available elsewhere.[34] I am more interested in how the institution of the café-concert was used to "rewrite the city" in ways that contradicted Haussmann's urban aesthetic. I am also interested in how the café-concert's open-ended geography and musical porosity resisted the "society of spectacle" propagated by the Second Empire.[35] In addition to being a venue for drink and song, the café-concert was an open space for social exchange—a media organization, to use contemporary terminology. In nineteenth-century terms, the café-concert acted like a newspaper *feuilleton* in spatial form, allowing patrons to share and absorb a spectrum of news and opinions.[36] We will return to the 1867 Eldorado season throughout the chapter, but the irony of performing classical-themed repertoire and parody in a café-concert needs to be underlined. By drawing on pre-nineteenth century classical traditions, Lorge and Haussmann both looked backwards to look forward. Yet a major difference between the two men was their attitude toward compartmentalization. While Lorge was amenable to presenting operetta, *grand-siècle* drama, and acrobats in a venue that was intended as much for gastronomic consumption as it was for theatrical performance, Haussmann wore his rigid sensibility on his sleeve, espousing an aesthetics of urbanism that reflected Napoleonic divisions of theatrical genre into neat categories. Thus from the outset, the nascent cafés-concerts were destined to be blemishes in Haussmann's sanitized conception of the city.

THE EARLY CAF-CONÇ

Chronologically speaking, the emergence of the café-concert aligns conveniently with the rise of Louis-Napoléon Bonaparte in 1848. Aside from being a revolutionary year in French political history, 1848 was a watershed year for the history of the café-concert. Theatrical censorship was suspended for five months, which allowed for a wave of bards like Joseph Darcier to push the limits of vocal delivery and lyric content. Darcier (whose real name was Joseph Lemaire) began his career as a performer in Paris's boulevard melodramas before transitioning to popular song in the 1840s. A champion of the singing societies known as *goguettes,* Darcier became one of the first "celebrity singers" on the café-concert stage. His performances at the famed venue L'Estaminet lyrique in 1849 inspired Hector Berlioz to gush about the singer's dramatic and lyrical talents. The article—showcasing Berlioz at the height of his journalistic powers—brings to vivid life the acoustic atmosphere of a typical evening at a Second Republic café-concert, and is worth quoting at length:

> If you liked the fantastical Hoffmann ... go to the Passage Jouffroy. There you will find an enormous tap-room where, every evening, two hundred pipes are at full blast while at one end of the room, dimly visible through the cloud and stench, six or seven vocalists on a little stage, accompanied by a tinkling piano, hoarsely dispense comic songs, nocturnes, romances, and character ballads. The roar of conversation, rattle of glasses and click of heels make them practically inaudible, but it covers up the wrong notes. At about ten, however, when the crush and smoke are at their densest, if you've managed to find a place near the stage you'll see a strange figure emerge. At the sight of

UN CAFÉ-CONCERT AUX CHAMPS-ELYSÉES
Dessin de M. MORIN, gravé par M. COSTE.

FIGURE 6. "Un Café-concert aux Champs-Élysées." In *Paris-guide, 1867: Par les principaux écrivains et artistes de la France, la science, l'art* (Paris: Librairie international, 1867), 996.

him there's a profound hush; the most fanatical pipe stops puffing, the cigars go out, the waiter stands stock still, clutching his bottles, like a Sisyphus who has forgotten to push his rock.... It's Darcier! Already his face has assumed the personality of the character whose dark or guileless or lamentable story he is about to sing you; he is in the part, acting, gesturing.[37]

Berlioz goes on like this for several pages. His famous sketch of Darcier represents what David Cairns has called Berlioz's "independent spirit" that fueled an "appetite for the oddities and curious corners of musical life."[38] But Berlioz was not alone in his fascination with the café-concert and the people it attracted. The quick succession of revolutions, regime changes, proclamations, and a *coup d'état* left its mark on Paris's literati in ways that challenged the very notion of a singular urban identity. To put it in Marxian terms, it is the atmospherics of Darcier at the Estaminet lyrique that generated in Berlioz the sense of alienation. The free movement of ideas and bodies anticipated the urban class antagonisms of the 1870s.

Indeed, the 1848 revolution marked an important moment in the urban history of the café-concert, as it led at once to an expansion of the institution and a restriction on its repertoire. Following the establishment of the Second Republic in February 1848, the new Prince-President, Louis-Napoléon Bonaparte, reinstated censorship, increased surveillance around the long-popular *goguettes,* and increased the responsibility of the Préfecture de Police to register and monitor new establishments.[39] Only with censorship and police firmly in place were cafés-concerts allowed to "multiply": that is, when the regime issued licenses (*privilèges*) to potential developers and proprietors. Summertime outdoor cafés blossomed during the Second Republic, flourishing along the tree-lined avenue des Champs-Élysées and occupying space previously occupied by rolling English gardens (perhaps a nod to the pastoral mythology of Hellenic "Elysian fields"—yet another Parisian ode to Antiquity). Thus from the onset, the summertime *concerts d'été* were marked as pastoral retreats of hedonism (figure 6). West of the city center, these outdoor *fêtes* represented a form of sociability more akin to the outdoor festivities of rural Frenchmen, the *paysans,* than the ritualized salon activities of *parisiens* and *parisiennes.* At a time when Parisian writers and painters increasingly turned to the built environment to sketch the structures of modern life, the *concerts d'été* provided a less scripted, less urbanized, indeed less structured form of sociability.[40]

CAFÉ ATMOSPHERICS

What *was* the café-concert to those who were offended by the genre-breaking performances at the Eldorado? How did it fit into the network of social spaces in the city? I pose these questions not to answer them succinctly, but rather to highlight the ontological complexity of the café-concert as an urban social space. The café-concert, born as an outdoor gathering area, never shed its outdoor identity even as it moved indoors. If the *embourgeoisement* of Parisian culture relied on the construction of the fetishized interior—think of Haussmann's endless rows of residential units—then at the opposite end of the spectrum remains the aesthetics of outdoor urban life, made resonant by those who made their living in the street (see chapters 4 and 5).

It takes a brief glance across the English Channel to gauge just how antisocial Paris's social spaces had become. British journalists commented on how Parisian sociability seemed homogenized into a society of spectacle. "There is no such thing as a public meeting," one disgruntled British journalist wrote. "There are not literary and mechanics' institutions in one sense of the term...

and in fact there is an intolerable sameness in Parisian relaxation. The *café*, the billiard table, the theatre, that is the triple chord which is not easily broken."[41] This review, reprinted in some dozen British newspapers, reveals as much about British sociability as it does about Paris. Life on the *grands boulevards* was a comparatively foreign phenomenon, as was the reliance on the theater for socializing outside the home. But the comment about the "triple chord" is striking: *embourgeoisement* was predicated on a controlled fetishization of certain urban spaces—in particular the theater, the salon, and the urban garden. Whereas the Eldorado attempted to hold its own against the homogenized monumentality of the surrounding urban landscape, the institution of the café-concert, defined by networks of anonymous peripheral and unvouched-for social spaces, did not strike the British correspondent as distinct from the city's nonmusical cafés and cabarets. Put another way, uninitiated foreigners did not know what to *do* with cafés-concerts, with the sole exception being those establishments like the Eldorado, Alcazar, and several others, which aspired to challenge the city's theater industry on its own terms.

Back in Paris, bourgeois criticism of the café-concert targeted its noisy bustle and unpredictable temporal structure. The café became—at least poetically—a reincarnation of the pre-Haussmannian street. Ross Chambers's concept of poetic "atmospherics" (in the work of Baudelaire) are useful in understanding how the café-concert cut against the grain of Haussmannian urban aesthetics. To speak of a poetic urban "atmosphere" is to speak of an "intuition one has, or rather the subliminal awareness, of a certain dimension of particularity, otherness, or strangeness that attaches to certain objects, places, or situations that in other respects are recognizable as ordinary, familiar, or not worthy of special attention."[42] A poetic urban atmosphere sets the tune of a city, but in counterpoint: one urban space negates, or confronts, or extends, another. The Haussmannian boulevard did not merely blaze the city into modernity. Rather, it networked all of the adjoining streets, buildings, cultural institutions, and liminal spaces.

It is a shame that Baudelaire did not write about the café-concert.[43] He did, however, write of a nondescript "new café" in his prose poem "Les Yeux des pauvres" (The eyes of the poor). Note that the café's very construction—barely opened, but already full of meaning—initiates an awareness of modernity that is ironically expressed by both the old poor and the newly rich:

> That evening, rather tired, you wanted to sit at a new café at the corner of the new boulevard, still full of stripped plaster but already gloriously presenting

its unfinished splendors. The café glittered. The gaslights themselves displayed all the ardor of a premiere and threw their beams on blindingly white walls, mirrors full of dazzling tablecloths, golden moldings and cornices. . . .

Right in front of us, on the sidewalk, was a fellow, fortyish, graying beard on his tired face, holding with one hand a little boy and carrying on the other a tiny creature not yet able to walk. As nursemaid he was giving his children the evening air. All of them in tatters. The three faces were extraordinarily serious, and their six eyes contemplated steadily the new café, with equal admiration, but nuanced according to age. The eyes of the father said: 'Beautiful! how beautiful! It's as if all the gold from the poor world had come to live in these walls.'—The eyes of the little boy: 'Beautiful! how beautiful! But it's somewhere only for those who are not like us.'—As for the eyes of the littlest one, they were too fascinated to express anything beyond a deep and stupid joy.[44]

Baudelaire paints a picture of the new café through the eyes of his urban onlookers. Yet its tone should not assume its presumed class reductionism at face value. Aimée Boutin notes the poem's ironic bent, as its "narration exposes the narrator's smugness" in delineating the border between the city, still under construction and treacherous, and the café, also under construction but already beautiful.[45] And David Harvey detects an "ambiguity of proprietorship, of aesthetics, of social relations, and a point of contestation for control over public space."[46] Baudelaire's poem is not only a metaphor for how Haussmannization was received from the street, but also how these new institutions operated from within. The ragpickers, street musicians, and glaziers of the street find their analogue in the acrobats, singers, and glassware-breaking waiters of the café-concert. As Chambers writes, the noisy workforce of the street "acquired a wisdom from their exposed existence that indoor dwellers—a metaphor for the *bourgeoisie*—are unaware of."[47] The many testimonies of bewilderment found in memoirs and guides reveal a bourgeois disconnect with the radically antispectacular aesthetics of the café-concert. We will dig into this claim further by exploring first the geographical and ontological bewilderment that typified early reception history of the café-concert, and later by examining how advocates feared—rightfully—that Haussmannian capitalist aesthetics would eventually eat away at the democratized sociability of this institution and create the conditions for the immersive popular spectacle that dominated the *fin de siècle*.

As far as nineteenth-century guidebooks were concerned, the interior of the café-concert was fertile ground for unpretentious sociability during the Second Empire. Authors of guidebooks and histories of cafés-concerts devoted considerable ink to detailing their atmospherics. This attention to atmospheric detail suggests that what was happening around the musical performances was at least of equal importance to the performances themselves. The café-concert comes to life in these texts as a microcosm of a city; people interacting in and moving in unpredictable ways, blurring the line between stage, seat, and street. Some guidebooks warned potential first-time visitors of their hectic nature. Take the 1862 edition of *Galignani's New Paris Guide for Travelers,* which instructs reticent Brits that Parisian audiences typically engage directly with performers: "A trifle is given to the performers, one of whom passes at intervals along the tables to collect the bounty of the audience."[48] An often-cited description of the café-concert atmosphere comes from Louis Veuillot's 1867 volume *Les Odeurs de Paris,* a searing account detailing how modern Paris—or more specifically, elite Paris—lost its moral compass. Veuillot's testimony of his first time at the Eldorado, with its blend of sensory experience and moral judgment, is worth a closer look:

> Passing through the smoke, we spotted two or three empty seats, which we reach not without difficulty. What an atmosphere! What an odor, a mix of tobacco, spirits, beer, and gas! It was the first time I entered this place, the first time I saw women in a smoking café. We were surrounded not only by women, but by Ladies.
>
> Twenty years ago, one searched all of Paris in vain for such a spectacle. Clearly these ladies dragged their defeated husbands here; the annoyed and confused looks of these wretches proclaimed that loudly. But these ladies seemed hardly out of place.... The presence of these 'well-to-do' women gave the audience a particular sense of unrest: social unrest![49]

Veuillot's turbulent account of the Eldorado does not center on music—he doesn't even mention it here, and only later comments on the clothing and vocal timbres of some of the singers. Nor was he concerned with the particular transactional relationship between singer, spectator, and bartender. What struck Veuillot—and irked the Goncourt brothers—was the socioeconomic disorientation of seeing women in a smoke-filled space presumably reserved for men. In fact, the roles were reversed; it was the *women* who dragged unwilling *men* to see and hear those lewd and raunchy singers, to whiff the pipe smoke, and to drink the spirits.

Responding to Veuillot's ungenerous and gendered characterization in *L'Opinion nationale* in 1867, Jules Claretie noted from first-hand experience that the Eldorado in fact skirted some of the traditional norms practiced in the *grands théâtres:* "At the café-concert (I saw it the other night at the

Eldorado) patrons could come and sit with their families, with their wife and children. They would all group around the same table, pressed together, listening and watching."[50] In contrast to accusations of moral decadence and the need for order, Claretie was struck by the equitable family dynamic on display, with women and children given the same rights to occupy the performance space as the men. The Eldorado was, in microcosm, the inverse of the Haussmannian ordered city. Whereas the passive spectacle of Haussmannization was on full display during the 1867 Exposition universelle, Lorge's Eldorado fostered a participatory aesthetic that featured wealthy and empowered women—Veuillot's "Ladies"—infiltrating male-dominated social spaces. If Haussmann's *nouveau Paris* monumentalized spectacles, Lorge recast spectacle as a carnivalesque reversal of societal roles.

Writers beyond the Second Empire pursued this notion that the café-concert was a sort of social wilderness. André Chadourne's *Les Cafés-concerts*, published in 1889, represents the first generation of reception history of these institutions based on second-hand experience. Chadourne, born in 1859, was too young to patronize the Eldorado during its heyday, but he was one of the first writers to document its atmospherics. He opens with a pseudo-ethnographic chapter on the *physioniomie* of the café: a rhetorical tactic that followed the long tradition of literary urban *tableaux* of the city, such as those in the work of Balzac. The "problem" with the café-concert as a social space, Chadourne explains, is that it essentially espouses proletarian values: "It is made available for those with the most modest purses; it counts neither etiquette nor dress code, and it caters above all to supporters of those special joys savored between the pipe and the beer mug."[51] With its ambiguously hyphenated name, the caf-conç seemed to cut across the worlds of café culture, nature, and the emergent society of spectacle: much to the chagrin of theater owners. Where imperial bureaucrats framed café-concert policy according to what it *lacked*—morality, structure, genre—Chadourne enumerates what it *offered:* an affordable barrier of entry, an unpretentious environment, and a diversity of musical and gastronomic vices. Above all, there was a sense of frenetic energy: "With every arriving patron there is an unimaginable disturbance. Spoons fall and glasses spill, knocked over by a frantic man's tailcoat."[52] Such noisy depictions help contextualize Cornélie's controversial performances of Racine and Corneille at the Eldorado. At stake was not merely the performance of classical repertoire. Rather, it was the environment in which this repertoire found itself. Slowness, monumentality, symmetry, conformity, repetition—these were all necessary conditions of the

Haussmannian urban aesthetic, but they were the antithesis of what the café-concert offered its patrons.

The more we read nineteenth-century reflections on the café-concert, the clearer these divisions between social and antisocial urbanisms become. Chadourne's book goes beyond mere voyeuristic description—the kind found in tourist guidebooks, for instance—and offers an analysis of gendered sociability as it was performed within the walls of the café-concert: "Paris is swarming with people, especially bachelors who, due to their jobs in offices, stores, and shops, cannot devote much time to *la toilette*. To that end, they need a pleasurable outlet that exhilarates them without condemning them to the requirements of the *salons*. . . . They are free to smoke, drink, chat, applaud loudly, ogle women: in short, to joke, prank."[53]

Cafés-concerts attracted stodgy husbands, their bored spouses, as well as Parisian *célibataires*, in particular single heterosexual and homosexual men. Freed from the imposing demands of salon decorum, bachelors used the café-concert as a semiprivate social club, thus inheriting the *goguette* tradition that by the 1860s was marginalized in Second Empire bourgeois society. These men, Chadourne implies were free to interact with one another, camouflaged by the din of applause, shouting, and singing. The success of drag performers like Arthur "the Countess" Belorget suggest that cafés-concerts were relatively safe spaces for both cross-dressing and same-sex sociability.[54] In a society that was increasingly partitioned and restrained along sociospatial lines—from the solidifying images of distinct *quartiers* to the enforced politics of genre in the theaters—the café-concert provided a microcosm of an urbanism in which the free and random flow of persons, ideas, and sexualities was a defining feature. In particular, the summer cafés-concerts along the Champs-Élysées were social refuges from bourgeois rigidity while also providing clientele a brief foray into nature.

Unlike the Paris Opéra and the other *grands théâtres*, whose halls were sealed off from the outside world and thus offered perennial programming, the Second Empire popular theater industry was seasonal. Jacques Offenbach's first success was in the poorly insulated Salle Lacaze, steps from the 1855 Exposition universelle. Seeking both a larger and warmer venue for the winter season, Offenbach eventually obtained a license to move his Bouffes-Parisiens to the Passage Choiseul, a company active to this day. Cafés-concerts likewise existed between seasonal venues (take the Alcazar d'été on the Champs-Élysées and the Alcazar d'hiver on the rue du Faubourg Poissonnière). And yet writers saw the outdoor cafés-concerts as more than convenient venues for warm weather. In stark contrast with the iron and macadam urbanization of the city, these summer cafés-concerts were often described in naturalistic terms, and their patrons like wild inhabitants. In the "Light" section of his *Arcades Project,* Walter Benjamin quotes a passage from Guy de Maupassant's 1887 short story "La Nuit: Le cauchemar" (The night: Nightmare), which reveals as much about the persistence of natural imagery in café culture as it does about manmade technologies: "I reached the Champs-Élysées, where the cafés-concerts seemed like blazing hearths among the leaves. The chestnut trees brushed with yellow light, had the look of painted objects, the look of phosphorescent trees."[55]

This poetic, almost synesthetic description of a café by night complements the *chiaroscuro* lighting suggested in the engraving above (figure 6). There are no borders between the natural and the artificial. The stage emerges from the brush, and the trees, along with the moon, provide as much illumination as do the gas streetlamps.[56] The café-goers know no borders, either; they are content, enjoying tableside service with their footwear touching raw earth. Visual and literary representations of these nocturnal gatherings paint the café-concert as a natural occurrence, an urban pastoral gathering: a stark contrast to the carpeted foyers, marbled floors, and paved boulevards of the city's subsidized theaters. Of course, these were institutions born directly out of the economic and social circumstances of urbanization. As such, the Second Empire café-concert not only provided an alternative social urbanism to the *embourgeoisement* of the boulevard and the theater, but also offered a refuge for working members of the Parisian theater industry.

BEHIND THE SCENES

While Chadourne cites invaluable witness testimonies of café-concert life from the patron's perspective, memoirs of famous café-concert performers offer a behind-the-scenes window on the atmospherics of these venues. Perhaps the most famous example are the memoirs of Emma Valladon, the café-concert performer who became famous under the stage name "Thérésa," and to whom Francisque Sarcey had compared the *tragédienne* Cornélie. The daughter of a street violinist, Thérésa was born in 1837 and spent her teenage years singing in the chorus of the Théâtre de la Porte Saint-Martin.[57] She began her early solo career as a *chanteuse* of serious parlor songs but soon found a knack for musical comedy. Her grimaces, accents, and contortions won her fame and spawned a much-imitated performance style known simply as *le style Thérésa*. Best known for her work at the Alcazar and the Eldorado, Thérésa was also a regular at the Café Moka, the Bouffes-Parisiens, the Gaîté, the Café des Géants, as well as several other theaters along the famous boulevard du Temple (before its theaters were razed in 1862). A master code-switcher, Thérésa championed the Parisian working class with rustic songs like "Fleur des Alpes," but also earned the respect of elites in the opera world, such as Alphonse Royer and the composer Auber, who frequented cafés-concerts during Thérésa's heyday in the 1860s. The singer who barked her way through "la chanson du chien" was also invited to perform at the Tuileries for Napoléon III.[58]

Published in 1865, the *Mémoires de Thérésa* are a collaboration between the singer and three journalists (Henri Rochefort, Albert Wolff, and Ernest Blum) who ghostwrote the majority of the text.[59] Veracity, then, was beside the point; in fact, Wolff disclosed in an 1879 article in *Le Figaro* that much of Thérésa's personal story was fabricated and exaggerated to fortify her rags-to-riches persona.[60] Large portions of the text—especially the broader meditations on Parisian life—were recycled versions of articles that the three journalists had published over the years. None of this was a secret to those in the café-concert community; as one songwriter-turned-chronicler put it, Thérésa's *Mémoires* "were written *by*—or rather *for*—herself."[61] Thérésa publicly endorsed her *Mémoires,* which enjoyed numerous positive critical reviews and remained in print through the end of the nineteenth century.

Though apocryphal in some parts and a pastiche of earlier journalistic accounts in others, the *Mémoires de Thérésa,* authorship notwithstanding, are a vivid document of the Parisian entertainment industry at midcentury. Thérésa the protagonist disappears for entire chapters, giving way to general reflections on boulevard life, social norms, and bourgeois values. In his review of the book, Paul Girard suggested that readers did not necessarily know or even care about the provenance of the book's stories and opinions: "One sees Parisians strolling the boulevards adorned with this popular book. It is discussed in the theater and out in the city. Many soirées have been canceled because housewives wanted to read it by the fireside."[62] The *Mémoires* promised to bring the café-concert into the salon, accommodating readers who wished to experience the "blazing hearth"—to again quote Maupassant—from the comfort of their armchairs.[63] While marketed as a personal tell-all, Thérésa's *Mémoires* are a valuable document of the urban experience as imagined by insiders to the entertainment industry. The ever-critical Timothée Trimm saw the book's appeal precisely in its ability to capture a snapshot of urban life in the midst of rapid change, linking the text to the rich literary history of *physiognomies parisiennes*.[64] When read as a street-level city guidebook, Thérésa's *Mémoires* reveal the extent to which spontaneous sociability was a marquee feature of café culture in general, and the café-concert in particular. Moreover, they offer a nostalgic, everyday counternarrative to the ordered, monumental modernism that Haussmann promoted in his own *Mémoires*.

Since the *Mémoires* were intended to both entertain readers and create a persona of a singer as engaged citizen, let us play along and read passages as if they were Thérésa's own words. The opening pages offer a glimpse of her dual reputation as café entertainer and serious artist. She writes that critics called her "la Rigolboche de la chanson," a comparison to the famous comedic dancer who had created a furor with her updated cancan, and who had penned her own *Mémoires* five years prior. On the very next page, Thérésa mentions another nickname, "la Patti de la Chope"—a reference to the famous Italian soprano Adelina Patti. In expressing her adulation for Hortense Schneider, Thérésa notes that the operetta star was often dubbed the "Thérésa of the theaters" and she the "Schneider of the café-concert." Thérésa frequently reminds the reader of her links to the musical elite through name-dropping and selective quotation. Remarking on her friendship with Alphonse Royer, she quotes the former director of the Opéra, who apparently told her that "le veritable Conservatoire, c'est le café-chantant." Whether Royer actually said this is unknown, but the fact that these words appeared in a bestselling memoir underlines the defense of the café-concert's integrity as a space of meaningful musical activity. In naming the actress Cornélie as the "Thérésa de la Tragédie," Timothée Trimm followed in a tradition of validating the world of the café-concert by identifying peers in the more "serious" theatrical arenas.[65]

Through comparison, name-dropping, quotation, and a confessional writing style, the *Mémoires de Thérésa* promise the reader access to the singer and her inner circle. But the text goes further, frequently offering opinions about working-class sociability in the city. These passages shift the tone from Thérésa as an object of fascination to Thérésa as an engaged citizen. Her third chapter contains a particularly vivid image of the city as both animated monster and inanimate machine: "Alas! In this immense Paris where nothing stands still, in this titanesque machine whose cogs turn incessantly, amid this tremendous continual clamor—like the breathing of a giant monster—who could have heard my first cry of pain?"[66]

From a present-day vantage point, this passage is, in a way, redolent of the urban literary musings of Sand, Stendhal, Balzac, Flaubert, and Zola, whose protagonists curse the city that has brought them heartache and disenfranchisement. The *Mémoires* transcend autobiography, functioning like a pamphlet in defense of café sociability. The reader is treated to direct and personal reflections on how the "titanesque" urban machine ground away the social and theatrical spaces that working musicians held so dear.

Thérésa's reputation, network, and personal voice were co-opted to comment on the urban conditions impacting creative working-class life. In one of many nostalgic passages, Thérésa pines for the boulevard that Haussmann demolished in 1862, displacing nearly every theater that lined it: "And where are you, poor boulevard du Temple, poor residents of all of its spaces, which today are sad and deserted?"[67] Thérésa resists a top-down view of the boulevard as a crowded and chaotic place. Such descriptions were often found in tourist guidebooks. Rather, she narrates from street level, focusing on the people who frequented those spaces—including herself. After a fruitless excursion to the theaters of Normandy, a young Thérésa returned penniless to Paris. She writes: "After getting off the train, I counted my money. I had four francs left. I had no home, no resources, and no hope for tomorrow. I ran to the boulevard du Temple, where I was sure to meet old friends."[68] One of the pervasive themes of the *Mémoires* is that cafés and theaters provided crucial patronage to destitute women, including sex workers and musicians. Thérésa devotes a whole chapter to the *filles de maison,* many of whom were aspiring female performers and courtesans for whom cafés served as community centers. For the more destitute women, cafés provided room, board, and training. Demolition of these cafés, especially the Café du Cirque, led to the displacement of these *filles de maisons*. Thérésa asks: "Where are they all now? Alas! I don't know. Poor girls, who lived on a memory, a regret, a hope!"[69] In one of her pithier turns of phrase, Thérésa writes that in many of these boulevard theaters and cafés, "on se tutoyait." The verb "tutoyer" is impossible to translate succinctly: it indicates a drop in formalities and a willingness to speak without presumed hierarchy. But the meaning here is clearly implied: Haussmannization was about monumentalizing boulevard life, but this monumentality came at the cost of community, in particular the community of working-class women.

As the city's boulevards stratified class divisions between center and periphery, so too did the demographics of working women change along spatial lines. Working-class men far outnumbered working-class women in the peripheries, largely due to the seasonal nature of available work.[70] Working-class single women took domestic servant jobs in the wealthier, western part of the city's Right Bank. The open boulevards may have increased safety for bourgeois strollers thanks to lighting and sightlines, but working single women would become vulnerable to the jeers of both women and men. These women, moreover, did not always have the benefit of traversing the illuminated openness of the daytime boulevards, and would navigate home, or to the next job, in the shadow of nighttime. Fearful of being mistaken—and approached—as prostitutes, these women gravitated to the back rooms of cafés-concerts, which served as de facto safehouses.

Of course, Parisian women were not a monolithic demographic. The novelist George Sand, writing from a position of relative financial and social privilege, found the newly widened boulevards aesthetically boring but ultimately liberating. In the monumental 1867 *Paris-guide,* Sand betrays the privilege of time and independence as she recounts the freedom granted by these broadened thoroughfares: "Now that broad avenues, too linear for the artistic eye but unquestionably safe, allow us to saunter at length, hands in our pockets, without losing ourselves and being compelled at each step to consult the gendarme at the corner or the amiable street grocer, it is a blessing to stroll along a generous sidewalk."[71] As her reference to hands in (trouser) pockets suggests, only in her gender-fluid attire was Sand spared the unwanted attention of gawking men. Nonetheless, the lived experience of the *grands boulevards* was not the same for all women, dependent as it was on the visible signs of class. Fashion, free time, and other visual and temporal markers of social status determined who had the right to the new city. Gender was an overt reason *not* to authorize a new café-concert. Among the many proposals for new *cafés* was one from a Mademoiselle Lehmann, who in 1866 proposed a café-concert in her home in Montmartre (opening a café-concert in a private residence was, in fact, common among many applications). In an internal letter, the Ministre de la Maison de l'Empereur et des Beaux-Arts, Jean-Baptiste Philibert Vaillant, explained his decision: "Cafés-concerts managed by women would leave much to be desired in terms of good upkeep and good administration."[72] While Sand spoke to her freedom to *consume* urban space as a bourgeoise, it was far more difficult for women to *produce* urban space of their own, regardless of means. Thérésa's views on boulevard culture thus suggest that the perceived safety of so-called seedy or liminal spaces, such as café-concert back rooms and alleys, depended on the outward performance of gender and class. If the gaudy façade of the café-concert promised dining, drinking, and entertainment, the back rooms offered the basic necessities of light, warmth, provisions, restrooms, and social support.[73] These liminal spaces, moreover, were the closest that women could come to owning a café-concert; to purchase and manage one was—at least unofficially—untenable.

LA LIBERTÉ DES CAFÉS?

The *Mémoires de Thérésa* are but one cog in the wheel of Second Empire café-concert reception history. As we have seen via both sympathetic and less amenable commentators, the café-concert became a mythological urban beast almost from the moment the hyphenated term first appeared in press in the 1850s. Myths, as Patrice Higonnet has shown, defined what it meant to be Parisian in the nineteenth century, and indeed, what it meant to be modern in Paris. Whether he intended to or not, Higonnet paraphrased Henri Lefebvre in defining the Parisian literary myth as "the way in which the city has been perceived, conceived, and dreamed."[74] One important deviation from Lefebvre's spatial sociology is the substitution of Lefebvre's notion of "lived" (*vécu*) experience for "dreamed." The café-concert did indeed become the stuff of dreams, and it lives an afterlife defined by Impressionist painters like Degas. Yet it is a mistake to reduce the café-concert to a stand-in for capitalist, imperial Paris. The two ideologies of liberalism and imperialism bore down on the theater industry in the 1860s during the empire's phase of deregulation. Here we can revisit the 1864 legislation known as the *liberté des théâtres* and its resonances in the café-concert industry. By the time Cornélie and Hervé completed their respective runs at the Eldorado in 1867, a group of critics worried that theater administrator Camille Doucet's recent deregulations regarding costuming would precipitate the café-concert's eventual obsolescence. By this logic, Lorge did not win a fight with the bureaucracy. He took their bait.

Already in January 1864, a debate erupted in the Parisian press around the future of the caf-conç in relation to the upcoming *liberté des théâtres*. Of particular note was "Article 6," quoted earlier in this chapter, which sparked the controversy around the Eldorado's costumed performances of *grand-siècle* tragedy and operetta.[75] The idea that playwrights, artists, and directors were henceforth free to pursue their careers across different theatrical genres was ostensibly a win; however, that law still did not consider the café-concert to be a theater. Small theaters could benefit from an influx of talent, but the city's singing cafés, which were increasing in number, could not open their repertories to more ambitious projects. Then as now, there was confusion about the ontology of the café-concert: was it a theater, or a drinking hall? While the authorities squarely defined it as the latter, journalists began to question the logic of such seemingly arbitrary compartmentalization.

Some critics resorted to fantastical speculation about the institution's future. In a widely reprinted article, Henri Gourdon de Genouillac asked precisely at what point a concert venue with a café becomes a "café-concert." Genouillac imagines winning a hypothetical permit to open a theater in the center of Paris that happens to have a café inside of it. This technically still constitutes a "theater" by French law. Patrons would buy a three-franc admission ticket, half of which could be reimbursed for a beverage. Still a theater. Waiters could shuttle between the dining and performance spaces, bringing small refreshments like drinks and ice cream. Not an unusual scenario. This is, after all, where the "aria di sorbetto" (sorbet aria) gets its name. In turn-of-the-nineteenth-century Italian opera—in particular the works of Rossini—secondary characters would be given an aria that would serve as a cue for patrons and waiters to initiate an informal ritual of chatting with neighbors, using the restroom, or ordering refreshments. The practice was therefore inscribed into operatic practice and in no way undermined the ontological stability of a performance of *Tancredi* or *Il barbiere di Siviglia*. Genouillac is still within the ontological boundaries of theater when he proposes that refreshments be brought to his hypothetical spectators. However, were he to install trays or tables on which spectators could rest their refreshments, such an infrastructural addition would push Genouillac's hypothetical venue into the category of "café-concert." He concludes his thought experiment by panning the law's assumption that the café-concert was somehow dangerous to the commercial theater industry: "Are the crowded cafés-concerts causing actual harm to theaters by robbing them of their audience? No, they simply created another one."[76]

Ontology was the topic on the table for those defending the cafés-concerts against the not-so-liberating "*liberté des théâtres.*" Notably, Genouillac's hypothetical dispute does not mention music. The regime's aim was never to create designated spaces where this or that genre could be performed in its purity. Rather, it seemed to fall along demographic lines: the café-concert was perceived as a threat in that it drew audiences away from theaters with its no-ticket policy. Theater deregulation was thus deployed as a regulatory tactic that would thwart cafés-concerts' ambitions to present larger-scale musical works. These policies amounted to a catch-22. By touting a free market and artistic autonomy, the regime installed a market-driven form of censorship, one that would throw café-concert owners into an existential crisis. If they stayed the course, then cafés-concerts would see their profits decimated by upstart *petits théâtres* whose bigger-budget productions would attract higher-profile performers. If they fought for the right to stage theatrical works, then cafés-concerts would render themselves redundant and thus obsolete.

The worst did not come true, and the café-concert exerted dominance over the Paris cultural scene through the 1860s. Nevertheless, defenders continued to fear the institution's imminent obsolescence through the end of the decade, likely fueled by the empire's unpredictable policies around censorship and deregulation. A short-lived newspaper, *Le Café-concert: Journal hebdomadaire,* was founded in 1867 as a public-facing arm of the recently created Agence centrale artistique, an agency tailor-made for songwriters and café singers and performers. Its contents reveal a collective attempt to raise the aesthetic and economic profile of the café-concert against the silencing effects of deregulation. A major theme through its yearlong publication run was a call to define exactly what a café-concert is and what it is not.

Le Café-concert was the brainchild of Paul Burani, who served as the newspaper's editor-in-chief, and Léopold Boyer, who served as managing editor. The first issue establishes the newspaper's premise: a forum for and by professionals within the café-concert world. Noting the rise of the institution of the past two decades, Boyer pans haphazard, directionless leadership of previous cafés-concerts and their publicity machines. He attacks them (without naming names) for their "pretentious inertia" and their lack of a progressive model. Boyer also goes after newspapers—this time, naming *L'Echo* and *Le Foyer*—for their lack of serious coverage of café-concert spectacles, in stark contrast to coverage of the city's more "serious" theaters. Indeed, "seriousness" is what Burani and Boyer demanded. At the heart of their newspaper's mission was a desire for artistic prestige. As Boyer emphasizes in caps at the end of his inaugural essay, "We want: a RESPECTABLE and RESPECTED Café-Concert."

Unsurprisingly, the editorial board of *Le Café-concert* took Cornélie's and Hervé's performances at the Eldorado very seriously. Yet not all were on the same page. One active contributor was Penna-Spada, who praised the bureaucrat Camille Doucet for his loosening of restrictions regarding costuming in the café-concert. Doucet's decision was a boon for the industry, and the bureaucrat's legislative change of heart was as "spontaneous as it was liberal."[77]

Of course, to be "liberal" in late 1860s France was to be in line with recent imperial policy regarding deregulation. A series of financial crises beginning in 1856 were exacerbated by costly military campaigns in Crimea and Mexico. In response to a series of rural food shortages and ballooning national debt—in no small part due to Haussmann's speculative financing for the urbanization of Paris—Napoléon III allowed increasing parliamentary control over the budget. While this "liberal phase" of the Second Empire allowed for a greater tolerance toward the press and the theatrical industry, the deregulation of key textile and agricultural industries resulted in an economy in which established firms preyed on smaller and upstart businesses. Liberalization became a means of transferring some of the emperor's power to the legislature and from there to the financial elites on whom those elected officials depended.[78] Thus advocates for the café-concert disagreed as to what *liberté* meant for their industry.

Whereas Penna-Spada praised what he called the "liberté des cafés-concerts" (a nod to the 1864 *liberté des théâtres* policy), Burani, for his part, was skeptical of the intrusion of theatricality into the café-concert realm. Complete deregulation—the kind that would force the Eldorado to situate itself amid the commercial theater industry—would erase what he thought was the café-concert's *raison d'être*: to uphold the French lyric tradition. Burani did not see the café-concert as merely an entertainment venue, but as a sort of "imaginary museum of musical works"—in this case, *chanson populaire*.[79] On the one hand, Burani wrote, there were the great bards of the early nineteenth century: Dupont, Lhuillier, Béranger. These names, as we will see in the next chapter, were elevated to canonic status in songbooks published after 1852, the beginning of the Second Empire. *Chanson populaire,* and the famous songwriters associated with it, were symbolic of a historical continuity stretching back from the medieval troubadour tradition.[80] On the other hand, there was the burgeoning *chansonnette* industry typified by successful musicians like Darcier, Hervé, and Villebichot. This industry, to Burani's chagrin, was utterly incompatible with the more refined *chanson populaire* tradition of Dupont and Béranger.

One culprit was the "star system," or the promotion of popular singers by agents and impresarios.[81] Thérésa, who positioned herself as a champion of old-school café sociability, entered Burani's crosshairs. He used the pages of *Le Café-concert* to rail against the singer, whose success spawned a generation of copycat stars (*étoiles*) who earned hitherto inordinate sums of money for popular song. To Burani, the "star system" was a war against national traditions of songwriting. It effectively marked a new era of popular music, one in which a performer's persona, and not their perceived quality of the performance, would be the main barometer of success. Such a barometer, he continued, outweighed the traditional need for counterpoint, theory, vocal training, diction, and other musical educational training. "War to the stars!" Burani proclaimed. "With Thérésa, their century has passed."[82]

Another topic of debate was genre. A major difference between the *chanson populaire* and *chansonnette* genres was political ideology. The state-approved *chanson populaire* repertory connected the cafés-concerts to the intellectually fecund *caveau* tradition. Burani feared that associating the café-concert with *chansonnettes* would be a gateway into the profit-driven world of theater, and which would inevitably lead to the café-concert's demise. Burani was not entirely wrong. By 1900, new institutions like the *music-hall* and *cabaret artistique*, made famous by figures like Yvette Guilbert and Aristide Bruant, would overtake the café-concert as the epicenter of counterculture in the city. But Burani's hardline stance pitting "serious" *chanson populaire* against "frivolous" *chansonnette* was met with pushback from more forward-thinking individuals—like Lorge himself. In an angry letter to Burani on April 14, 1867, right in the middle of Hervé's run of *Le Retour d'Ulysse* and in the wake of Cornélie's classical recitations, Lorge attacked Burani's unwillingness to adapt to new audiences. Here, Lorge betrays himself as a capitalist first and director second. Theater deregulation, as we have seen, was but another element of the Haussmannization of the city. The city became "modern" only after a complete and systematic rejection of financial oversight and conservation activism. Lorge did to the café-concert what Haussmann did to the city's medieval quarters: he bulldozed the fragile walls of tradition, rethinking the café-concert not as a porous space of spontaneous sociability, but as a monument to popular spectacle. If the early cafés-concerts were microcosms of a democratized, pre-Haussmannian city, Lorge's Eldorado aspired to be a temple to classical spectacle, cementing the café-concert's fate as a secondary theater.

URBAN PLANNING LESSONS FROM THE CAFÉ-CONCERT

The café-concert has always been a tricky institution to define. Its hyphenated name betrays the fact that no one—not bureaucrats, censors, impresarios, performers, nor architects—could come up with a better one. The café-concert's rise and decline seemed to align with the rise and fall of the Second Empire. But by no means was the café-concert the *epitome* of Second Empire Parisian life. Despite the formation of organizations like the Union des artistes lyriques des cafés-concerts and the Agence centrale artistique that offered support like medical subsidies and pensions for performers, and despite the efforts of the café-concert's advocates to legitimize the institution *vis-à-vis* Paris's larger theaters, there was no consensus around what the café-concert *was* as a social and performance venue, nor what it *should* be. The reason, as we have seen, is that the café-concert was not a monolithic institution. Just as a city is a loose and at times arbitrary conglomeration of neighborhoods, natural spaces, and communities, so too was Paris's theater and leisure industry a network of institutions with different aesthetic and financial ambitions.

The theatrical deregulation initiatives between 1864 and 1867 did not result in *liberté* for the café-concert in its original iteration as an intimate, *sans-gêne* space for song and socializing. The lethal cocktail of censorship, deregulation, negative publicity, and policing allowed the empire to successfully mitigate the café-concert's influence on social life in the city and indeed, in the rest of France. By the late 1860s, the smaller *concerts de quartier* were rarely written about by the city's chroniclers, marginalized as they were geographically and financially. This erasure, writes historian Martin Pénet, has caused an unfixable historiographical problem, as the names and repertoires of these cafés are all but absent in the archive. Smaller, peripheral venues like the Café de l'Annexion (La Chapelle), the Café de la Réunion (Belleville), and the Concert des Oiseaux (Ménilmontant) survive only as seedy *bouis-bouis* in the press and lack the archival richness of the larger venues in the city center.[83] Much like deregulation policy in the modern neoliberal era, the late Second Empire's deregulatory schemes were in fact an assault on the autonomy of localized social spaces. Following the 1864 *liberté des théâtres*, it was, in theory, easier for one to apply to open a theater or café. But most of these requests fell on deaf ears. Furthermore, the financial and geographic advantages of affluent venues like the Eldorado set new standards for the industry regarding staging, costuming, licensing music, and hiring stars.

At stake was the café-concert's "right to the city," or the right for urban spaces to exist and flourish regardless of political or aesthetic discrepancies with other urban spaces. Henri Lefebvre reminds us that cities are necessarily co-created spaces. Imposed class structures give the illusion that those in power have the right to produce, destroy, or unilaterally regulate urban space according to the imagined rules of a dictatorship, free market, or some other hegemonic force. The right to the city is the therefore the right "not to be classified forcibly into categories which have been determined by the necessarily homogenizing powers."[84] Read through the lens of Lefebvre's spatial sociology, the café-concert fought for its right to exist as separate from the theatrical complex that it purportedly threatened. Theater deregulation did not result in true *liberté*, but rather in an authoritarian, centralized decentralization, benefiting some but not all. Far from granting freedom of expression, the so-called *liberté des théâtres* struck a dull but fatal blow to the café-concert, as it forced the hand of impresarios like Lorge to innovate and compete in order to survive. Despite the success that Lorge enjoyed with inviting new genres and new stars to his stage, the Eldorado's 1867 season, with its introduction of operetta repertory and nods to a Hellenic past, signaled the end of an era for the café-concert as an antidote to the immersive spectacles found in the city's commercial and state-sponsored theaters. Lorge had effectively invited the twin beasts of canonicity and capitalism into a space that until then had offered a dizzying array of ephemeral but topical songs. These songs, as the next chapter shows, were not confined to indoor performance spaces, but roamed freely and largely unhindered throughout the city.

FOUR

Street Music

BETWEEN REGULATION AND LIBERATION

IN 1867, THE CRITIC, TRANSLATOR, and bureaucrat Charles Nisard (1808–89) published *Des Chansons populaires chez les anciens et chez les Français* (Popular songs ancient and French), a two-volume history of Parisian street songs. This ambitious publication followed his earlier work from 1854, *Histoire des livres populaires et de la littérature du colportage* (History of popular books and peddled literature), in which Nisard used historical and sociological analysis to ultimately censure the literature it studied. The second volume of *Des Chansons populaires* opens by describing how street songs pervaded both the visual and sonic landscape of the city:

> There is not a person who, while walking along the quays, does not notice from a distance the rows of little booklets of equal dimensions that are spread over the guardrails and weighted down by pieces of flint. There is not a person who, in certain neighborhoods where there are still gardens, does not notice those same booklets suspended from strings along walls, flapping in the wind in opposite directions. One also sees them in construction zones, spread out over the rubble or lining fences that cordon off work zones.... These little booklets are street songs.[1]

Street songs, Nisard implies, were both seen and heard, a ubiquitous piece of Parisian cultural life. Even more than the "larger" works of music heard in the city—the operas, the symphonies, the cantatas—street songs permeated outdoor urban life as a visual spectacle. They belonged to what Esther da Costa Meyer calls the "urban semiotic," or the sea of visual signs that covered public architecture.[2] Haussmann, who obsessed over details, adorned his new boulevards and squares with all sorts of urban furniture, including urinals or *pissoirs,* kiosks, benches, lampposts, fountains, and Orientalist-inspired advertising towers or *colonnes*. But as soon as these new structures were installed, they were covered in all sorts of printed discourses, including theater announcements, work opportunities, bazaar advertisements, and hundreds of song texts. Haussmann's effort to curate the urban sensorium by curbing the unsanctioned printed materials scattered throughout the city failed. Nothing seemed to have changed since the eighteenth century, when Louis Mercier, in his *Tableau de Paris,* complained of the incessant plastering of Paris: "The placard! It covers, colors, it clothes Paris [. . .] one could even call it *Paris-affiche,* to distinguish it from other cities of the universe by its most striking garb."[3] This guerrilla-style paper advertising did not cease under Haussmannization; in fact, itinerant peddlers now had more surface area to cover. Yet to focus solely on the visual skirmish between planners and peddlers is to miss an important distinction between plastered street songs and other visual debris: songs existed in the Parisian urban imagination through both sight and sound. The latter, then, would necessitate an entirely different mode of curation and policing.

This double-edged urban presence was, I believe, part of Nisard's skepticism toward the ubiquity of popular songs in the city. For if placards were the antithesis of bourgeois décor—unsupervised, unrefined, and unsophisticated in their messaging—so was the culture of popular song divided between the placarded song texts and the published *chansonniers* enjoyed indoors. Michel de Certeau has written critically of Nisard, citing his work on street culture to argue for a skepticism of class-based social science. It is tempting to consider urban popular culture in binary, vaguely Marxian terms, with upstart street musicians on one hand and an unrelenting police presence on the other. But as de Certeau warns, the question that the historian must ask is "not one of ideologies, or of options, but that of the relations of an object and its associated scientific methods to the society that sanctions them."[4] The criteria of aesthetic autonomy do not apply to street pamphlets, popular songs, and other crumbs of popular cultural historiography. Street songs are as hard to define generically as the café-concert was hard to define geographically, as was argued in the previous chapter. Yet these sonic artifacts of popular culture belonged to the conversation over how Paris would sound under Haussmannization.

Popular song traversed the city in many formats. Publishers printed song texts on cheap paper as *feuilles* (single leaves, akin to British broadsides) or as pocket-sized collections known as *cahiers, receuils,* or *chansonniers.* In most cases, these songs were contrafacta: new words were fitted to a pre-existing tune, usually from the widely circulated *Clé du caveau* anthology. Generally speaking, the *Clé du caveau* is to nineteenth-century French popular song what the *Great American Songbook* is to the twentieth-century United States. Both exist as printed publications, but they primarily function as orally transmitted "canons" of popular tunes, repeatedly covered, adapted, and referenced. Beginning in the early nineteenth century, singing societies known as *caveaux* (cellars) began anthologizing the popular tunes used by *chansonniers*. The *Clé du caveau* was compiled by the members of the *Caveau moderne* under the direction of Pierre Capelle. First published in 1811 and reissued regularly through the nineteenth century, the *Clé du caveau* contains over eight hundred indexed melodies, known as *timbres*. Many songs were therefore published without sheet music but included the name of a *timbre* or tune to which the singer would perform the song, suggesting a prevalence of contrafactum text setting in popular music.[5] Song texts, and the tunes to which they were meant to be sung, were blown up on posters and plastered on walls, fences, and along construction sites and reprinted in magazines, newspapers, and calendars. Thus on any given day a Parisian could hear a chanson performed at a café-concert, listen to it bellowed by a *marchand de chansons,* and sing or play it at home. Hundreds of such chansons were performed, busked, and printed in Paris every month of the Second Empire. This ubiquity made the *chanson* repertoire a potent element of the Parisian soundscape as a form of entertainment, a conduit of information, and an ambient reminder of modernity's persistent presence in the French capital. Song was more a part of Parisians' lives than any other musical genre, even more than the state-sponsored *fêtes impériales* discussed in chapter 2 of this book. This "festive muse," as Nisard labels songs, sprouted "in the cafésconcerts, in the music halls, and in the cabarets, where the proprietor offers it like a product to the consumer."[6] Nisard is suggesting that song was both commodity and currency. But whether it flourished as a cultural attribute or festered as a moral dilemma depended on a range of issues, from performance context to geography to questions about the role of street culture in the urbanizing city.

The previous chapter indicated how the café-concert—the popular song institution *par excellence*—was by design incompatible with Haussmann's aesthetics of spectacle. Turning now to the music itself and the people who performed it, this chapter explores the myriad ways that popular song captured the contradictions between popular culture and imperial urbanism. From inane earworms to fanfares for the empire to nostalgic odes, songs—especially those peddled in the street—open a window to the politics of representation in Haussmann's Paris. Street music and street musicians continue to be analyzed in tandem with the urban spaces that produce and sustain street culture. As Romain Benini observes, the street and street music mutually defined each other poetically, geographically, and sociologically.[7] Yet in order to grasp the full extent of popular music's role in shaping social life, we must also consider the *policies* of representation to account for the human labor that produced, disseminated, and policed music in public social spaces. Later we will encounter some of the musicians who were repeatedly represented as an urban subculture in newspaper reviews, cartoons, guidebooks, and memoirs. Songwriters, performers, and publishers were beholden to external social forces, such as policing, censorship, and perceptions of morality. Yet despite the efforts of Nisard and others to lump them into single urban community, Second Empire street musicians faced a contradictory terrain of policies, regulations, and reputations. On the one hand, street musicians were regarded as iconic urban heroes whose lowly stature and haggard appearance undermined the manicured and pretentious habits of Second Empire high society. On the other hand, tourist guidebooks and police decrees cast these musicians as hindrances to the flow of urban life, while literary elites blamed street songs for the overall dumbing-down of Parisian musical culture. These contested attitudes reflect the widespread ambivalence toward Haussmann's urbanization of Paris in the mid-nineteenth century and the distinct brand of fast-paced, mass-produced urban culture that it precipitated.

Street songs have long played a decisive role in constructing spaces of congregation and organization for Paris's sociopolitical communities. Indeed, their strong ties to discourses about modernization extend back to the French Revolution. Rarely was it possible, for political reasons, to say exactly what you wanted in song. Rather, meanings were obscured and refracted, and depended as much on the contexts of performance as on content and authorial intent.[8] Unlike orchestral concerts of the early nineteenth century, which, as James Johnson has argued, became less about socializing and more about aesthetic contemplation, the culture of popular singing consisted of several interrelated elements: the choice of space, the freedom (or lack thereof) to participate, the means of distributing the music, and the bureaucratic relations between songwriters, patrons, and censors.[9] Haussmannization, as we have seen, extended well beyond demolishing and rebuilding into musical acoustics and aesthetics. It also, in no small way, involved rezoning the listener. Second Empire bureaucrats—Nisard and Haussmann among them—sought to control all infrastructure networks of musical circulation by any means necessary. Though overlooked in most musical histories, Second Empire song was a potent social force. Its malleability, accessibility, and ubiquity allowed song to infiltrate Parisian social worlds in ways that concert or stage music could not. To wrap our minds around just how ubiquitous song was in Second Empire Paris, we begin with a song that was as influential as it was inane.

A UBIQUITOUS TUNE

Popular song's perceived lack of seriousness and artistic merit allowed its creators and users to smuggle all sorts of topics into their lyrics, from working conditions to tourism to city planning. There was little correlation between audience and class, and therefore little opportunity to take personal offense. Songs glossing working-class life were particularly welcome in factories and taverns. Catchy tunes and picturesque images of street life allowed workers to see themselves as part of the mainstream urban conversation.[10] During the Second Empire, songs of all varieties circulated both indoors and out; the same song could be heard on a street corner, in a tavern, in a café-concert, or in a theater. Contemporary observers did not hesitate to regard even the most frivolous songs as markers of Parisian identity.

One such song was the August 1864 hit "Hé Lambert!," written by Félix Baumaine and set to the tune of "La Belle polonaise."[11] Baumaine's verses, which repeatedly ask if anyone has seen a man named Lambert, sold a hundred thousand copies within days of being sent to the *marchands de chansons,* putting a tremendous strain on the printers.[12] The song's popularity swelled after singer Alexandre Legrand gave an infectious performance at the Concerts du XIXe Siècle, a café-concert on the rue du Château d'Eau in the tenth arrondissement.[13] The refrain shows the extent to which repetition was a driving factor in the song's catchiness:

> Have you not seen Lambert,
> At the rail'way station?
> Have you not seen ...
> Lambert? (*5 times*)
> Did he go swimming in the sea,
> Is he lost in th'desert?
> Who's seen Lambert?
> Lambert? (*4 times*)[14]

The song is identified in the print version as a *scie parisienne,* or "Parisian saw." A *scie* was a type of song that bordered on sense and nonsense, featuring a catchy, easy-to-remember refrain repeated *ad nauseam.* According to the 1863 edition of the *Dictionnaire de la langue française,* a *scie* was a "refrain of premeditated monotony, to be repeated all the more often if it seems to irritate the person it intends to aggravate."[15] The famously moody critic Timothée Trimm penned a front-page article titled "Hé! Lambert!" in *Le Petit journal.* He begins by defining the *scie* as "a repetition of a word, a sentence, or a question with the aim to exasperate the reader, to try his patience, to disrupt his solace."[16] Some of the most popular Parisian café songs of the latter half of the nineteenth century were *scies,* such as "Le pied qui r'mue," which appeared in 1862 (words and music by Paul Avenel), and "L'amant d'Amanda," which appeared in 1876 (words by Émile Carré, music by Victor Robillard). The enduring taste for *scies* from the 1860s through the end of the nineteenth century suggests an inverse relationship between perceived aesthetic value and mass popularity. *Scies* were lucrative because they were mostly nonsensical and thus less prone to censorship, making them all the easier to distribute and perform. Derek Scott, evoking Henri Bergson, has attempted to explain that the humorous appeal of the *scie* was its machine-like repetition "rather than something emanating from a thinking, living human being."[17] Yet some nineteenth-century critics argued that the *scie's* monotonous verses were meditative and allowed one to think freely while humming. Writing for the *Mercure de France* in 1898—two years before philosopher Henri Bergson published his famous treatise on comedy, *Le Rire*—the journalist Jean de Tinan defended the *scie* as "an indispensable safety valve under the conditions of modern intellectual life."[18] By tracing its circulation through Paris, however, I interpret *Lambert's* ubiquity as an exercise in human agency, a sort of fanfare for the common Parisian: an example of the citizenry seizing control, however briefly, of the urban sensorium.

Contemporary accounts offered conflicting origin stories of the "Hé Lambert!" verse, which only further added to the song's mystique. In his article, Trimm recounts a crowded scene at the Bois de Vincennes where a hundred thousand people gathered to watch a fireworks display. Amid the noise of cannons and firecrackers, an old woman shoved through the crowds looking for her misplaced husband. In a piercing soprano she bellowed "Hé! Lambert! Où est-il?" ("Hey! Lambert! Where is he?") The crowd, there to have a good time, began to repeat the woman's beckon. Cries of "Hé! Lambert!" resonated in the trains from Vincennes all the way to the city center and echoed in the streets of Paris through the night. For the rest of the month of August, Trimm adds, "Lambert" was shouted by men, women, children, soldiers, butchers, and servants. Spectators in Paris's theaters would chant it between—and during—performances. The songwriter Jules Renard referenced the Lambert episode—as well as Trimm's front-page coverage—in a song titled "On n' s'amuse qu'à Paris" (One has the most fun in Paris).[19] After quoting the Lambert cry directly in a sung verse, Renard recounts the origins of "Hé Lambert!" in a spoken section of the song, observing that such trivial pleasures could only be found in Paris: "Well, one could boast about knowing Lambert. I heard him beckoned from the Bastille to the Champs de Mars, in every street, on every corner. He hid somewhere, surely.... When buying the *P'tit journal*, I asked my vendor: Have you seen Lambert?—Gone like a canary, she replied.... Decidedly one has the most fun in Paris."[20]

The *New York Times* reported it differently, claiming that the woman lost her husband *on* the train:

> A few days ago a very gross and especially a very grotesque woman named LAMBERT missed her husband on a train of cars on which there happened to be a large number of fast young men going boating at Asnières, and the frantic cries of this grotesque woman after 'Monsieur LAMBERT,' gave the start to this singular word.... Foreigners were alarmed, and but for the laugh which accompanied the exclamation, would have beat a retreat for fear of a revolution.[21]

Both Trimm and the *Times* correspondent used Lambert to highlight Parisians' knack for noisy, improvised spectacle. Both interpreted distinctly urban social spaces—the park and the train car—as fertile sites for festive soundscaping, just for the sake of it. But there is another story to report here, as well: Parisians employing their collective voices in a playful yet subversive way, using song to reclaim Parisian spaces increasingly occupied by tourists. Guy Debord's well-known concept of *dérive* or "drifting" is useful. While modern infrastructure networks like the railway and omnibus shuttled passengers to and from monumental squares via monumental boulevards, the presence of song within these networks unsettled the curated, touristic image of the ordered city. As a sonic *dérive*, "Lambert" was not so much symptomatic of spectacle as it was evidence of urban communities' desire for participatory urban place-making. As radical acts of collective expression, *dérives* involve "playful-constructive behavior and awareness of psychogeographical effects, and are thus quite different from the classic notions of journey or stroll."[22] Assuming the form of a *scie*—catchy and vapid, but also slogan-like—"Lambert" granted citizens a playful means for renegotiating their experience of urban space, drifting out of passive spectatorship back into an active participation in city life.

Shortly after its exploration as an oral phenomenon, "Lambert" was transplanted into the commodified realm of notated sheet music. Despite its hazy provenance—or because of it—the "Lambert" slogan spread like a virus through Parisian popular musical circuits, spawning not only Alexandre Legrand's chanson but also instrumental arrangements. The conductor and arranger Henry Marx published a piano quadrille titled "Eh! Lambert!!" in 1864. Quadrilles were incredibly popular at the time, providing consumers with catchy melodies, rhythmic variety, and relevant subject matter. The cover indicates that orchestral and four-hand arrangements were also available for purchase. Marx's quadrille follows the typical five-movement structure, with each respective movement named after a famous *contredanse* from the early nineteenth century.[23] The first "Pantalon" movement consists of a leaping G major melody over a galloping accompaniment in duple meter. The second "Été" movement is also a duple-meter dance but with a melody in the dominant D. The third "Poule" movement, also in D, is a rocking jig in 6/8. The fourth "Pastourelle" movement, also in 6/8, features a stepwise melody in C. The fifth "Finale" movement returns to duple meter to bring the quadrille to a close in G major. In short, Marx's quadrille unfolds through the same rhythmic and harmonic changes as do all quadrilles of the day. It is unremarkable on all accounts, save for one: Marx embeds the "Lambert" cry into a quasi-choral passage in the "Pastourelle" (example 5). The rising and descending passage underscored with the words "Lambert! Lambert!" echoes the hordes of curious Parisians depicted on the cover of the sheet music. As if to capture the mocking tone of the chanters at the Bois de Vincennes, Marx repeats the quasi-modal passage up an octave and diminishes the rhythmic value from dotted quarter notes to eighths. This "echo" effect is clearly marked in the score so as to avoid any confusion regarding the passage's humorous intentions. The "Lambert" cry, through its many forms, not only pervaded the Parisian streetscape, but also became a sought-after commodity in Paris's salons and parlors.

Critics from both France and abroad worked to rationalize "Lambert's" evolution from an urban earworm to a commercial hit. In their journal entry on August 20, 1864, Edmond and Jules de Goncourt called for governmental intervention in bringing the fad to an abrupt end: "at this time in Paris, there

EXAMPLE 5. Henry Marx, *Eh! Lambert!!* Movement 4, "Pastourelle," measures 17–25.

is an epidemic of idiotic cries, of *Ohé Lambert,* such that they need to be stopped by the police."[24] In a far more sympathetic take on street song, the critic Henri Gourdon de Genouillac deployed language redolent of Baudelaire in his essay *Les Refrains de la rue.* After a mere eight days of popularity, observes Genouillac (albeit exaggerating), "it was over, faded, out of fashion."[25] Others commented on how the cry reflected how the Parisian public often disregarded tact for the sake of amusement. Nisard observed that the "Lambert" craze accurately summarized contemporary urban sensibility and was an inevitable by-product of *la vie parisienne:* "Nothing is more consistent with the temperament of the people of Paris."[26]

News of the song's popularity soon made its way to London critics, many of whom pounced on the chance to compare Victorian and Second Empire sensibilities. The magazine *Temple Bar* featured a six-page exposé on "Lambert," in which the anonymous author used the song as a pretext to praise Parisians' taste for silliness (and to bemoan the relative snobbishness of Victorian London). Referring to the August 15 Saint-Napoléon festivities, the author explains how the "Lambert" craze disarmed the solemnity of the event by adding a dose of absurdity to the festivities: "Neither the French nor the English have a monopoly of snobs who hate that the mass of the toilers of the earth should have a holiday; who think enjoyment was made for them, and perpetual labor for the 'lower classes.' God help us all, and forgive us our class selfishness."[27] This juxtaposition of "high" and "low" festivities gave an illusion of democracy to an otherwise authoritarian French government. While Napoléon III's regime regulated urban space by staging organized parades, processions, concerts, speeches, and coordinated chants of *Vive l'Empereur,* the ubiquitous presence of "Lambert" offered passive Parisian onlookers a chance to participate in the spectacle: "In the Tuileries gardens we are just in time to catch a glimpse of the Emperor on his balcony, bowing his acknowledgments of the greeting... and then we turn and find ourselves in fairyland. If it were not for *As-tu vu Lambert?* we would look for elves and 'wee folks.'"[28]

If *Temple Bar* painted a jovial picture of the "Lambert" craze, the *London Review of Politics, Society, Literature, Art & Science* offered a more sobering interpretation of Parisian mass culture.[29] The review explains how *Lambert* was used as a protest cry against the emperor and empress during the August 15 festivities—an anti-fanfare. Led by a group of Parisian street urchins, a crowd of rowdy onlookers greeted the imperial cortège with cries of "Vive Lambert! Vive Madame Lambert!"—much to the chagrin of the police authorities. The *London Review* reporter notes that such irreverence was also heard during the final years of the *ancien régime,* when protestors bombarded Louis XVI's and Marie Antoinette's carriages with shouts of "À bas Capet! À bas Madame Capet!"[30] This collective desire to nickname the emperor after a passing street fad betrays a distinctly Parisian impulse to stage everyday life as if it were a spectacle—and, indeed, to regard the city of Paris as one giant theatrical space. Following this account, the anonymous author launches into a diagnosis of modernity that is too prescient not to quote at length:

> The little incident, however unimportant from a political point of view, throws light, nevertheless, on the way in which Paris regards the Second Empire. For the present, it almost seems as if Paris had ceased to be a city of politicians: it has become a city of spectators. The Empire is to the population of its great metropolis not so much a sad or joyous reality as a spectacle of pomp and magnificence. It is an institution, just as the rue de Rivoli, or the Cirque Impérial, or the boulevard des Italiens is an institution—something rich, and tangible, and flashing, which adds to the gaiety of the day. As the Emperor rides along the street he is received, not with flushed cheeks and beating pulses, but with open mouths. His progress excites neither respect nor indignation, but simple curiosity. When France receives her elected Emperor with an extemporized *charivari,* it is plain that she is not in the habit of connecting his name with any particular idea.... He is in their eyes something to be looked at, and, for anything they care, they can pleasantly receive him with the comical cry, '*Voilà, Lambert!*'[31]

The "Lambert" craze of 1864 epitomized a pervasive urban narrative associated with Second Empire life: the ephemerality of fashion and taste. This narrative, of course, stems from Baudelaire and his "Painter of Modern Life." Legions of students and scholars have defined Parisian modernity on Baudelaire's terms, citing his three adjectives as necessary conditions— ephemeral, fugitive, contingent. To summarize bluntly: modern life moves fast, and so modernity is an awareness of that speed. The second half of Baudelaire's oft-quoted statement, however, is more revealing. These three qualifiers are but *half* of his conception of modern art, "whose other half is eternal and immutable."

Baudelaire's modern Paris, then, rests in a dialectic between the visible and the invisible, the here and the not-here. Popular song would ostensibly belong to the "fleeting" half of modernity, but as "Lambert" proves, its porosity and mutability blur this division of presence and absence. Just as there were multiple Parisian narratives of modernity playing out simultaneously, so too there was not one "Lambert," but many: the missing husband, the train rumor, the street cry, the song, the spinoff quadrille. "Lambert" infiltrated Parisian minds by occupying Parisian spaces. The public parks, the train cars and stations, the cafés, the salons—these all constituted the dense network of infrastructures that Haussmannization hoped to streamline into a single file. Haussmannian modernity, with its broadened streets and sidewalks, large department stores, and cavernous performance spaces, promoted a no-touch society. The popularity of "Lambert" spread not through curated mass spectacle but through makeshift forms of oral transmission like spontaneous refrains. Thus ephemerality, in the Baudelairean sense, was also a physical and spatial phenomenon. In the previous chapter I argued that the café-concert's potency rested in its sonic and spatial porosity. This chapter sees a similar porosity in popular music. Helen Abbott has recently noted that the perceived ephemerality or durability of a song, and the subsequent value judgment of that song, depends on its ontological stability. Reflecting on the negative press that *chansonnettes* received in the nineteenth century, Abbott reminds us that "it may be hard not to make value judgements about works based on their impermanence," and I would add that impermanence could also be viewed as malleability and translatability.[32] With their ability to adapt within different spheres of public and private life, songs offered listeners, practitioners, and promoters an opportunity to narrate urban experiences alternative to those imposed by *status quo* journalists and bureaucrats.

PORTRAIT OF A STREET MUSICIAN

As we have seen, street song's impermanence was its greatest asset. But as Haussmann continued his campaign to homogenize the sensory experiences of the city, street songs—and those who performed them professionally— became a liability to the Second Empire's monumental urban aesthetic. The "Lambert" craze demonstrates how a single melody could infiltrate urban spaces as diverse as train stations, parks, living rooms, public squares, and theater boxes. As Genouillac writes in *Les Refrains de la rue*, the most popular hits were "ground on barrel organs, tapped on the pianos, and scraped on violins."[33] Perhaps no other musical community better understood modern urbanism than that which made its living outdoors. Of the three instruments mentioned by Genouillac, it was the barrel organ, or *orgue de Barbarie*, that most symbolized Second Empire street life. The exact origins of the instrument's name are contested, but the most widely accepted, if apocryphal, version is that an Italian organ maker named Barberi or Barbari brought a prototype from Modena at the end of the eighteenth century.[34] This portable organ, which requires little skill on the part of the player, soon became a staple of the Parisian soundscape. In the 1830s and '40s, organ grinders cranked out tunes from the Italian operas and French opéras-comiques currently in vogue.

Although these musicians helped introduce many working-class pedestrians to the operas of Vincenzo Bellini and Adolphe Adam, authors of bourgeois Paris guidebooks regarded them disparagingly: "how miserably he cranks out the duo from *Puritains!* How he abuses parts of *Favorite* and *Postillon de Longumeau!*"[35] Following the collapse of the Second Empire, the organ grinder became a poster child for anti-Haussmannian sentiment. As *La Lanterne* reported on February 8, 1870, "The renovations of Paris have dealt a terrible blow to street performers who, little by little, disappear from public spaces."[36] The press continued advocating for street musicians even as the government gradually tempered their presence in the streets of Paris. Sentimental images cast organ grinders as old, destitute, or both; among many from the period, Honoré Daumier's tragic depiction (figure 7) shows an organ grinder and a street singer performing like automatons for a small, unimpressed audience. For anti-Haussmannian preservationists, organ grinders were embodiments of the Paris that had been stripped from them at the expense of relentless urbanization. Like so many other *types parisiens* mythologized in guidebooks, magazines, and memoirs, organ grinders

FIGURE 7. Honoré Daumier, "Le Joueur d'orgue de Barbarie," ca. 1860. Image: Musée des Beaux-arts de la Ville de Paris.

provided a means of negotiating the inevitable disappearance of *le vieux Paris* and the people who epitomized it. The complexity of this nostalgia will emerge as a main theme in the next chapter.

Street musicians rarely attained the level of renown as did café-concert stars like Thérésa, Susanne Lagier, or Joseph Kelm. This, as the previous chapter explored, was by design: the "star system," the Société des auteurs, compositeurs et éditeurs de musique (SACEM), and the Agence centrale artistique all played a hand in Paris's burgeoning industry of popular musical spectacle. However, due to the increasing popularity of literary *flânerie* in the 1850s and 60s, ambulant musicians became mythological figures of the Parisian streetscape, and writers depicted them as at once heroes, villains, and victims. In "The Painter of Modern Life," Baudelaire mused that the modern urbanite marvels at "the amazing harmony of life in the capital cities, a harmony so providentially maintained amid the turmoil of human freedom."[37] Harmony here could mean many things: cooperation between urban institutions, a utopian sense of community, or in a musical sense, a polyphonic experience of outdoor din. The journalist Charles Yriarte shared Baudelaire's fascination with the street performer and her role in harmonizing the city. A devoted *flâneur* who was deeply moved by the destructive effects of Haussmann's urbanization on street life, Yriarte maintained that street performers helped define the city as a conglomeration of picturesque, strange, and diverse urban spaces. "Tomorrow," Yriarte lamented in his book *Paris grotesque: Les célébrités de la rue*, "it will be too late to write a book such as this." Urbanization would instead cleanse the Parisian street of its most unique and enduring characters: "Farewell to the gaiety of our public squares, farewell to the gaudy costumes, to the strange songs, to the open-air dentists, to the street musicians. . . . I swear to you, gentlemen, that Paris will become dull; it will be filled with nostalgia for the picturesque."[38]

Some street musicians, aware of bourgeois guilt and nostalgia, did manage to earn renown and income in the music publishing industry. One of the most famous street singers was Eugène-Théodore Baumester, who penned the ode to the boulevard du Prince-Eugène discussed in this book's introduction. The son of a respected *chanteur des rues*, Baumester was singing in the streets of Paris by the age of four; at his peak in the 1850s, he was most often seen and heard outside the cirque d'Hiver.[39] The busy intersection was home to the circus as well as public bathhouses, making for an ideal spot to attract pleasure-seeking pedestrians. Baumester resisted the stereotype of the panhandling street musician, and instead sought to project himself as an enterprising musical professional. He was successful. Between 1832 and his death, Baumester published hundreds of original chansons either as single-leaf *feuilles* or as bound notebooks or *cahiers*. While his earlier publications were largely funded by his father, Baumester later worked with high-volume publishers such as Durand (*Chansons du peuple,* 1848), Vert (*La Chanson des rues,* 1850), and Tassus (*Le Siècle du progrès musical,* 1864).[40]

Despite his success, Baumester never attempted to conquer the café-concert stage. Instead, he continued to attract street crowds into the second half of the century, selling collections of his printed music as well as the popular chansons of his contemporaries, to which he was often given sole publishing rights. In 1869 the daily periodical *L'Orchestre* called Baumester "the doyen of Parisian street singers."[41] Baumester's confidence was high; in the 1870s his published song collections, titled *La Chanson des rues,* included the epigraph: "Despite those jealous, villainous, fools/ The people continue to listen to my songs with pleasure."[42] The covers of these collections (figure 8) featured this epigraph beneath an illustration of an organ grinder. Unlike Daumier's image of an aging grinder, Baumester's youthful organist is the center of attention. Surrounded by a diverse and attentive crowd of onlookers, the organist grinds with one hand and sells sheet music with another. The posters in the background feature the names of famous French *chansonniers* from the eighteenth and nineteenth centuries, as if suggesting a lineage that linked Baumester to bards like Pierre-Jean de Béranger.[43] Baumester used this type of imagery as a mode of promotional self-fashioning; unlike the café singer, whose success was in essence "manufactured" by the impresario, the street singer needed to work hard in order to resist the haggard image that was so popular among poets and illustrators.

Often depicted as urban curiosities, street musicians possessed considerable agency. Baumester both wrote and performed music, which meant that he had both a platform and an audience for self-expression. He had relationships with printers and bureaucrats at his disposal. Yet nearly all of Baumester's compatriots are now forgotten or, in fact, have never been acknowledged in the first place. A major reason for this marginalization was policing. Although some evidence of these forgotten musicians survives in the form of identity cards and police summonses, the Second Empire succeeded in lumping street performers into a single category, thereby making them easier to monitor through policy. The Préfecture de Police effectively wrote their own narrative of the city by treating the regulation of the urban soundscape as a moral issue.

FIGURE 8. Cover image of *La Chanson des rues: Recueil de romances, chansonnettes comiques, gaudrioles, barcarolles, chansons grivoises, etc., etc. Entièrement inédites, publiée par Eugène Baumester, auteur et chanteur* (Paris: E. Vert, 1850–74).

STREET MUSIC AND THE POLICE

The history of nineteenth-century street music is closely tied to the policing of Parisian urban space. Throughout the nineteenth century, street performers dealt with an ebb and flow of police regulations; in general, a relatively stable government meant relaxed restrictions on what and where they could perform, while the years surrounding revolutions and regime changes meant more severe regulations. Each of the French regimes of the nineteenth century regarded uncontrolled street music as a potential threat to general moral welfare.[44] A police decree passed on July 4, 1816, two years into the Bourbon Restoration, demonstrates the severity with which both the municipal prefecture and the state ministry treated undocumented street musicians. Following a series of reports submitted to (or by) the police, street musicians were accused of causing discord either because they sang "licentious" songs or because they caused congestion in public.[45] As a result, the Bourbon police issued a new law requiring all organ grinders to obtain a license from the prefecture and renew it yearly. Any musician caught without documentation, the decree continues, would be "severely punished."[46]

Licensing became the primary means of controlling the number and geographic distribution of street musicians in Paris. The annual renewal process detailed in the 1816 decree became every six months in 1830—the year the July Monarchy was established—and every three months in 1853—the first full year of the Second Empire.[47] Yet this increased bureaucratic pressure did more than just hold street performers accountable: it reflected a desire to tighten street regulations as the city was being urbanized. According to a police report dated December 14, 1831, street performers were no longer allowed to roam freely around Paris. Rather, they were for the first time restricted to specifically designated intersections, squares, and boulevards. Other spaces that musicians had frequented for centuries, such the famed Pont Neuf connecting the Île de la Cité to the Left and Right Banks, were henceforth off limits.[48] The increased emphasis on licensing coincided with the increasing instability of the Parisian landscape. As the streets changed shape, so too did the laws regulating them.

Shortly following Haussmann's appointment as Prefect of the Seine in 1853, the laws regarding street performers underwent a series of substantial reforms. A police decree issued on November 30, 1853 grouped four distinct professions under the same legal category of "street performer": clowns, barrel organists, street instrumentalists, and singers.[49] As a result all extant certificates were annulled, requiring street performers to reapply to the Préfecture de Police for their licenses and medallions. Applications also included a comprehensive list of designated public performance spaces. After 1860, street musicians had sixty-three options across Paris's twenty arrondissements.[50] Performers were strictly forbidden from congregating on sidewalks, in front of market entrances, or near other designated *voies publiques*. The large majority of acceptable spaces were intersections, squares, and along certain sections of the newly widened boulevards.

Nor could these musicians leave and work elsewhere. Thousands of workers remained in the Paris center during and after Haussmann's renewals, as the cost of housing needed to be weighed in conjunction with wages, transportation, proximity and access to food, and other economic factors; one worker, Antoine Granveau, argued that "many families would rather pay 400 to 450 francs inside [the city center], near their work, than 300 in the outskirts."[51] Cheap housing solutions, known as *garnis*, packed tired workers into filthy rooms. Fearing police altercations, street workers, including musicians, traveled by night to these crowded lodgings or spent their evenings in workers' cabarets near Les Halles, like the infamous Cabaret de Paul Niquet.[52] Inevitably, drunkenness and slovenliness went hand-in-hand with urban labor, as these were the side effects of urbanization that benefited some but not all. Police, eager to maintain moral order along the "renewed" Haussmannian boulevards, targeted these *garnis* and cabarets, completing the vicious circle.

By Haussmann's standards, to be itinerant in his city was a sign of moral failure. Despite being attacked for his disparaging remarks toward the working class, Haussmann doubled down on his convictions regarding the true purpose and function of the modern city. "Paris belongs to France," he wrote in his *Mémoires*, "and not to those Parisians by birth or by choice who reside here, nor above all to the mobile population of its lodging houses, . . . nor to this tribe of 'Nomads,' according to an expression for which I was reproached, but whose accuracy I maintain."[53] While Haussmann and the Prefecture of the Seine concerned themselves with demolition and construction, the Prefecture of Police was tasked with establishing a new moral order within *le nouveau Paris*. Those street performers who wished to reapply following the 1853 decree now needed to provide a "certificate of good moral standing."[54] New curfew hours placed stricter regulations on both kinetic and aural activity outdoors: between October 1 and April 1, clowns, barrel organists, street instrumentalists, and singers could only perform between eight in the morning and six in the evening and during the warm months, between eight in the morning and nine in the evening. Other measures were taken to prevent performers from exploiting children; the 1853 decree prohibited children under sixteen years of age from performing in the streets for money, or even accompanying performers of legal age. Together, these measures represented the empire's systematic efforts to regulate street activity according to an implied code of conduct. To the regime, Haussmannization was as much a moral project as it was a geographic one. If songs represented the cultures of urban space, then policing those songs thus constituted policing urban space, as well.

For many proponents of Haussmann's *nouveau Paris,* the epitome of moral licentiousness was Carnaval, the indulgent Catholic celebration directly preceding Lent. In Paris, the place to celebrate Carnaval was Belleville, the historically working-class commune in the hills to the east of Paris, which was annexed by the city in 1860 as part of the twentieth arrondissement. The main celebration in Belleville was the *descente de la Courtille,* the "descent to the Belleville courtyard," a festival that was accompanied by heavy drinking and partying. The July Monarchy and (later) the Second Republic police tried to prevent the merriment from bleeding into the central *arrondissements,* but these attempts were largely unsuccessful. Year after year, composers, playwrights, and songwriters glorified the event through vaudevilles, symphonic works, and chansons.[55] Even Richard Wagner participated in the festivities, composing a short work for chorus and orchestra titled *Descendons gaiement la Courtille.* Wagner composed it as incidental music for a vaudeville-ballet-pantomime by Théophile Marion Dumersan and Charles-Désiré Dupeuty that played at the Salle Ventadour during the 1841 Carnaval season.[56] A main draw was the low price of alcohol; before its annexation into Paris, Belleville sat outside of Paris's *barrières,* or gates, and thus was part of a different taxation scheme. Ultimately, the Second Empire Prefecture of Police quashed the *descente* once and for all, first by expanding the radius of the *octroi,* or city tax, then by outlawing the celebration once Belleville officially became part of the city of Paris.

The gradual suppression of the *descente de la Courtille* had a devastating economic impact on working-class community organizations in Belleville, especially those centered on communal song and drink. Supporters lamented the government's taxing what was regarded as a cultural institution. In 1864, Alfred Delvau commented on how the suppression of the event sapped the "festive spirit" of the Parisian working class: "The *descente de la Courtille* is about to give up the Parisian ghost that it had taken in the wrong direction. This tradition diminishes from year to year, like everything else that is at the mercy of our tastes, and yet we do not gain in morality."[57] Others complained that canceling the event damaged the economy of Paris's outer neighborhoods. One chanson from 1858 titled "Hommage au choral de Belleville" (set to the tune "Marchons à la frontière" by the noted *chansonnier* Charles Gille) addresses not only the dissolution of the *descente de la Courtille,* but also the alcohol tax hike that followed.

> Truly, to not toast
> The choirs of Belleville
> Would be to act
> In an uncivil manner.
> Fleeing the big city,
> Fearful of the atmosphere,
> Cordiality
> Is exiled to the periphery.[58]

Although the government regarded the celebration as a site of morally bankrupt drunkenness, this chanson alludes to an artistic working-class culture that economically depended on sociability around low-priced drink. *Hommage au choral de Belleville* was premiered at a *chansonnier* banquet on December 18, 1858, by the community chorus of Belleville.[59] Far from being a group of drunks, this chorus was in fact an established lyrical association that won annual medals in Orphéon choral competitions.[60] The song's final stanza, which laments the rising tax and the wane of organized social events in Belleville, was a polemic aimed at the empire's unforgiving attitude toward working-class café culture:

> This joyous dinner
> Will remain in our memory;
> But to coronate it
> Let us drink;
> Because the Paris border tax,
> Extending its reach,
> Will raise the price
> Of the wine of the [Parisian] peripheries.[61]

Hommage au choral de Belleville is an example of how street songs were deployed for a variety of uses, entertainment, homage, and protest. Songs provided a means of spreading a message into a diverse set of urban public and private spaces. This multivalence was precisely what made chansons at once attractive and dangerous, and which make the genre a crucial component of understanding music's role in the nineteenth-century urban imagination. Ontologically unstable, geographically mobile, songs were vital to the city's infrastructure networks of sociability—the city's "lifeblood," as Michel Colardelle and Florence Gétreau have aptly observed.[62] When viewed as both sources of entertainment and as conduits of information, Parisian street songs offer a window into the everyday opinions, customs, and ideologies underpinning Second Empire society. Though never explicitly subversive, songs offered Parisians multiple perspectives on a variety of urban-centered topics, such as the new boulevards, the influx of tourists, the middle class, and demolitions. The remainder of this chapter offers a snapshot of songs about Paris: in praise of it, nostalgic for it, critical of it. I have selected these songs to highlight how the popular musical repertoire articulated the perceived clash between Haussmann's new city (*le nouveau Paris*) and the erosion of the old urban landscape and its culture (*le vieux Paris*). It would be a monumental and unreasonable undertaking to catalog every song published during the Second Empire in this chapter (though it would make for a groundbreaking digital humanities project). Rather than pretend to be comprehensive, I offer instead a walking tour of some of the most popular songs about the city that circulated in its streets and cafés. Penned by wandering songwriters and musical elites, these songs represented Paris as a multiplicity of geographies, demographics, and temporalities.

NEW PARIS, IN SONG

During the 1850s and 60s, when the modernization of Paris became Napoléon III's primary domestic agenda, publishers issued countless guidebooks, memoirs, and songs with "Paris" in the title. Those songs simply titled "Paris" typically presented the city as a singular object of fascination and desire. In Eugène Baumester's "Paris," set to the tune of "Mon âme à Dieu," the narrator bids a romantic adieu to a city that provided happiness in an otherwise troubled personal life:

> Farewell, adored city of Paris,
> Where my poor heart was once happy.
> I now go tread once again
> The dusty soil of my sad homeland [*contrée*].
> I leave you, farewell, my idol,
> My eyes, you see, are moved.

> With you I leave behind happiness
> And my joy remains in Paris. (*bis*)⁶³

Baumester fashioned himself as a modern-day troubadour, lacing oblique references to urbanization into what is ostensibly a lament about lost love and departure. The word "contrée" is especially loaded with multivalent meaning. It can mean "region" or "countryside," but in this context the land is metaphorical: the return to "dusty soil" does not necessary mean that the narrator has traveled far. Rather, it is Paris that is both a welcoming and unforgiving landscape. Whereas some of these odes to Paris, like Baumester's, evoked a romanticized connection between narrator and city, others focused more concretely on politics, emphasizing human freedom and praising the imperial family. The Conservatoire professor and *Prix de Rome* winner Antoine Elwart (1808–77) wrote a chanson that depicted the French capital as an urban "paradise." Elwart's "Paris!" appeared in his 1867 *Oeuvres musicales choisies*, a collection consisting of fifty chansons, melodies, and cantatas for solo female voice.⁶⁴ Following a quasi-recitative introduction in which the narrator thrice asks why he loves Paris, the song proper begins by explaining that Paris is a haven for free expression and individual liberty:

> [Paris], this enchanting place
> Where the soul, free and proud,
> Can hide its misery
> And retain its liberty.⁶⁵

Set over a waltzing E minor accompaniment (example 6), the first verse assumes a folk-like simplicity through the open fifths in the vocal part and a repetitive, dactylic rhythm that appears in every measure. Whereas Baumester's song looks inwards, Elwart's has an extroverted sensibility with its pastoral motifs and simplistic optimism. Following a piano interlude, the tonality shifts to the relative G major, and the narrator reveals his political leanings. Paris, after all, was the sacred site where the emperor's only child was baptized:

> It was in Paris that the genius boy
> Received his holy baptism;
> And his supreme power
> Radiates throughout the country!⁶⁶

This shift to the relative major highlights the song's intended audience: not passersby or fellow bards, but rather the imperial audience. By beginning

EXAMPLE 6. Antoine Elwart, "Paris!," measures 1–9.

with the city and ending with the country, Elwart frames Paris as a sacred space of consecration, much like the exhibition cantatas discussed in chapter 2. These two chansons by Baumester and Elwart, through both titled "Paris," demonstrate the wildly different interpretations of what the city could signify to its people; while Baumester's street song oozes with personal nostalgia, Elwart's composition focuses on themes of patriotism and imperial allegiance. In short, we see two different cities: one community-oriented, romantic, sociable; the other imperial, monumental, sacred.

Indeed, "Paris" proved to be a kaleidoscopic theme that inspired all types of songwriters from Conservatoire professors to street musicians to café celebrities. As the café-concert industry burgeoned in the late 1850s, impresarios would feature these "odes to Paris" in boulevard variety shows known as *revues*. These shows, which attracted a diverse audience of urban bourgeois, rich provincials, and tourists, featured a trivial plot, topical humor, and upbeat musical numbers. *Revues* were, by design, potpourris of familiar pieces of music, and any newly composed music would serve as incidental music. Scholars are only recently looking to these *revues* for their connections to the city's elite musical communities.[67] As with cafés-concerts, *revues* were not contained within the walls of their theaters. The more successful numbers were circulated out of doors as part of the street music market. One such number was "La Vie de Paris," a *ronde* with text by Lambert-Thiboust and Alfred Delacour, music by Sylvain Mangeant.[68] It appeared in a *revue* titled *Souvenirs de jeunesse,* which ran at the Théâtre des Variétés during the 1860–61 season. The text addresses the delicate balance between work and play in the city. The narrator reflects on urban life in a deeply personal way, even referring to Paris in the familiar second-person "toi":

> Splendid and proud city,
> Always welcoming,
> If there is on this earth,
> If there is a paradise,
> It's you, noisy city,
> Where ardent youth
> Works, dreams, and sings. . . .
> Yes, it's you! . . . It's Paris!
> Long live folly!
> And may pleasure
> Leave in our life (*bis.*)
> A joyful memory. (*bis.*)[69]

The description of Paris as "noisy" runs like an *idée fixe* through nineteenth-century literature, from novels and guidebooks to poems and song texts. Although guidebooks tended to deride the city's noise levels, songs featuring the word "bruit" praised the city for its vibrancy. As we have seen, the government cited excessive noise as a major excuse to patrol the streets. But "bruit" also encompassed activities such as eating, smoking, theatergoing, and walking. The *chansonnette* "Paris la nuit," the enduring title song of a five-act stage play by Dupeuty and Eugène Cormon that premiered at the Théâtre de l'Ambigu-Comique in 1842, places the listener in the midst of a bustling scene replete with cafés, diners, and smokers. The song's final stanza cites noise as a means of signaling the end of the nocturnal celebration and the beginning of the workday. Whereas the beginning of the song focuses on café chatter, here the narrator hears the din of construction: another signifier of a thriving metropolis. Sound functions as both an indicator of time and class, as the workers' toil signals bedtime for the narrator:

> But I hear, in the City,
> The clock tolls. . . . Ah! Morning.

> For the agile worker,
> It is already morning.
> Hammers and pincers
> Begin to work.
> One wakes, one works. . . .
> Quick, to bed!
> Such is, my friends, Paris by night, etc.[70]

The city comes alive as an assemblage of people and objects working in time. Through its temporal account of street noise at different times of day, "Paris la nuit," offers what philosopher Henri Lefebvre would evocatively call a "rhythmanalysis."[71] I propose that we riff on Lefebvre's musical metaphor and listen to Parisian songs for soundscapes they are constructing. As we have seen, these songs were not composed with a specific intent, audience, or venue in mind. Their mobility throughout the city meant that their identity was as malleable as the street and boulevards where they were heard. Thinking of songs this way allows for the multiple meanings and dualisms to emerge. The multiplicities that these songs explore—temporal, social, geographic—reveal the extent to which Parisians of different socioeconomic statuses interacted with one another through shared sonic cultural objects.

Songs about Paris and Parisians often imagined interactions between rich and poor, old and young. The songwriter Léon de Chaumont explored the lives of the Parisian rich and poor in his chanson "Paris qui rit et Paris qui pleure" (Paris laughing and Paris weeping). Self-published in 1852 on a single sheet with text and an accompanying drawing—likely intended to be placarded on a wall—the chanson captures vignettes of Parisians with contrasting fates and fortunes. Set to a tune by Béranger, the song describes a newlywed and a widow in the first stanza, two conversing husbands in the second, a rich nephew and a poor nephew in the third, a winemaker and a drunk in the fourth, and two daughters with different musical capabilities in the fifth. Chaumont notes that the city is both "heaven" and "hell." Indeed, the song's first verse dwells on this contradiction. Two people on the same Parisian street could experience two parallel realities:

> The same lodging, often at the same hour,
> Will have a mix of sobs and joyous outbursts.
> Long live Paris, where one laughs or one cries;
> Paris, what paradise, and what hell![72]

Binaries of rich/poor, old/new, and young/old pervade the contemporary accounts of Parisian life. They also view the city as a multiact spectacle in which everyone played a supporting role. Many songs featured colorful and hard-to-translate vocabulary that described types of Parisians: *trottins, flâneurs, badauds, gandins, dandies,* and *grisettes* were all fodder for entertainment, and were terms that categorized a "mass public" of urban consumers.[73] With the exception of the *badaud*—the "gawker" who does not engage critically with his surroundings—the other terms denote a person who treats Paris as an aesthetic object, traversing the city's public and private spaces with open eyes and ears.

Thanks to the writings of Baudelaire and Benjamin, the *flâneur* has emerged as the archetypal—but by no means only—Parisian modernist figure.[74] In an 1870 magazine article, the poet and chansonnier Alexandre Flan (1827–70) discussed the word *flâneur* in French popular usage (although never with regard to his own surname). Flan argued that the word first appeared in the eighteenth century, at which point the action of urban walking (the verb "flâner") became a veritable occupation for the aspirational bourgeoisie. In the first decade of the nineteenth century, the *flâneur* became an increasingly visible presence on theatrical stages. According to Flan, the title character in M. L. B. Picard's 1803 comedy *M. Musard* was the first onstage *flâneur*. Other examples of theatrical *flânerie* from the early nineteenth century include Dumersan's, Théaulon's, and Dartois's *Les Bêtes savantes* from 1813, which features a character named M. Flanard.[75] Although this particular *type parisien* has served as "the emblematic figure of modernity," *flânerie* emerged well before Baudelaire's "painter of modern life."[76]

Casimir Ménétrier's chanson "Le Flâneur" was first heard in 1816 at the Société de Momus, a *goguette* of which Ménétrier was a founding member.[77] We do not know much about Ménétrier. He made his living as notary clerk in Paris but gained a degree of respect in musical circles as a traveling violinist, songwriter, and café-going *bon vivant*. His political allegiances seemed to be based more on opportunism than on ideology; he composed songs celebrating Napoléon Bonaparte, and after his demise, the reascent of Bourbons under Louis XVIII. His "Le Flâneur" was a hit. It appears in song collections in the 1840s, 50s, and 60s with illustrations and with a piano accompaniment arranged by the composer and Conservatoire professor Hippolyte Colet (example 7). The tune, a straightforward trot around the first three scale degrees, is an apt choice for a song about walking. Colet's easy-to-play accompaniment provides harmony in the right hand and bare fifths and octaves in the left, as if to assure that the *flâneur* proceeds at a regular pace. The text is a first-person account of a Parisian urbanite who spends his days shuttling between cafés, the riverside *quais,* and theaters. As the refrain states, the *flâneur*'s main goal is to be everywhere so as to not let any new detail slip him by:

EXAMPLE 7. Casimir Ménétrier, "Le Flâneur."

Proudly I stroll;
Whether one approves or condemns me!
Proudly I stroll,
I see everything
I am everywhere.[78]

Ménétrier's depiction of carefree strolling is a far cry from the self-awareness behind Baudelaire's "man of the crowd." As the words and illustration suggest, *flânerie* was as much about pleasure and sociability as it was about aesthetic rumination. What Baudelaire's and Ménétrier's *flâneurs* have in common, however, is their fascination with the ritual of walking through the city. Haussmann's concentrated urbanization projects only amplified this fascination, as elements of the city landscape could potentially change from day to day, or even hour to hour. The Paris of the *flâneur* embodied the metaphor of the city as a palimpsest: by walking, one saw the familiar constantly confronted with the new.[79]

Yet outdoor urban sociability was not exclusively a male activity. Music scholars continue to revise narratives of musical success in the nineteenth century by considering the distinct economic challenges faced by women.[80] Street song thus not only offers a conduit for exploring responses to urbanization across socioeconomic lines, but also across an arguably broader rift in nineteenth-century life: that of gender. It is well-known how the *Code Napoléon*, established by Napoléon Bonaparte in 1804, severely limited the civil rights that women had previously enjoyed. These regressive policies, as Annegret Fauser points out, diminished women's opportunities in the musical public sphere, including their ability to vie for prizes like the *Prix de Rome*.[81] Women spanning the entire socioeconomic spectrum had to take several steps back during the nineteenth century.

Perhaps for this reason, all of the street songs that I have been able to find were written by men, including those about women. The chansonnier Eugène Pégand tried to capture the female Parisian's unique perspective in "La Grisette du quartier Latin," a chanson published by Joubert in 1860 that remained in café repertories into the next century. The *grisette* is an archetypal female figure of French bohemia. She was mythologized in novels by Eugène Sue, George Sand, Henri Murger, and Victor Hugo and adapted to the opera and operetta stage on numerous occasions: famous operatic *grisettes* include Musetta in Puccini's *La Bohème*, Magda in Puccini's *La Rondine*, Valencienne (in disguise) in Léhar's *Die lustige Witwe*, and Ninon in Kálmán's *Das Veilchen vom Montmartre*. Much has been written on the *grisette* as a product of the male literary imagination. In a classic study of bohemian Paris, Jerrold Seigel sees the free-spirited and artistically minded *grisette* as the polar opposite of the *bourgeoise*, who from a young age is taught to wait on suitors in order to secure financial and marital success.[82] "La Grisette du quartier Latin" is notable for how it offers agency to the working-class woman *vis-à-vis* her bourgeoise counterpart. While the fictional *grisette* often appeared as the object of the male gaze, Joubert narrates the song from her perspective, and conveys the famous free-spiritedness that made later heroines like Bizet's Carmen so notorious. Both Carmen and Joubert's *grisette* evoke the image of an *oiseau* (bird) to visualize their independence from men:

> The night beckons me to another riverbank;
> Quick, let us flee work and boredom;
> Let us reach the threshold where each night I arrive
> To fill myself with Pleasure and with noise.
> Ah! Though beautiful, I was once also wise!
> But now, from evening until morning,
> I'm off, like a wild migratory bird
> To drink punch in the Latin Quarter![83]

Songs about *types parisiens* often mixed gender stereotypes with generalizations about class. In other words, Parisians were grouped by how they dressed and by what they owned. Among the many composers who capitalized on Second Empire materialism was the young Léo Delibes (1836–91). Today Delibes is best remembered for the work he composed during the Third Republic: the ballets *Coppélia* (1870) and *Sylvia* (1876) and the opera *Lakmé* (1883). But during the first decade of the Second Empire, Delibes composed short, comic stage works for Hervé's Folies-Nouvelles and Offenbach's Bouffes-Parisiens. Light fare sustained him both artistically and financially; beginning in 1856 he wrote roughly one new stage work a year for fourteen years, collaborating with librettists such as Ludovic Halévy, Hector Crémieux and Théodore Barrière.[84] During this time, Delibes also wrote *chansonnettes*. Music scholars have not taken kindly to these songs, passing over them as musical juvenilia; Frits Noske, for example, notes with a touch of disparagement that "just as [Delibes's] operas and ballets show vestiges of his early operettas, so the piquant tone and charm of Delibes's serious *mélodies* may be traced to his *chansonnettes* dating from the Second Empire."[85] A broader tendency in biographical musicology often frames a composer's shift from "popular" to "serious" work as a teleology. For example, Hugh Macdonald writes that "the more ambitious scale and elevated tone of his later works may be attributed to a determination to break out of Offenbach's milieu and prove himself as a composer of ballet and opera."[86] This is a fair point—except it implicitly brands "Offenbach's milieu" as a steppingstone to a "superior" realm of musical success, namely that of serious concert and stage works. In writing about many lesser-known names in this book, I do not intend to pit them as underdogs against the omnipotent Opéra and Conservatoire. Such an approach, as Ellen Lockhart and others have recently shown, only betrays the cultural historian's own condescending fascination with the lesser-known and little-noticed—a phenomenon known as "quirk historicism."[87] Popular song highlights the musical ecosystem of Second Empire Paris as a network of interlaced communities that shared the same infrastructure—personnel, genres, venues—regardless of any perceived "high/low" aesthetic categories attributed to this period *ex post facto*. Common to these musical communities, moreover, was a willingness to create what Philippe Darriulat calls "social utterances," or music which, in one way or another, allowed authors to cope with the diverse ideas that constituted urban modernity.[88]

One way that Parisians coped with these pressures was through imaginative human typology. Literary archetypes—*dandies, flâneurs, grisettes, lorettes*—were also deployed to prescribe how class, gender, and culture were to play out in everyday life. We encounter a wealth of these ideas in "Le Code fashionable," a song with words by Antoine Vialon and music by Delibes from 1857 (example 8). The narrator lists specific visual signifiers that distinguish the modern-day "dandy." What is striking here is the *galop* rhythm and the "heroic" key of E-flat major. Far from the detached, *blasé* demeanor associated with the dandy, the music tells a different story. This dandy is determined—destined, even—to take the city by storm. Indeed, the marchlike accompaniment offers a comical sense of heroism to the superficial description of the strolling gentleman. The oscillating leap of a major sixth in the couplet melody, in B-flat major, provides refreshing contrast to the punctuated tonic-centered delivery of the refrain. In the first couplet, Vialon describes the dandy's "armor." The list of clothing is typical of comic songs in both popular and operatic spheres. In addition to giving the verse rhetorical pace, the text offers critique of how Parisian youth dress:

> Straw-colored gloves,
> Tight-fitting trousers,
> A coat whose waist
> Would make a child uncomfortable;
> Next shoes that shine with patent-leather;
> That's how they dress
> Now, our social lions.[89]

It is not just clothing that defines Vialon's Parisian "heroic" gentleman. The repeated last line of the first couplet, beginning at the C major secondary dominant chord of the penultimate line, notes that this "social lion" also employed abiding servants:

> [A *Beau* needs to] lead with skill
> and with no hesitation
> A negro [*nègre*], who ceaselessly
> Crosses his arms.[90]

Slavery was abolished in mainland France in 1794, but colonial enslavement remained legal until 1848, so this last line implies that the fashionable dandy is assisted by a nonwhite, colonial subject, likely against the latter's will. The line is cringeworthy; it is unlikely that this song will ever be performed or recorded again. But the casual racialized dynamic painted here suggests that ownership—of clothing, objects, or human services—was, as both song and operetta suggest, a distinguishing feature of the Parisian bourgeois male.

EXAMPLE 8. Léo Delibes and Antoine Vialon, "Le Code fashionable: Chansonnette," measures 1–12.

Another form of ownership appears in the song's second couplet: the sense of sight. Vialon turns to urban sightseeing, which, as we have seen, was an activity that allowed Parisians to claim ownership over their city. Yet for Vialon's "Dandy," the actual ability to see clearly is not a given:

> You're not a 'gentleman'
> If you have good eyesight.
> It's essential to have seen a painting
> Exhibited at the Salon,
> Or better, at the Arc de Triomphe,
> By quickly donning a pince-nez.[91]

Vialon's dandy is deeply concerned both seeing and being seen. The visually impaired *flâneur*, whose *raison d'être* was spectatorship, thus attracted attention to himself by turning the act of seeing itself into a bourgeois ritual. Vialon and Delibes's song reveals that the Second Empire bourgeois was obsessed with an imaginary audience. *Flânerie* was not merely the isolated ruminations that Baudelaire imagined. The emerging city plan of open vistas, straight lines, and cavernous spaces thus did not only allow citizens to see their city more clearly. It also allowed for the city to see them.

OLD PARIS, IN SONG

While many Second Empire chansons explored what was new in the city, a substantial number addressed what was being destroyed.[92] Songs featuring phrases like "le vieux Paris," "les démolitions de Paris," or "les ruines de Paris" offer a window on how chansonniers critiqued Haussmannization without falling victim to censorship. Nostalgia functioned as a rhetorical tactic through which chansonniers could voice their concerns about urbanization without overtly attacking the regime. I take up the subject of nostalgia more fully in the next chapter, but here I wish to return to Charles Nisard, with whom we began this chapter.

Just as modernity constituted a skirmish between old and new ideas, so too did songs reflect on both new and old versions of the city. Albeit obliquely, Nisard addressed Haussmannization in the first volume of his *Des Chansons populaires*: "Man seems born to destroy. From the most tender age, he destroys his toys, his clothes, and generally any fragile object he gets his hands on.... Without fully considering the retaliation that could be staged against him, he follows his primitive instincts with abandon, and becomes a child as before."[93] This passage is striking. Not only does Nisard frame urbanization as a form of social Darwinism at the infrastructural level, but he also hints at a skepticism toward his own regime. The utopian dreams of the Second Empire's public works project translated into an inevitable fate for the old city, a natural selection of neighborhoods and communities. Demolition became a fetish, something that even an insider bureaucrat could see. Cryptically, Nisard follows this narrative with a workers' song by Eléonore Pecquet titled "Les Démolitions de Paris, ou les joyeux maçons" (Paris demolition, or the happy masons). Set to the popular tune "Le Petit bleu," the chanson text treats the demolitions as a source of pride for workers:

> Let us live worry-free,
> Let us work with courage
> By singing a gay refrain
> Our work keeps moving along.
> They see us climbing gleefully
> On our scaffolding.
> Let us sing together
> Long live our jolly masons![94]

Ostensibly this song is nothing more than a bucolic workers' tune. But its placement in Nisard's text—immediately following a veiled lamentation about urban modernity—gives this text a distinct frame, and indeed an ambivalent meaning. As the song continues, this optimism turns into justification:

> May the demolitions
> In our capital
> Allow the masons to refurbish homes.
> At the [place de] Grève and at the Louvre, and also at Les Halles,
> One only sees them demolish
> But it's so they could rebuild.[95]

Nisard does not disclose the provenance of this song, nor where it was most widely heard. But the song itself offers a cartographic snapshot of "old Paris": the place de Grève is the pre-1800s name for the place de l'Hôtel-de-Ville, or Paris's city hall in the fourth arrondissement. As we have seen, popular songs permeated different contexts and venues, but they also permeated different temporalities. Songs, like city plans, were palimpsests, capable of accumulating meaning over time. What was once a space where the poor could apply for work eventually became an imperial hub and Haussmann's lavish residence. Popular song's ontological instability thus allowed for such layers of meaning to accumulate.

It was not until the final tumultuous years of the Second Empire that chansonniers began to publish songs that directly confronted the financially disastrous behaviors of Baron Haussmann and his coterie. This wave of anti-imperial songwriting was largely inspired by the republican statesman Jules Ferry, who in 1868 published a pamphlet titled *Les Comptes fantastiques d'Haussmann* (The fantastic accounts of Haussmann).[96] The title is a play on words of the popular book *Contes fantastiques d'Hoffmann* (The fantastic tales of Hoffmann), which in two decades would become the basis of

Offenbach's famous opera. Ferry lambasted Haussmann for his ruthless parceling-out of Parisian urban space to private speculators, and for his scheme of borrowing money (hence "comptes," or bank accounts) against government equity. Above all, Ferry's pamphlet aimed to deflate the myth that the Second Empire was the torchbearer of prosperity. Elsewhere in the pamphlet, Ferry critiqued Haussmann indirectly, by evoking nostalgia for "Old Paris" and the intellectual tradition that it represented: "This old Paris, the Paris of Voltaire, Diderot and Desmoulins, the Paris of 1830 and 1848— we weep for it with all the tears of our eyes, in view of the magnificent and intolerable hostelry, the costly disorder, triumphant vulgarity, and frightening materialism we bequeath to our heirs."[97] Such a critique cut directly into the intellectual heart of the Haussmann project. Whereas the prefect rooted his own urban aesthetics in both Napoleonic monumentality and Enlightenment order, Ferry's nostalgic critique devalued Haussmannization as a hollow fanfare to materialism and imperialism.

As we saw in chapter 1, Haussmann owned the label of "demolition-artist" (*artiste-démolisseur*), as it validated his confidence as both aesthete and administrator. He not only took credit for public works but intentionally engineered the concept of "Haussmannization" as an infrastructural, moral, and aesthetic campaign to modernize the city by turning to classical ideals of structure and beauty. Haussmann propagated what historian Pierre Pinon has dubbed a "double myth" around his own reputation and the city he worked to transform.[98] By memorializing his achievements in his *Mémoires* and by promoting the use of the neologisms *haussmannisme* and *haussmannisation*, Haussmann maintained that he was the *first* to initiate urban reforms of such a magnitude, and that Paris was the *only* city in which such ambitious public works projects could take place.

In 1868, the same year that Ferry published his pamphlet, the famed songwriter Gustave Nadaud (1820–93) toured Paris's salons with "Osmanomanie," a razor-sharp satire of Haussmann and his penchant for demolition. Nadaud never mentions the prefect directly. Instead, he toys with the French pronunciation of Haussmann's name (pronounced "ohss-mahn") and recounts the destructive nature of Osman (pronounced "ohzz-mahn"), the fourteenth-century founding figure of the Ottoman dynasty.

> Osman, prefect of Bajazet,
> Became taken by a strange delirium:
> He demolished in order to build,
> And he built in order to demolish.

> Is this madness? I deny it,
> One need not be mad to be a Muslim.
> Such was Osman,
> Father of Osmanomania.⁹⁹

"Osmanomanie" and the myriad other songs we have explored offer documentary evidence of opposition to the empire's modernist ideology. Although many chansonniers sang the empire's praises and embraced Haussmann's vision, others provided an alternate mythology: a Paris that more closely resembled a falling Atlantis than it did a rising Utopia. Parisian urbanization, as the songs in this chapter suggest, did not benefit all. While *chansonniers* and singing societies were often depicted with their backs against the wall, Paris's itinerant street vendors and merchants became the most romanticized of the working-class *types parisiens* of the Second Empire. The cries of street hawkers, as we will see in the following chapter, became for preservationists a sonic reaffirmation of the popular and apocalyptic slogan *Paris s'en va* (Paris is vanishing).

FIVE

Street Cries

CONSTRUCTING THE OLD CITY

STREET HAWKERS—ITINERANT SALESPEOPLE who peddled goods from produce to scrap metal—populated Paris's streets from at least the thirteenth century to the beginning of the twentieth. They advertised their products by shouting to attract passersby and lure customers away from the indoor markets and boutiques. Guidebooks referred to these outdoor merchants by a variety of names: whereas the most common was the French word *colporteur*, others included *petits métiers, industriels nomads, gagne-petits, marchands ambulants, crieurs,* and *camelots*. They became known collectively as the *crieurs de Paris*, and their chantlike melodies formed a curious sonic repertory known as the *cris de Paris*. Hawkers provided a wide variety of goods and services: the *marchand de journaux* shouted the day's headlines, the *marchande des fraises* advertised the freshness of her produce, and the *marchand de contremarques*—the nineteenth century's ticket scalper—announced the low price of admission for that night's theater performance. The *marchand de robinets*, who sold faucets and taps, was especially known for using percussion and brass instruments that musically mimicked the clanging sounds made by his merchandise as he walked. This din, when blended with the perpetual concertizing of Paris's street musicians, undoubtedly made for a noisy commute. Like their musician counterparts, hawkers were an active and ubiquitous element of the city's economy, and their cries—at times melodious, at times raucous—formed a distinct part of Paris's auditory environment.

As Haussmann began to "bludgeon the city into modernity," hawkers faced stricter zoning laws, and the liminal spaces where they dwelled vanished from the map.[1] A proliferation of books, poetry, and musical works about hawkers reveals a middle-class collective mobilization to thwart the eventual disappearance of the city's iconic sights and sounds. As we will see with the musical centerpiece of this chapter, Jean-Georges Kastner's *Les Cris de Paris* (1857), nostalgic counternarratives filtered into the emerging idea of *le vieux Paris,* a concept that became the subject of numerous memoirs, guidebooks, and sociological studies published during the 1850s and 60s.[2] Yet the *vieux Paris* label did more than sell books. The emergence of an imagined "old city" provided an ideological check on the Second Empire's utopian, capitalistic urbanism. Hawkers, like the street musicians explored in the previous chapter, were subjected to policing and zoning on one hand, and sentimental romanticizing on the other.

Ironically, the subject of Parisian street cries has inspired recent work by literary historians but has largely eluded musicological study.[3] The 1850s and 60s were decades when urbanization, emerging cultures of capitalism, and shifting epistemologies of sensory experience became catalysts for new formal structures in poetry and painting. Over the course of the nineteenth and early twentieth centuries, the *cris de Paris* became increasingly associated with noise pollution as the city refashioned itself according to bourgeois demands for quiet. Texts like Charles Baudelaire's poem "Le Mauvais vitrier" and Marcel Proust's novel *La Prisonnière* (the fifth volume of *À la recherche du temps perdu*), both discussed later in this chapter, directly pitted sound made by a hawker against the inability of a bourgeois listener to sleep. These and other literary works suggest that hawkers existed in a different spatial and temporal urban environment than did those who heard them. They worked in the mornings when others slept; they wandered outdoors when others sat or lay indoors near open windows; their belongings were portable, whereas others cultivated interior spaces isolated from rest of the urban fabric. As a community, street hawkers were not merely objects of literary fascination. They were also deemed an urban policy problem. An examination of the intertwined literary, musical, and material history of the *cris de Paris* offers the missing link between the soundscape as *perceived* and *policed,* and the unwritten experiences of those hawkers whose voices, unbeknownst to them, were co-opted as fanfare for a disappearing urban culture.

The "urban historical musicology" proposed in this book's introduction links music to the production of urban space. It balances real and fictionalized accounts of city life and gives equal weight to the biases and inherited traditions of diverse urban communities. Indeed, Paris's musical elite betrayed a long-standing preoccupation with the voices of hawkers, making the soundscape a subject of both musical and moral discourse. In the eighteenth century, Grétry, Mercier, and Rameau wrote of the ubiquity of hawkers in discussions of vocal pedagogy, public health, and the future of operatic composition. The nineteenth century brought a more imaginative, romanticized attitude toward the city's urban subcultures. In the literate middle-class imagination, the boulevard was not only a venue for political dissent and capitalistic *flânerie* but also a sacred site populated by ghostly figures of the past. Indeed, hawkers under Haussmann were inadvertently performing what Gavin Steingo would call "immaterial musical labor": a production system that valued affective responses to urban pictorialism over the actual goods being sold.[4] The bourgeoisie's fascination with the *cris de Paris*—an aestheticized hearing of sonic labor—thus represented an attempt to "echolocate" the modern city through the working class.[5] Under Haussmann, the sonic practice of hawking became an aesthetic ends and not an economic means. The Second Empire street cry was urbanized, in effect, by becoming a commodity; alienated from the crier, the cry's value morphed into the exchangeable visual and musical products explored in this chapter.

From a musicological perspective, no other nineteenth-century city—not even London—shared the burden of being at once a homogenized capital and a culturally diverse metropolis. London, for that matter, had its own storied tradition of auditory street commerce. Seemingly immune to turn-of-the-century changes in taste, the so-called *Cries of London* had become a pervasive trope between the 1600s and the 1800s, spawning popular engravings such as those by William Hogarth and William Marshall Craig and polyphonic musical works such as those by Thomas Weelkes and Orlando Gibbons.[6] As Nicholas Mathew writes, songs, images, and other fashionable re-hearings of the London streetscape were among "the stylized ways in which Londoners aestheticized (and eroticized) urban experience—by discriminating, extracting, and refining those sonic dimensions of London's street life that lent themselves to tasteful citation."[7] Parisians' nostalgic fascination with street commerce thus highlighted a rupture in the city's urban ethos: despite the regime's best efforts to institutionalize urban space, Paris remained a place of vibrant outdoor activity. Whereas Haussmannization was, among other things, an exercise in socioeconomic segregation, preservationists like Kastner seized the opportunity to hear the city across class lines. By transcribing urban noise into more marketable media such as guidebooks, prints, and sheet music, writers, illustrators, and composers appropriated an "outdoor" urban phenomenon—one strongly associated with the beleaguered laboring class who for decades lived and worked in central Paris—and transferred it into the newly constructed bourgeois interior spaces.

GUTTING THE CENTER

By Haussmann's own estimation, 13 percent of the city was leveled between 1851 and 1859.[8] Yet of all these demolition projects, one that made a particularly noticeable impact on the city's image was the near-leveling of the Île de la Cité. Best known today as the island on which the cathédrale de Notre-Dame stands, the Île de la Cité had been Paris's central working-class district since the Carolingian eighth century. Haussmann, however, conceived of the island not as a residential neighborhood but as a thoroughfare between the Left and Right Banks. By the outbreak of the Franco-Prussian War in 1870, the residential population on the island had dropped from fifteen thousand to five thousand, reflecting Haussmann's broader campaign to reconfigure inner Paris as an exclusively bourgeois space.[9] Yet Haussmann's razing of the Île de la Cité did not only involve slum clearance. Between 1789 and 1889—with a noticeable spike during the Second Empire years—no fewer than sixteen churches, convents, and other historical religious structures were pulled down.[10] The "imperial vandalism" of Haussmannization, as Esther da Costa Meyer called it, did not begin with Haussmann. Nevertheless, the prefect was instrumental in overseeing a century's worth of inner-city demolition to its eventual conclusion.

The idea to streamline the Île de la Cité, a key episode in the history of Haussmannization, was not Haussmann's own. In the 1840s, disciples of the utopian socialist Charles Fourier (1772–1837) coalesced around the idea that a premeditated urban plan not only facilitated transit and air flow, but also provided a "public utility" that directly impacted both public and moral health. The economist team of Victor Considerant and the pseudonymous Perreymond each authored a series of works in the 1840s extolling workers' rights to clean urban space. In a coauthored article, they effectively explained the need for systematic urban studies, a field that had not yet been formulated. Calling for greater control over what today would be called an organic urban plan—infrastructure emerging as needed from a central node, like a square or a church—Considerant and Perreymond rationalized a top-down approach to public works: "We believe that the Department of the Seine should be considered as ... a *systematic ensemble,* and that the projects that are currently executed piecemeal by the communes ... should be combined, centralized, and brought into line, each in its own way and location with a general plan encompassing the unity of the department in its entirety."[11] What Paris needed was a central figure to play the metaphorical role of orchestrator and conductor: a unified vision for harmony in the city, and an iron grip on curbing deviations from this harmony. Despite their roots in worker-oriented Fourierist ideology, Considerant and Perreymond's proposals, namely to remove the dense "decay" of the Île de la Cité and erect a series of large institutions "for the public good," employed workers while displacing them in the process. By 1853, the recently self-anointed Napoléon III had inherited Fourierist rationale for urban renewal from the inside out. But the emperor's selective take on urbanism as social good—an approach endorsed by Haussmann, who rarely disagreed with his superior—would obscure the workers' right to the city. Centralized urbanization extending from the center served the broader, symbolic role of consolidating power through the destruction and production of urban space. Fourier's dreams of a functional city became, in Napoléon III's urban imagination (and in Haussmann's hands) a city of spectacle. And spectacle of this magnitude is most immersive—most Wagnerian—when the work is hidden from view.

Demolition of Paris's central island lasted through the 1860s. The Préfecture de la Seine issued a decree on May 22, 1865 to raze the entire eastern part of the island apart from Notre-Dame and the streets around the rue Chanoinesse, the rue du Cloître Notre-Dame, and the quai aux Fleurs. The hundreds of little buildings that had dotted the island were replaced by three monumental governmental edifices: the new hospital (L'Hôtel-Dieu), the police headquarters (La Caserne de la Cité), and the municipal court (Le Tribunal de Commerce). In addition to taking down some hundred residential buildings and shops, the demolitions also claimed churches and historic buildings such as the largest orphanage in Paris (L'Hôpital des Enfants-Trouvés).[12]

Though devastating to workers, demolition padded the pockets of Parisian speculators—a phenomenon famously documented in Émile Zola's 1872 novel *La Curée* (translated to English as *The Kill*). Members of Paris's literary community, however, were ambivalent. This was, after all, the generation that had read Henri Murger's 1851 *Scènes de la vie de bohème,* which mythologized—and, to an extent, invented—a social class that was intellectually wealthy but financially poor, and who were at once regarded as exotic and quintessentially Parisian. As more new boulevards and buildings emerged from the rubble, writers situated *le vieux Paris* as an integral part of *la vie de bohème;* from year to year, as Patrice Higonnet so poetically observed, more and more Parisians "began to weep for old Paris, with its placarded walls and noise-filled streets."[13] Between 1850 and 1870 dozens of mass-produced publications revisited the subject of Parisian history as a conflict between past and future. The engraver Léopold Flameng (1831–1911) published a bimonthly periodical entitled *Paris qui s'en va, Paris qui vient* (The Paris that is disappearing, the Paris to come), which featured illustrations and articles about historic Parisian sites. On the title page of each issue, Flameng prophesied the fate of Paris's landmarks: "Those intersections, those public spaces frequented by generations [of Parisians]. In a few years, it will all be gone! A new city will have sprung up like magic: no ruins, no landmarks, not even a humble inscription to explain what was where!"[14] Shorter pamphlets and essays also expressed remorse while obliquely critiquing the government's cavalier approach to urban renewal. In 1860, the archaeologist and historian Adolphe Berty (1818–67) published a street-by-street historical overview of the Île de la Cité. Berty explained that the leveling of the old Hôtel-Dieu had prompted him to undertake a history of a neighborhood that would soon vanish: "The disappearance of an old monument makes it urgent to preserve its memory; when a city undergoes radical transformation, it makes sense to try to see the city as it once was."[15]

The *cris de Paris* were as dear to literati as were the crumbling buildings of the Île de la Cité. Yet it was not just demolition that disrupted street commerce; the new public works projects coincided with new modes of policing that ushered in stricter regulations and increased surveillance. As we will see, this increased policing of street vendors only intensified middle-class fascination with the sonic relics of a mythical "old city." As objects of transcription, ethnographic exploration, caricature, and criticism, the *cris de Paris* featured prominently in debates about whether urban modernity could coexist with urban cultural preservation. Furthermore, growing nostalgia for the "old city" during the 1860s led to a reframing of street hawkers from perpetually menacing Others to disenfranchised Parisians. These conflicted attitudes about what it meant to be "Parisian" encapsulated broader nationalistic and colonial notions of French identity. As Jann Pasler has shown, there was little consensus regarding a singular notion of "Frenchness" during the nineteenth century. This precipitated the widespread use of terms such as *race* and *outre-mer* ("overseas") as generalized indicators of musical and cultural difference.[16] It is thus striking that these issues of vilifying/lionizing Others were also apparent within Paris's city limits. The perceived disappearance of these *cris*—and of *le vieux Paris* as a whole—is symptomatic of what Eric Hobsbawm would call an "invented tradition" of the nineteenth-century cultural imagination, which took visual and sonic artifacts from everyday life and instilled in them a historical, even legendary, significance.[17]

HAWKERS IN POETRY, FICTION, AND SONG

Nineteenth-century poets drew on the *cris de Paris* to explore the negative effects that urban change could wreak on the collective psyche. Yet a literary reception history of the *cris de Paris* would be incomplete without comparing the well-known poems with the now-forgotten *chansons populaires* that captured the streetscape in both word and sound. In his prose poem "Le Mauvais vitrier" (The bad glazier), Charles Baudelaire places the narrator in direct contact with the abrasive cries of a window cleaner. Baudelaire's "discordant" and "insalubrious" soundscape paints a grim picture of inner-city life. At the same time, Baudelaire's rejection of verse for prose reflects the influence of the urban experience on poetic form. Midway into the poem, Baudelaire recounts the meeting:

> The first person I noticed in the street was a glazier whose cry, piercing, discordant, came up to me through the oppressive and dirty Parisian atmosphere. Impossible for me to say why this poor fellow roused in me hatred as sudden as despotic.
> '—Hey there!' and I yelled for him to come up, meanwhile reflecting, not without amusement, that, my room being on the sixth floor and the stairs very narrow, the man would find it difficult to make his ascent, to maneuver at certain spots the corners of his fragile merchandise.[18]

Here, Baudelaire chooses against transcribing the glazier's shrill cry into prose. Rather, as Aimée Boutin has observed, the poem captures the "sensation of sound as a mental construct and the behaviors sounds elicit" in the reader.[19] From the safety of the window, Baudelaire's narrator summons the hawker with an unceremonious "hey!"—as if the glazier's very presence resists empathy.

We find a far more sympathetic tone in an 1855 Parisian café song entitled "Ferraille à vendre! Chiffons!" (Metal scraps! For sale! Rags!), with words and music by Léon Peuchot.[20] The song is an ode to the *chiffonier* (ragpicker), one of the oldest street trades in Paris. The *chiffonier* was paid by the city's sanitation department to pick up scraps of metal and wood, rags, clothing, paper, or other residue off the streets, selling the more useful items for a profit. A crucial component of Paris's urban ecology, the *chiffonier* at once cleaned the streets and provided raw materials to independent contractors and secondhand boutiques. An illustration published along with the song's text and music demonstrates why the ragpicker was, by many contemporary accounts, the most destitute tier of street labor (figure 9). The twisted fingers of her left hand are shown holding some recently acquired rags. Her haggard dress and undone bonnet are a stark contrast to the *bourgeoise* onlooker behind her, as if to highlight the middle class's condescending fascination with street culture. The song was also published with a preface, in which Peuchot describes the ragpicker's cry in terms remarkably redolent of Baudelaire: "Scraps for sale! Rags! Surely, those who have lived in Paris are familiar with this piercing yet plaintive cry. After a few seconds, it begins to attack the eardrum in a very unpleasant way."[21] The "piercing yet plaintive" cry, as well as the clanking pieces of scrap metal, pervaded Peuchot's imagination long enough to merit aesthetic contemplation.

In the first verse of "Ferraille à vendre! Chiffons!" the narrator regards the ragpicker, "Madame Ourlier," with both chagrin and empathy: she is so old as to be deemed "eternal," and yet her services remain valuable:

Look at that old hag,
That eternal Madame Ourlier,
Who clears out my workshop
Of old rags and scraps.
Alas, scavenger covered in filth!
Your skills have much value.
Ah! Leave those rags and scraps,
Go sell some fried potatoes.
I honorably leave you be.
Scraps for sale! Rags!
Clothes, hats, ribbons![22]

Whereas the song's verses revolve around the ragpicker and her trade, the refrain serves as a musical transcription of the "strident and plaintive" cry itself (example 9). Here the piano drops down to single chords on the downbeat, and the singer is instructed to "almost speak." Fermatas over the words "ferraille" and "vendre," coupled with the expressive marking *crié*, likely encouraged the singer to bellow in their best "outdoor" voice. Given the

FIGURE 9. Image accompanying Léon Peuchot's "Ferraille à vendre! Chiffons!" in *Paris en chansons, sous la direction de Comte* (Paris: P. H. Krabbe, 1855).

EXAMPLE 9. Peuchot, "Ferraille à vendre! Chiffons!," measures 22–35.

second-person perspective of the verses, is this outcry an instance of the singer ventriloquizing, or even mocking, the hawker? Or does the song capture the hawker's own perspective as she gazes into a mirror and delivers a self-disparaging judgment?

The social codes embedded in Peuchot's preface, cover image, text, and score expose the bourgeoisie's fascination with the Parisian working class. In this case, difference was inscribed not through place but through privilege. In Marcel Proust's *La Prisonnière*, published 1923 (and known in English as *The Captive* or *The Prisoner*), this particular cry of "Chiffons, ferrailles à vendre" suggests something out of step with urban modernity: a mystical evocation of medieval plainchant. Proust's novel captures the meandering thoughts of a narrator whose jealousy around Albertine, his friend-turned-mistress, leads to aggressive inquisition and suspicion of her romantic involvements with other women. His obsessive behavior eventually leads to Albertine leaving him. Albertine is particularly fond of the *cris de Paris,* and the narrator wakes early one day to listen to them and to stare at her in voyeuristic solitude. It is here that Proust quotes "Chiffons, ferrailles à vendre," among many other street cries. Commenting on the drawn-out inflections of the ragpicker, leather tanner, and orange vendor, the narrator compares these cries to the Latin liturgical call to prayer that typically precedes the Pater Noster:

> 'Praeceptis salutaribus moniti et divina institutione formait audemus dicere,' says the priest, ending sharply upon 'dicere.' . . . [I]t is of that 'dicere' that this rag vendor makes one think when, after drawling the other words, he utters the final syllable with a sharpness befitting the accentuation laid down by the great Pope of the seventh century: 'Chiffons, ferrailles à vendre' (all this chanted slowly, as are the two syllables that follow, whereas the last concludes more briskly than 'dicere') 'peaux d'la-pins.' 'La Valence, la belle Valence, la fraîche orange.'[23]

Why this particular passage of Latin chant, with its hanging clause leading directly into the Lord's Prayer? To Proust's narrator, the slow, monotone incantation of "dicere"—a verbal invitation to prayer—parallels how the ragpicker suggestively intones "à vendre"—a verbal invitation to buy. The narrator, imagining a monk while hearing a ragpicker, picks up on the consistencies between the two: a call to community, an acoustic production of space (sacred and commercial, respectively), and—especially in ragpicker's case—an announcement of continued existence and relevance. Though unlikely companions, Baudelaire's poem, Peuchot's song, and Proust's novel all reveal that the image of the solitary hawker represented an uncertain urban present at odds with the city's disappearing past. This mode of nostalgic representation marked a drastic break with previous practices; the ubiquity of vendors in pre-1800 Paris made them an easy target for satirical, exoticized treatment of the city's gritty underbelly.

STREET CRIES IN *LE VIEUX PARIS*

Poets had mined the *cris de Paris* for their lyrical potential since the Middle Ages, but these depictions tended to treat street merchants as a homogenous unit—not unlike the street musicians we met in the previous chapter. One of the earliest literary representations of street peddlers is found in Guillaume de la Villeneuve's thirteenth-century poem "Les Crieries de Paris."[24] Villeneuve's Paris resonates with the sounds of hawkers selling a wide variety of goods: produce, bread, fish, cheese, as well as odds and ends. Lines that describe the ubiquity of the cries—heard in the streets from morning until night—are interspersed with direct quotations of the cries themselves. Villeneuve's poem, as Emma Dillon has observed, captures the spontaneous and ephemeral nature of street commerce.[25] Like the perishable products they advertised, the hawkers' cries had short shelf lives, with one voice blending into another and leaving the listener with a dizzying number of products from which to choose. Villeneuve's image of Paris as a perennial space of noisy energy translated rather easily into the realm of polyphonic music; two examples, the Montpellier Codex motet *On parole a batre/A Paris/Frese nouvele* and Clément Janequin's *Voulez ouyr les cris de Paris,* remain favorites in early music history courses for their crafty contrapuntal depictions of a fictionalized, unified urban soundscape.[26]

Within musical communities in the late eighteenth and early nineteenth centuries, the *cris de Paris* began to appear in serious arguments about class definition, morality, and the aural experience of urban life. One major point of contestation involved musical pedagogy: namely, whether sustained exposure to the *cris* could do harm to the cultivated ear. In 1760, Jean-Philippe Rameau insisted that singers could learn from listening to street hawkers. "Listen to those who sing street cries," Rameau writes. "Nothing will be better proof of the effectiveness of nature."[27] Rameau believed that a beautiful and natural vocal tone is not born from inspiration or learnedness, but rather from the singer's corporeal awareness. The street hawker, therefore, represents the human, singing body in its most natural and uninhibited state, and as a result, is able to produce tones that are agreeable to the ear.[28] As if to refute Rameau, André-Ernest-Modeste Grétry used the street hawker as a scapegoat to warn singers at the Opéra that poorly articulated consonants and arcane, provincial vocabulary can obstruct the understanding of the words. The result is a drastic misunderstanding of the intended message. "Listen to the street criers," Grétry wrote in his *Mémoires*, "you cannot find ten that you would be able to comprehend. From my room, I hear three cries: *Parjure, iras-tu?* I hear another one: *i, a u*. Another one yells: *Belles pêches*. But these *belles pêches* are actually mousetraps; *i, a, u*, are actually bundles of wood, and *parjure, iras-tu?* are actually old clothes for sale."[29]

Grétry's warning articulated the rift between the cultivated elite who patronized the Opéra and the uneducated workers who populated the streets. But Enlightenment-era writers also tied street cries to shifting epistemologies of urban acoustics—as if overpopulation obfuscated both aural and geographic navigation through the city. In his multivolume *Tableau de Paris* (1782–88), Louis-Sébastien Mercier worries that newly arrived foreigners will immediately associate the incessant noise with the chaotic medieval plan of Paris's inner districts: "No, there isn't a city in the world where criers' voices are sharper and more piercing. You have to hear their voices soaring above the roofs. Their throats overpower the noise of the streets. It is impossible for a foreigner to comprehend any one of them. . . . [A]ll of these discordant cries form an ensemble that one can't imagine if one has never heard it."[30] For Mercier, street cries were distasteful—even dangerous—because they represented a social class whose sound was marked by incomprehensible language. By documenting his negative sensory experience of street noise, Mercier distances himself from the hawkers that surround him in the street. The main reason why hawkers are "unable" to vocalize properly, he contends, is their lack of refined, homegrown, *Parisian* urbanity: "These [provincial] people are excessively noisy by nature. One hears their hoarse, sharp, and muffled cries from every corner."[31] It is crucial that Mercier does not mention specific racial or ethnic origins in this passage. Rather, their "natural" vocality permanently marked their status as a marginal urban community.

By the mid-nineteenth century, street cries became a subject covered in travel literature. Pamphlets and guidebooks offer a glimpse into the negative reception of street cries and the noise of the industrialized city in general. An 1840 booklet titled *Les Embarras de Paris: Quel horrible fracas, quel tumultes, quel cris* (The annoyances of Paris: What horrible noise, what commotion, what cries) details the frustration caused by the onslaught of loud outdoor commerce.[32] The author—one Lanterelu, who adopted the unequivocally modern pen name "J. C. M. le Flâneur"—describes how his eyes and ears are overwhelmed by the streetscape: "Cage welders, produce vendors, ambulant glaziers, newspaper vendors, barking dogs, barrel organs, street musicians on every corner, all of these distract you while attacking your eardrum.... [I]t's a perpetual concert, rather pleasant if one is lucky enough to already be deaf, but at least we [the rest of us] can keep hoping to attain that state."[33]

Lanterelu's "deafening" account resembles Antoine Le Roux de Lincy's description of the rue Saint-Martin in an 1855 tourist guidebook.[34] In preparation for the Exposition universelle held in Paris later that year, Haussmannization had already pushed much open-air commerce out of the central arrondissements, but the rue Saint-Martin remained a popular venue for street markets, fairs, and itinerant hawkers. De Lincy notes that the noisy shouts of street hawkers from morning to afternoon, amplified by the perpetual din of carriages, could be a potential terror for uninitiated foreigners: "Soon, as in previous centuries, these little merchants appear, each with a particular cry that is incomprehensible to those not accustomed to it. These cries are barely muffled by the deafeningly noisy carriages of all kinds; their increasing numbers block traffic until midday. Woe to the foreigner if chance or business leads him to this street."[35] To be a nineteenth-century urbanite, it seems, was to be made figuratively numb from sensory overload. Acoustic quantity overwhelmed any arguably positive quality. The noisiness of the city was thus deemed a threat to well-being: a moral public health crisis. The Second Empire police were more than happy to step in, implementing a series of decrees that not only curtailed criers, but also prepared the streets for Haussmann's streamlined plan for the French capital.

PEDDLERS AND THE POLICE

We have seen how the police infiltrated Parisian spaces of work and leisure, often on the grounds of controlling sound. They lurked in the spaces of the World's Fairs, serving as hired *claqueurs* during the emperor's speeches. They tempered the natural porosity of the singing cafés by making themselves seen and heard with clocklike regularity. But it was the outdoor economy that most felt the ubiquitous presence of law enforcement. Between 1850 and 1900, a series of police decrees systematically increased the surveillance of *marchands des comestibles*—those who sold meat, produce, fish, etc.—as well as those who peddled *écrits*, such as daily newspapers, magazines, and pamphlets. Police regulations made it systematically more difficult to obtain commercial licenses. This increasingly specific interpretation of *what* and *how* things ought to be sold effectively stripped the street cry of the communicative power it once possessed. On October 6, 1851, the Second Republic government of the soon-to-be Napoléon III issued a set of regulations that rendered all previous decrees obsolete, and generally viewed vendors as a disturbance to everyday traffic and commerce. The new law prevented hawkers from moving freely within the city, subjecting them to strict licensing and zoning requirements: "No one shall circulate through public thoroughfares to sell merchandise or food on display devices [such as stands or stalls] or by any other means."[36] There was immediate backlash. A group of angry peddlers stormed the prefecture with a petition carrying fifty thousand signatures, and they flooded the daily press with polemical open letters. But the police prefect upheld the decree. The October 1851 decree irrevocably affected the aural component of street commerce. As vendors could no longer accost customers, they increasingly turned to visual advertising. As a result, many of their cries, stripped of their communicative function, were rendered obsolete.

Subsequent police decrees placed further restrictions on public spaces in which street peddlers could sell goods. In the early 1860s, the police increasingly cracked down on vendors who stopped to sell goods in Paris's *voies publiques*, or "public thoroughfares." A decree posted on July 25, 1862 effectively forbade merchants from obstructing pedestrian flow by occupying sidewalks. Instead, they were to find spaces away from foot and vehicular traffic, such as the tips of street corners. Vendors were often accused of turning bridges, streets, and squares into full-blown markets, which resulted in traffic jams and occasional accidents. Yet empty spaces were increasingly difficult to find, as the congested streets, alleyways, and squares that defined the geography of pre-Haussmann Paris were systematically replaced by the long boulevards of seemingly endless sidewalks. In addition to easing urban flow, these regulations of public space also sought to defend brick-and-mortar boutiques and markets by banning peddlers from operating within a hundred meters of indoor businesses where similar products were being sold.

Other police measures reveal that Haussmann's notion of modernity included a segregation of old from new, center from periphery, and regulated sound from unregulated noise. During the years of the Second Empire, all

FIGURE 10. Medallions worn by street vendors to denote registration in "new" and "old" Paris. Image: APP, Box DB 194.

street vendors who applied successfully to the Préfecture de Police were issued medallions. According to a police ordinance issued on December 28, 1859, "Street merchants who have obtained a permit will receive from the Prefecture a brass medallion engraved with the last name and first initial, as well as the permit number. They are required to wear the medallion and make it constantly visible in public spaces to exercise their trade."[37] To passersby, these medallions were a visual reassurance that the products sold were at least partially vouched for by the government. To the police, the medallions indicated that vendors stayed within their designated zones. Following the enlargement of Paris in 1860 from twelve arrondissements to twenty, street vendors were assigned specific parts of the city in which they could do business. To facilitate policing, medallions came in two shapes: bell-shaped or circular (figure 10). Bell-shaped medallions indicated zone 1, or *ancien Paris,* which represented the central neighborhoods of the first through the eleventh arrondissements. Circular medallions indicated zone 2, or *nouveau Paris,* which consisted of the outer ring of communes (arrondissements twelve through twenty). The town hall of each arrondissement set a cap on how many vendors could congregate in a single public space, and implemented further restrictions based on the vendor's age and disabilities, if any.

Through mandatory licensing and branding, and by rezoning the newly added Parisian neighborhoods, the municipal government remapped outdoor commercial activity by creating two distinct Parisian identities: one "old" and one "new."

Policing, coupled with the annexation of the outer communes in 1860, brought about a redistribution of human bodies that directly affected outdoor commerce. Memoirs and book-length essays published in the 1850s and 60s, most notably by Fournel and Kastner, proposed a preservation of sonic urban heritage: readers were instructed to seek out criers before they all vanished. This narrative of disappearance, argues Boutin, was a way of creatively coping with the times; nostalgia offered a means of expressing ambivalence toward modernity without critiquing structures of power.[38] As hawkers saw their economic circumstances become more perilous, they increasingly became muses for songwriters, composers, librettists, and spokespeople for *le vieux Paris*. No evidence exists that hawkers were compensated for playing this outsized cultural role. While they continued to populate song lyrics and opera libretti, they were also increasingly present in police records. One of my goals in these last two chapters has been to think of policing as a historiographical category. Press reception histories and close readings have been the bread and butter of musicological inquiry into the French nineteenth century, but the documents and historical actors that we hold as witnesses to our stories have always been beholden to the shifting pressures and priorities of legal authorities.

Keeping in mind the extent of the police's impact on sensory experience in the city, we can now turn to our musicological bread and butter—the reception of published musical works—to analyze how street sound infiltrated the elite musical mind during the Second Empire. The remainder of this chapter is devoted to one particularly fascinating attempt to make historical and musical sense of the *cris de Paris*. The ebb and flow of sonic street policy inspired a push and pull of interest in hawkers. Perhaps unbeknownst to them, their cries—born of necessity—came to mean more than sales pitches. For as much as the Second Empire Parisian bourgeoisie heard the din of their city, they did not seem interested in *listening* to what the hawkers had to say about their own situation. In this absence of key witness testimony, we are left to interpret the sonic archive with a critical ear toward the effects of policing sound, and so we must listen carefully to where the hawker's call ends, and the musician's imagination begins.

KASTNER'S PARISIAN VOICES

It took a particularly idiosyncratic musical imagination to hear the street cry as something more meaningful than caricature or *couleur locale*. Enter Jean-Georges Kastner (1810–67), a polymath composer, theorist, and critic who wrote a proto-ethnomusicological treatise on the urban soundscape: a "sound student," as Jonathan Sterne would put it.[39] Of all the guidebooks, travelogues, and memoirs detailing life on the boulevards, Kastner's *Les Voix de Paris*, published in 1857, offers the most synoptic account of the *cris de Paris*. Kastner supplements his prose with samples from musical works featuring street cries, including Janequin's 1530 polyphonic composition *Voulez ouyr les cris de Paris*, as well as transcriptions of cries that he purportedly had heard himself. Yet Kastner went further than any predecessor in setting Paris's cries to music: he concludes his volume with a fully scored, three-movement symphony for orchestra and chorus titled *Les Cris de Paris*, which sets a text by Édouard Thierry and uses street cry transcriptions as motivic material. This monograph-score, or *livre-partition* as it was dubbed in the printed edition, reveals two aspects of Kastner's views on urbanization and his musical aesthetics. On the one hand, he is a scholar, penning a historical essay that treats the street cry the way an ornithologist would treat birdsong. On the other hand, he is a humorist, composing a musical work in which a sleepless bourgeois and an amateur pianist are respectively interrupted by brazen vendors shouting from the streets. Despite the work's inherent humor, critics nonetheless were struck by the essay's nostalgic tone. Kastner's book, its critical reception, and its influence on subsequent opera composition all point to a historiographical—and market-driven—demand for nostalgic sonic histories of the "old city."

Les Voix de Paris is divided into two parts. Chapters 1 through 4 survey musical and poetic representations of street cries in chronological order. Chapters 5 through 7 discuss the vocal differences between various *petits métiers*, the ways in which street cries have been discussed by writers in the past, and how Paris's *cris* compare with street noise in other cities and countries. Although most of his statements regarding the specifics of street commerce rely either on previously published French or German sources or on sweeping generalizations, what is enlightening is the way in which Kastner approaches the subject of street cries as sonic relics to be cherished and not destroyed. The more personal and philosophical passages of his book shed light on how Second Empire musicians experienced everyday sound in the midst of massive urban change.

For a citizen of the nineteenth century, Kastner shows remarkable awareness of the human labor needed to make a capitalist city run. In the introductory chapter, Kastner invokes the Parisian soundscape in linguistic terms, arguing that commonly heard and uttered sounds have the power to define communities: "Large cities have a language; they even have their own sort of—if I may use the term—music that expresses, at all hours of the day, the movement and evolution of life that is joyous or somber, laborious or peaceful, which comprise home.... There is something characteristic in this sonic chaos that cradles the pleasures that make up activity in the Parisian behemoth."[40] The ambient noises of the street, he implies, are not the concealed pit orchestra, but rather the epicenter of the urban drama. As Kastner notes, "these cries taken as a whole, are like the voice of the people, and in certain civilizations become symbols or traditional formulas of certain groups or certain distinct professions."[41] Kastner's attitude toward street cries clearly alludes to Rousseau's ideas about modern language as directly descending from ancestral cries. Kastner does not cite Rousseau or his *Essai sur l'origine des langues,* perhaps remembering that the *philosophe* famously disdained the noisy din of inner Paris. But just as the French Revolution produced the very notion of an *ancien régime,* so too was the notion of *le vieux Paris* a byproduct of Haussmannization.[42] To Kastner, street cries are not noisy obstructions to civilized living, nor are they mere sonic curiosities. Instead, Kastner used his ears to write a nostalgic urban narrative that sought to reclaim the boulevard as a communal space.

As Rousseau and other eighteenth-century interlocutors have informed us, sensory distaste signified class, likening the frail ear to delicate hands relieved of manual labor. Kastner thus suggests that his own privileged, trained "voice" as a member of the Académie was no more prominent than the unrefined, utilitarian voices belonging to his everyday urban community:

> Yes, without a doubt, the Paris resident, disturbed while sleeping or while studying, could curse these unwelcome noises. But if he leaves his dwelling for a while, all of these noises will charm him upon his return. They will no longer seem like the sharp and discordant voices that tore at his eardrum. They will be intimate and friendly voices that seem to celebrate him; they will be the sweet voices of home.[43]

Rather than dismiss street cries as intrusive and amoral impositions on the bourgeois ear, as eighteenth-century commentators tended to do, Kastner argues that these sounds comprise—literally and figuratively—the collective "voice" of the Parisian community. Orchestral timbre functions as an index of the familiar. Kastner's nostalgia for hawkers translates into a "sweet" and inviting vocal sound. In the orchestral score of *Les Cris de Paris,* nostalgia translates into an accessible tonal language which, for an orchestral work of the late 1850s, was particularly sparse in Wagnerian/Lisztian chromaticism. Although Kastner demonstrates great inventiveness in orchestration to bring the urban soundscape to life, I read this reserved approach to harmony as a sign of his familial sonic relationship with the street cry.

THE SYMPHONIC STREET CRY

Kastner's description of the disgruntled Parisian resident turned enthusiastic listener aptly summarizes the program of Kastner's programmatic symphony *Les Cris de Paris: Grande symphonie humoristique.* Cast in three parts—respectively titled "Paris by Morning," "Paris by Daytime," and "Paris by Evening"—*Les Cris de Paris* consists of a sequence of solo numbers alternating with orchestral dance movements and choruses. Technically the work does not fit the formal conventions of a symphony at all; rather, the work is more akin to a nineteenth-century secular cantata given the diversity of its musical material.[44] A brief overview of the work will show how Kastner bypassed the exoticized tropes typically linked to the street cry. Instead, his musical choices reveal his own comfort with hawkers and the subterranean culture they presumably represented.

As if to pay homage to *ancien régime* operatic convention, the first movement opens with an evocative aria by the muse Titania, in which the soprano bids farewell to the quietness of night and welcomes the sights and sounds of dawn: "Do you hear the rooster crow in the distance?/ A cool air skims the earth./ Shadows are shifting on the horizon,/ Light dreams; it is morning."[45] A clarinet in C evokes a distant birdsong, which is later echoed in the flutes and English horn. Kastner then turns to the Parisian street at morning; the high woodwinds give way to percussion instruments—anvil, cymbals, whip, jingle bells, and timpani—to render the noises of workers and merchants preparing for the day (example 10). The written instructions in the score give a sense of the desired effect: "Various noises. The shops opening up, the milkman's trumpet, the blacksmith striking an anvil, the coppersmith striking copper, etc., etc."[46]

The music unfolds as a gradual ebb and flow of sound. Following a quiet pedal tone on G in the clarinets and double basses, the strings exchange a

EXAMPLE 10. Orchestral interlude in part 1 of Jean-Georges Kastner, *Les Cris de Paris, grande symphonie humoristique vocale et instrumentale.*

EXAMPLE 10. *(continued)*

EXAMPLE 10. *(continued)*

sextuplet ascending motive, creating a sense of quiet but frenetic energy. Repeated triplets in the horns further reinforce the workers' business at dawn. There is no discernible melody in this passage; it is not the cries themselves that we hear, but rather the sounds of the city as heard by a pedestrian. The passage is built on a dynamic arc that suggests movement through space, beginning pianissimo and ending in near silence with a quintuple piano marking in the penultimate measure. Although the symphony's other movements contain musical structures and idioms conventional in mid-nineteenth-century French composition, such as a ternary cavatina form and an orchestral polka, this brief passage is an outlier in its minimal motivic development and atmospheric orchestration. Indeed, this passage makes a case that Kastner's symphonic work is more than a mere playful *symphonie humoristique*. The interlude, with its programmatic instructions and substantial percussion battery, reveals a serious attempt to connect the *cris de Paris* to the mechanized sounds of the industrialized city.

This orchestral interlude sets the atmosphere for the cavatina that initiates the symphony's program. Édouard Thierry's text recounts the awakening of a troubled sleeper (simply named "Dormeur") by street noise in the first part, his profession of love for a piano-playing neighbor in the second, and his transition from angry auditor to committed *flâneur* in the third. Thierry's text alternates between octosyllabic and alexandrine verse; following the sleeper's cavatina, in which he wishes away his insomnia, several street hawkers interrupt the second verse. Kastner does not present hawkers on their own as free-standing objects of alterity, but rather writes a duet that situates street cries vis-à-vis the listener. Although the sleeper perceives this as an abrasive intrusion, the hawkers humorously complement the sleeper's song by maintaining the versification and concluding on the same end-rhyme:

SLEEPER: Stay put, my faithful dreams! . . .
A VOICE: Nuts! Nuts! Come eat these new nuts.
SLEEPER: [My dreams] hear me; they seem to speak . . .
A VOICE: Knives, scissors, ironing![47]

Kastner sets this soliloquy as a rocking barcarolle, with the alto saxophone presenting the main melody. As the sleeper then takes over the melody, the saxophone continues as an *obbligato* line. In the reprise of the cavatina, the hawkers interject through sporadic *parlando* outbursts, which create an illusion of spatial distance between the bedchamber and the street (example 11).

Unable to ignore these sounds any longer, the sleeper erupts in what can only be called a "rage aria" (example 12). Following a series of exclamatory remarks, he describes the unpleasant timbre of the criers' voices as "yelping" and "bellowing." This ternary-form movement is the "noisiest" passage of Kastner's work. The rapid juxtaposition of *piano* and *forte*, the chromatic weaving of the singer's melody, the tremolo strings, and the piercingly high range of the first flute all underscore the singer's unrelenting hatred of street noise: *Paris, c'est l'enfer!* (Paris is hell!), he laments.

EXAMPLE 11. Hawkers' interjections in part 1 of Kastner, *Les Cris de Paris*.

EXAMPLE 12. The sleepy protagonist's "rage aria" in part 1 of Kastner, *Les Cris de Paris*.

EXAMPLE 12. *(continued)*

If the street noise drove the "Dormeur" to sing a rage aria, then the following section—a tightly woven polyphonic chorus of street cries—betrays a radically different attitude toward Paris's morning sounds. The final chorus of part 1—*À deux liards les reinettes!* (Apples for two pennies!)—is in essence "heard" through Kastner's own sympathetic ears. Hawkers do not disrupt or distract; rather, each entrance of the SATB chorus corresponds with a motive heard in the orchestra. Composed in a sprightly C major, the chorus unfolds through a series of lyrical or declamatory motives. We hear a total of sixteen distinct street cries, with one of them—*à deux liards!*—functioning as a recurring cadential figure. Although the cries are not strictly linked with a specific tonality or melody, each recurrence does retain a basic rhythmic and melodic contour. In the final measures, four distinct cries come together in harmony to bring the choral number to a close.

No street cries appear in part 2: "Le jour." Indeed, the middle movement is more an interlude about urban domesticity. The sleeping protagonist—now fully awake in his apartment—listens to his female neighbor accompanying herself on the piano ("Sa fenêtre est sous ma fenêtre"). As she begins her "warm-up," we hear two simultaneous sonic phenomena: an onstage piano plays a rising and falling E major scale, while the protagonist, accompanied by a second onstage piano, sings an ode to his invisible neighbor. Once she completes her warm-up, the neighbor begins to sing a three-verse romance in the key of E: "Oh Dona Flor, flower of the court,/offer love to the beggar!"[48] Yet this is by no means a "duet." There is no indication that the neighbor hears the protagonist, or that she is even aware of his presence. Rather, the protagonist plays the role of what Boutin would call an aural *flâneur:* he manufactures a reality in which her singing voice, unbeknownst to her, provides fodder for a romantic interchange. Kastner plays with the acoustic and social distance between the two characters by calling for two pianos to be positioned at opposite sides of the stage; one piano recreates the daytime soundscape of an apartment building while the other represents the protagonist's wishful imagination. Whereas the first movement of *Les Cris de Paris* features a direct contest between street hawkers and the insomniac protagonist, "Le jour" presents a sonic rendering of two domestic spaces. If the first movement establishes outside noise as an interruption to the protagonist's inner thoughts, the sound of a practicing piano is music to his ears. In "Le jour," Kastner doubles down on the overarching thesis of *Les Voix de Paris:* that unsolicited environmental sounds need not be categorically dismissed.

The third part of *Les Cris de Paris,* "Le soir," sees our protagonist leave his bedchamber and enter the street. As if to reflect on the carnivalesque diversity of boulevard life, "Le soir" features a compilation of five mini-movements: a ternary aria, a choral number, an orchestral polka, a hunting chorus for brass, and a final sung chorus. The narrative trajectory of *Les Cris de Paris* effectively concludes with the aria of "Le soir," since it is the last time we hear the main character. Singing in a barcarolle rhythm, the protagonist—whose name has changed in the score from "Dormeur" to "Promeneur" (walker)—offers a tender serenade about Paris by night. Recalling part 1, the street criers—this time a group of *crieurs de journaux* (newspaper vendors) and a *marchand de contre-marques billets* (ticket scalper)—interrupt the song right before the final cadence. In the E minor section that immediately follows, the band of hawkers shouts the names of the newspapers for sale. Instead of expressing annoyance as before, the fully awake protagonist seems content with or even pleased by the hawkers' presence. Kastner uses this humorous union of musical forces to obliterate the distinction between melodious singing and intrusive crying; rather than interrupt or disturb the stability of the aria, the hawkers complement the protagonist's melody. Although there are no stage directions, we can imagine the sleeper-turned-*flâneur* parading through the streets of Paris alongside his hawking compatriots. Kastner's aforementioned "sweet voices of home" find their symphonic parallel here: by deploying counterpoint, rocking barcarolle rhythms, and obbligato melodies, Kastner presents a sonic landscape of a city that treats hawkers not as intrusive Others but as welcome elements of the urban sensorium. *Les Cris de Paris* can thus be heard as a symphonic triptych on the moral imperative of listening to disenfranchised voices. The work presents a series of programmatic vignettes that musically outline the main ideas that Kastner proposes in his prefatory essay, propositions for how to become an active, listening member of the new urban environment. Listen without prejudice—without Proustian, referential rumination—and you will realize that the sounds of the city *are* the city as conceived, represented, and experienced.

As of this writing, Kastner's *Les Cris de Paris* has never been performed in its entirety, despite the full score being freely available in the public domain.[49] In Kastner's lifetime, fragments were arranged as piano parlor pieces soon after its publication. The third movement *polka carnavalesque* in particular made its way into the celebrated Musard concert series; the conductor and pianist Émile Desgranges arranged the polka first (presumably) for his orchestra, and then for solo piano. The piano arrangement, a fairly accurate and banal transcription of Kastner's orchestral music, was published by G. Brandus & S. Dufour. Pianists continued to transcribe Kastner's polka into the next decade; Emmanuel Baumann's 1865 arrangement is a more pianistic rendition, featuring octave arpeggios and precise pedal markings, evidence that even semi-serious pianists consumed street cries in their salon musicmaking.[50]

The warm critical response to Kastner's *Les Voix de Paris* suggests that the volume made its way around the Parisian musical and theatrical communities. Taking note of the book's reception, François-Joseph Fétis observed in his 1866–68 edition of the *Biographie universelle des musiciens* that *Les Voix de Paris* "generated as much astonishment for the originality of the idea, as for patience of the research."[51] Writing in the *Revue de beaux-arts* in 1857, Antoine Elwart commended Kastner's efforts to historicize street cries: "[Kastner] set out to highlight the intimate rapport between the sonorities of outdoor commerce and the state of our history. He also sought to demonstrate that these cries, which are all too often perceived as insignificant chaos, hold keys to understanding the traditions and intentions that touch upon the most problematic and delicate issues of our musical heritage."[52] In other words, the *cris de Paris* belonged to both linguistic and musical narratives of history, and as such, they merited a study like Kastner's to secure their place in French cultural memory.

Joseph d'Ortigue was more direct in connecting *Les Voix de Paris* to ongoing debates about urban demolition in Paris. In a lengthy essay published in the *Journal des débats* on March 19, 1858, d'Ortigue looked past the inherent humor of the musical work and situated it as a serious critique of urbanization's deleterious effects. *Les Voix de Paris*, d'Ortigue claimed, should interest those who specialize in the history of the French capital and who are witnessing "the architects' hammer demolishing what remains of old Paris."[53] Under such devastating urban conditions, he continued, the vibrant practice of hawking was at serious risk of being annihilated from Paris's cultural memory: "In a few years, no traces will remain of these old cries, just as no traces will remain of the old city. Both will be replaced by constructions and 'compositions' which are perhaps more regulated, but which will be far from presenting the same character."[54] D'Ortigue drew a direct parallel between urban construction and musical composition, and he implies that Haussmann's symmetrical urbanism and Kastner's symphony are two ways of disciplining the urban experience.

I alluded to these contrasts—between the ordered world of bourgeois interiority and mobility of the outdoor hawker—at the beginning of this chapter. As we have seen, Baudelaire's poem "Le Mauvais vitrier" suggested how the audible "improvisations" of the street vendor disrupted the narrator's carefully "composed" acoustic interior. As Thomas Christiansen notes, d'Ortigue heard in the *cris de Paris* the conservation of ancient tonality, whereas for Kastner it was their overall vocal naturalness that stood the test of time, thereby adaptable for a modern, tonal urban soundscape.[55] To listen to cries is necessarily to organize them, to link them to past vocal traditions of singing, chanting, and declamation.

While I do not know if Proust knew about or read Kastner's *Les Voix de Paris*, his extended meditation on the "medieval" character of street cries is worth revisiting at this point. As explained earlier in this chapter, *La Prisonnière*'s narrator awakens early to listen to the sound of the street, while his lover, Albertine, sleeps next to him (in stark contrast to Kastner's "Dormeur," who is reluctantly awoken by what he perceives as noise). Just as Kastner and d'Ortigue both detected antiquated vocal techniques in nineteenth-century cries, so too does *La Prisonnière*'s inquisitive narrator. Elongated, plaintive street cries, such as "ferrailles à vendre," evoke in him the modalities and cadences of Gregorian chant. But in the same paragraph, the narrator proceeds to associate the punctuated delivery of cries with syllabic declamation in modern opera, namely those of Mussorgsky and Debussy: "[The street cry] differed from song as much as the declamation—barely colored by imperceptible modulations—of *Boris Godunov* and *Pelléas;* but on the other hand recalled the psalmody of a priest chanting his office of which these street scenes are but the good-humored, secular, and yet half liturgical counterpart."[56] How could a street cry generate such disparate sound worlds? As Christiansen notes, Kastner's street cry transcriptions do not suggest direct connections to medieval modality in ways that his contemporaneous critics had envisaged. Kastner no doubt translated many of his cries into a "modern," nineteenth-century tonality, one that would be legible at the piano. Moreover, the "transcriptions" in the early chapters of *Les Voix de Paris* also sit alongside quotations of operas in which the cries of vendors were detected (such as Gaspare Spontini's *Fernand Cortez*). Thus what appears on the printed page may not necessarily be what was heard on Kastner's street in 1857, nor for that matter during Proust's writing of *À la recherche du temps perdu* in the 1910s and 20s.

What Kastner and Proust seem to have in common, then, is that they were not merely listening *to* street cries, in some sort of isolated, phenomenological chamber of perception. Kastner and Proust—a generation apart but deeply aware of the process of urban change—were listening *for* something. In Kastner's case, it was to prove his argument that the aggregate sounds of Paris's cries were the sounds of home: a shared collective memory of Frenchness, of Parisianness, a common diatonic vernacular, a desire to signal a fanfare for the "old city." To Proust, hawkers signaled something more personal. The cries themselves, and what they intended to signify, mattered little to the narrator. Being bourgeois, neither he nor his love interest, Albertine, relied on hawkers exclusively for their daily nourishment. Rather, street cries, despite being quoted and detailed so vividly in the pages of *La Prisonnière*, amount to an *idée fixe:* the bourgeois pleasure of patronizing an anachronistic form of commerce. Albertine claims to find hawkers' oysters brinier, their lettuces crisper, their confections sweeter. As she confesses, "What I like about these foodstuffs that are cried is that a thing which we hear like a rhapsody changes its nature when it comes to our table and addresses itself to my palate."[57] Proust's narrator cares neither for the oysters nor the lettuces nor the confections, but rather what all of this gustatory and aural sensation grants him: access into Albertine's elusive desires.[58]

What was once a public utility—an actual way of cheaply feeding and clothing people—had, by the turn of the century, become an aestheticized rhapsody, a literary leitmotif. Kastner's conception of "home," of which he and the hawkers were a part, was in the end an imagined space in which hawkers did not sell, but rather sang, to the pleasure—or frustration—of bystanders. As the physical markets, squares, and alleys were demolished and Paris's working communities were displaced to the city's outer rings, "the old city" emerged as a nostalgic but ultimately fictional place, ripe for poetic, novelistic, and operatic treatment, but uninhabitable for those who helped construct it in the first place. Cries didn't necessarily fade away, but their social function changed irrevocably. Use value ceded to exchange value; the communicative cry became nostalgic fanfare, or, as some commentators put it much later, folklore.

UN PEU DE FOLKLORE

One year after the publication of *Les Voix de Paris,* Jacques Offenbach and librettist Armand Lapointe quoted Kastner's street cry transcriptions in *Mesdames de la Halle,* a one-act opérette-bouffe that premiered at the Bouffes-Parisiens on March 3, 1858. Set in Paris's historic Marché des

Innocents during the reign of Louis XV, the operetta features an opening chorus of street vendors who advertise their wares to passersby. Indeed, each distinct street cry heard in the chorus could be traced to specific examples in Kastner's book—an observation that d'Ortigue made in the same essay in which he reviewed *Les Voix de Paris*.[59] But it is the operetta's setting in the Marché des Innocents that begs our attention, as it spotlights one of the most celebrated outdoor markets that was slated for demolition. In early 1858, Haussmann closed the Marché des Innocents to make room for a giant, indoor marketplace known as Les Halles Centrales. The glass and iron edifice designed by Victor Baltard, which Zola later dubbed "The Belly of Paris" in his eponymous novel of 1873, was to represent Second Empire modernity at its peak. The closure of the Marché des Innocents meant that the bustle of surrounding outdoor commerce would give way to indoor pavilions, fixed prices, and visual advertising. In "modern" Paris, then, transactions became interactions between customers and signs, with vendors serving as silent mediators. This Kastner-inspired operetta can thus be read as a gentle pushback to Haussmann's monument-driven urbanism. Satirical musical works by Offenbach, Kastner, and others deserve merit as documents of urban history. They offer a balancing counternarrative to Haussmannian utopianism and Baudelairean pessimism: two narratives that have dominated the historiography of Second Empire France.

Amid heavy police crackdowns on street commerce during the nineteenth century, writers, composers, and critics situated street vendors on a historical continuum, with "old Paris" and its alleyways and street carts on one side, and "new Paris" and its boulevards and department stores on the other. The many debates, reflections, and creative acts inspired by the *cris de Paris* highlight the rift between urban change and collective care for the municipal past, but they also reveal a horizon of experience that has eluded the predominantly opera-centric scholarship of the period. As a cultural phenomenon, Haussmannization redistributed social activity from a diverse array of intimate spaces and interactions to monumental boulevards, stores, and markets. The *cris de Paris* thus represented an antiquated, haphazard exchange economy that was at odds with the new, homogenized vision of the city. Haussmannization, after all, was as much about curating sensory experience as it was about executing public works projects. Street hawkers provided far more than passive *couleur locale* to Offenbach's *Mesdames de la Halle*, and later, Giacomo Puccini's Parisian *verismo* operas *La Bohème* and *Il tabarro*, Frederick Delius's symphonic nocturne *Paris*, and Gustave Charpentier's

Louise.⁶⁰ Rather, hawkers constituted yet another urban community whose prevalence in the economy inspired nostalgia in the preservationists—and ire in the Préfecture de la Seine.

Notwithstanding the ultimate success of these attempts to "preserve" the memory of outdoor urban commerce, the *cris de Paris* played a substantial role in the folklorization of *le vieux Paris*. Today, the ubiquitous presence of Parisian street criers is a thing of the past, although some produce vendors will still advertise bargains by hawking the price—in euros—to passersby. But the phenomenon of the *cris de Paris* has been literally folded into history: at the Archives de la Préfecture de Police, nineteenth-century police decrees are tucked into twentieth-century newspaper clippings reminiscing on *le vieux Paris*. Buried in an archival box is a 1976 clipping from the newspaper *Le Parisien* that asks: "The cries that once animated the street of Paris are gone. Is that for better, or for worse? Opinions are divided. A bit of folklore (*un peu de folklore*) has disappeared, steamrolled by commercial codification."⁶¹ Folklore—along with related concepts such as *patrimoine* (heritage formation), mythology, homage, preservation, ethnography, historicity, and nostalgia—belonged to the broader discursive practices of nineteenth-century Parisian modernity. And as Ross Cole observes in a book-length study, the concept "the folk" continues to be co-opted by a spectrum of ideologies, from the reactionary to the revolutionary.⁶² This loaded appearance of the word "folklore" in the 1976 article suggests that oral histories of Paris were fueled by nostalgia for a community perceived to be lost. The fanfare around *le vieux Paris* emerged in parallel with Haussmannization as a way to reclaim a sense of community in an industrializing metropolis. The "old city," as celebrated by Kastner and others, was a quintessential cultural product of the mid-nineteenth century, a nostalgic painting of modern life.

Epilogue

ON OCTOBER 25, 1870, without any fanfare, the boulevard du Prince-Eugène became the boulevard Voltaire. The provisional mayor of Paris, Étienne Arago, had quietly made an announcement that the city would replace the statue of the emperor's uncle with that of the Enlightenment *philosophe*, subsequently renaming the boulevard itself. In stark contrast to the media frenzy around the boulevard's inauguration in 1862, Arago's announcement was buried in the "press communications" sections of the Parisian daily newspapers. *Le Temps* and *Le Figaro*, for example, both published the same canned, one-sentence notice on their respective second pages on October 26, stating succinctly and matter-of-factly that Arago had made the decision in consultation with the *maire* of the eleventh arrondissement, Arthur de Fonvielle.[1] Soon, the place du Trône would become the place de la Nation, and the place du Château d'Eau would be renamed—for political reasons—the place de la République.

Those political reasons were dramatic. The ongoing Franco-Prussian War had broken out on July 19, 1870, and would last until January 28, 1871. By the fall of 1870, the French prospects in the war were bleak, and the empire's demise was all but assured. The Battle of Sedan, which was fought in early September, resulted in over ten thousand Frenchmen dead and wounded, and over one hundred thousand captured—among them a beleaguered Napoléon III. This capitulation led to the Siege of Paris, a drawn-out blockade of the city by Prussian forces, and the bombardment of the city in January 1871. By the end of the month, with the city in flames and its people starving, an armistice put an end to the siege. But Paris would soon witness more violence. By May, the Paris Commune had ended with tens of thousands of Communards slain by the national French army.

The silent announcement of the boulevard Voltaire was a stark contrast—almost conspicuously so—to the spectacular inauguration of the boulevard du Prince-Eugène in 1862, described in the opening pages of this book. During the bloody events of the Franco-Prussian War and the Paris Commune, there seemed to be little taste for spectacle or commemoration. It took the Parisian government many years to account for the mass murder of its own citizens; it was only in 1983 that the wall in Père Lachaise cemetery against which many Communards were shot became a historical monument. In 1871, however, no public mourning took place; the *Te deums* that rung from church bells were not for the fallen Parisians but for the city's archbishop, Georges Darboy, who was executed by Communards on May 24, 1871, a casualty of a botched hostage exchange.[2]

Given all the loss of life between the years 1870 and 1872, it might seem frivolous to check in on the city's musical infrastructure. And yet, many of the musical spaces described in this book played critical functions in the relief effort, their interiors adjusted to fit the circumstances. While Paris's musical industry did not grind to a complete halt, there was indeed a noticeable decline in musical activity in late 1870. Theaters that closed for the summer remained shuttered through the fall. Many orchestral musicians, as well as composers like Georges Bizet, Vincent d'Indy, Jules Massenet, and Camille Saint-Saëns, enlisted in the National Guard against the Prussians, leaving little time for new music. The nineteen-year-old d'Indy was particularly moved by the sounds of the war, even detailing with morbid precision that the Prussian guns were tuned to B-flat.[3] The musical press, too, went silent; the two major periodicals, *Le Ménestrel* and *Revue et gazette musicale de Paris*, both went on hiatus between September 1870 and the fall of 1871.[4]

Despite this lapse in musical and celebratory events, the larger performance spaces did not remain empty for long. The Palais de l'Industrie, once the crowning glory of the nascent Second Empire, became an artillery facility, an infirmary for the wounded, and the home base for the relief society known as the Société de secours. As evidenced from sketches housed at the Bibliothèque historique de la ville de Paris, artists rushed to depict what must have been a striking recontextualization of palatial space: thrones, stages, sculptures, and flags were cleared off to make room for rows of cannons, piles of sandbags and cannonballs, and hospital beds. One can even imagine that the Palais's decorative items, like the marble statues and drapery, might have been repurposed as weapons and bandages.

The Palais was not unique in this wartime reuse of space. As Delphine Mordey has detailed, Charles Garnier's still-unfinished opera house was refashioned into a military storehouse, its roof outfitted with an observation deck and its cellars flooded to create a reservoir for fire engines.[5] This sudden shift from spectacle to storehouse indicated the end of the *fête impériale,* the two-decade reliance on monumentality and sensory curation to propagate power. Sound worlds were reversed; the large performance spaces lost their acoustic brilliance as innumerable bodies and raw materials filled them, while outside, explosions, gunfire, and calls-to-arms generated violent urban rhythms not felt since the revolution of 1848.

The *fin de siècle* marked a referendum on the preceding empire's spaces of spectacle: what would stay, what would go, what would be repurposed. In 1897, the Palais de l'Industrie was demolished to make room for the new home of the 1900 Exposition universelle, the Grand Palais, a building that occupies space along the Champs-Élysées to this day. Unlike the Second Empire's penchant for ephemeral and liminal architecture, the present-day Fifth French Republic has made a commitment to the Grand Palais, designating it a *monument historique* in 2000. Nothing remains of the Palais de l'Industrie, save for Élias Robert's entrance statue, "France crowning Art and Industry," which sits tucked away in the suburban Parc de Saint-Cloud. Aside from that, photos, illustrations, prose descriptions, concert programs, and cantata and song texts are the only documents we have to imagine how the Palais might have looked—and sounded—in its heyday.

The Eldorado also fell silent during most of the Franco-Prussian War and the Commune. These disturbances would bring the administrative reign of Charles Joseph Éleazar Lorge to a premature end, as he stepped away from his duties and into retirement. Having rescued the Eldorado from financial ruin in the 1858, Lorge transformed it into one of the Second Empire's most sought-after entertainment venues. Workers, petty bourgeoisie, families, critics, composers—all were welcome to enjoy the venue's food, drink, diverse musical entertainment, and free-flowing mode of sociability. Lorge's post-1864 efforts to raise the Eldorado to the same status as the *grands théâtres*—first by hiring the classical actress Cornélie, then by staging, in full costume, Hervé's Greco-Roman spoof *Le Retour d'Ulysse*—generated heated debates about what the café-concert was, and what it ought to be. These debates continued into the early 1870s. In a long report circulated among members of the Ministère d'État, L. Casslant, inspector general of the Opéra, lambasted the encroachment of the café-concert into the realm of theater. As he saw it, all cafés-concerts were the same, and they did little more than spread propaganda, encourage vice, and "atrophy public taste."[6] Responding to the landmark 1864 decision to "liberate" theaters from licensing and generic restrictions, Casslant argued that the broader liberalization of the 1860s-era Second Empire needed to be reversed: more censorship, more policing, a recentralization of performance venues. In short, Casslant desired greater control over what had become a diffuse theatrical landscape.

As I have argued in chapter 3, cafés-concerts were never the theater-breaking menace they were made out to be. Indeed, the Eldorado's desire to compete head-on with the larger theater would set an unsustainable standard for the network of cafés-concerts as a whole. Though "liberated," cafés-concerts would eventually buckle under the weight of big-budget theatrical programming, particularly that of staged operetta and vaudeville. By 1880, they would cede their carefree, fluid status to the *cabarets artistiques* of Montmartre, such as the Chat Noir. The wordsmithing of the repetitive *scies* would make way for the gritty storytelling of the *chansons réalistes*. Thérésa, having defined what it meant to be a "star" in the nebulous world of the singing cafés, now had descendants, each with their own unique personality, singing style, and relationship to the city and its audiences: Bruant, Guilbert, Paulus, Piaf. Granted, the larger cafés-concerts did survive well into the twentieth century, and some are still operating as "popular" entertainment venues today. Outfitted with fixed seating, orchestra pits, projection screens, and audiovisual control booths, these veritable "theaters" no longer resemble the porous extensions of boulevard life that they were in the 1850s. Lorge, for his part, would play no further role in "liberating" the café-concert for a new Third Republic. In August 1871, he formed a business partnership with the chansonnier Paul Renard, who became the Eldorado's chief artistic director and operating officer.[7] Lorge thus ended his reign over the Second Empire's most lavish café-concert in a quiet, but lucrative, fashion.

As for Baron Haussmann, the political consequences of his vastly expensive urban reforms eventually caught up to him. Jules Ferry itemized Haussmann's speculative financing in damning fashion in his pamphlet *Les Comptes fantastiques d'Haussmann*, a text discussed in chapter 4. In 1869, facing pressure from an emboldened republican legislature, Napoléon III asked Haussmann to resign from his post, which he refused to do. This shortly led to Haussmann's dismissal as Prefect of the Seine, an episode he recounts with indignation in his *Mémoires*. In the early 1870s, while his former emperor lived in exile, Haussmann stayed out of the public eye in his family château near Bordeaux. He therefore did not witness Paris's Hôtel de Ville—where he conducted his most consequential urbanistic work and where he hosted his beloved musical soirées—burning to the ground. He returned to public office in 1877 when he moved to Ajaccio, Corsica, to serve as a Bonapartist delegate until 1881. Though he continued to advise Parisian bureaucrats who wrote him regularly on all matters of state and business, he never regained the power he once held, and he devoted his final years to reflecting on his life and work.

Dubbed a musical amateur and *mélomane* by contemporaries, Haussmann enjoyed early musical experiences which, along with his polymath interests, informed his aesthetic perspectives on the art of urbanism. Despite his early encounters with Reicha, Cherubini, and Berlioz, and his later financial support of the conductor Jules Pasdeloup during the Second Empire, the self-described *artiste-démolisseur* once wrote off musical study as a "distraction." Be that as it may, the "distraction" appeared to sustain him for the rest of his life. According to a postmortem inventory of his Bordeaux château conducted in 1891, Haussmann and his wife, Octavie de Laharpe, owned an Érard upright piano and a bookcase of musical scores. A mountain of receipts suggests that the piano was serviced regularly.[8]

It was inevitable that Baron Haussmann would want a boulevard named after himself. In 1857, Haussmann oversaw demolition for what would become the boulevard Haussmann, an east-west thoroughfare that would stretch from the quartier du Faubourg-du-Roule in the first arrondissement, over the site of the future Palais Garnier, into the ninth arrondissement. Building stalled between 1874 and 1926, and daily newspapers like *Le Figaro* regularly invoked "the incompleteness of the boulevard Haussmann" like a leitmotif of the disfunction of the empire's final years.[9] In an event symptomatic of twentieth-century Paris's complex relationship to the "capital of the nineteenth century," the boulevard Haussmann was inaugurated on January 15, 1927 (figure 11). The President of the Third French Republic, Gaston Doumergue (born in 1863, a year after the inauguration of the boulevard du Prince-Eugène) rode down the completed boulevard, not on horseback, but in a motorcade. Tricolor flags lined the thoroughfare, in contrast to the imperial imagery of the previous century. No *arcs de triomphes* were erected for the occasion, but the *art nouveau* arch of the new metro station signified the new mode of subterranean urban planning that would unite the city from below—much like the sewer system had in the nineteenth century. Billboards lining the thoroughfare are a reminder that by the 1920s, the boulevard

FIGURE 11. The inauguration of the boulevard Haussmann, January 15, 1927. Image: BnF.

Haussmann was already home to the department stores that rendered the city's itinerant street hawkers obsolete.

Plus ça change. Military officials lined the boulevard to greet the president, just like they had for the emperor. But their uniforms signified a different era: the Gardes républicains, wrote one newspaper, looked dapper in their signature helmets, boots, and white breeches. The crowds that gathered between the neighboring boulevard des Italiens and the rue Drouot, mostly men, sported classic 1920s bourgeois style: black top hats and capes. Choirs and mounted brass players provided a soundtrack for the motorcade procession. To commence the official inauguration ceremony, Victor Charpentier (brother of the composer Gustave) led the musicians in the French national anthem, *La Marseillaise,* a song banned during the Second Empire. The musical number that followed paid tribute to the "folklore" of the city and its dwellers, as explored in chapter 5: the "Marche des cris de Paris" from Gustave Charpentier's 1900 opera *Louise.* Like his imperial predecessor, President Doumergue gave a rousing speech to an enthusiastic crowd; among the guests of honor were the descendants of Baron Haussmann. Rather than a giant curtain revealing the vista, Doumergue opted for the more modest gesture of cutting a ribbon. The musical postlude to the ceremony was a staple of nineteenth-century ceremonial music, Berlioz's *Apothéose* from the *Grande symphonie funèbre et triomphale,* the same work that featured during the Expositions universelles.[10] In his speech, Doumergue paid homage to the boulevard's namesake urbanist, but his remarks also touched on the importance of urbanism in forging French republican identity. The Paris of the Third Republic would realize, then reframe, the urban reforms begun under the previous imperial regime. The musical juxtaposition of Berlioz's *Apothéose,* Charpentier's *Louise,* and the *Marseillaise* amounted to a fanfare for a twentieth-century city, a republican metropolis grappling with its nineteenth-century past, a city in recovery from the violent events of 1870–72—as well as those of 1914–19.

Despite the Third Republic's splintered relationship with the regimes of the preceding century—a relationship far beyond the scope of these final pages—the commitment to greeting new boulevards with fanfare suggests several tiers of cultural continuity: from empire to republic; from realism to surrealism; from the *fête impériale* to *les années folles.* Third Republic values of public utility and beauty were inscribed in ornately decorated buildings and diversely programmed cultural events. During the Third Republic, as Jann Pasler has shown, beauty and utility were interdependent.[11] This was also true of the Second Empire. In reading song and cantata texts, libretti, scores, published testimonies, fiction, and police records—against the grain and with open ears—it becomes evident that French regimes, from *ancien* to *moderne,* all understood the power of sound resonating in space, and the need to curate both.

This book has argued that in nineteenth-century Paris, urban politics both shaped, and were shaped by, musical discourses and practices in the city. As I hope to have shown, there is not one singular Parisian soundscape to study, reducible to a set of concepts, ideologies, institutions, behaviors, and artistic proclivities. For that matter, "Second Empire Paris," too, resists homogenization as a music-historical category. Napoléon, Haussmann, Offenbach, Berlioz—these names reappear in musical and urban histories of the period, but the period cannot be reduced to names alone. Shifts in musical practices and policies were conditioned by shifts in urban infrastructure, but as we have seen in case studies of imperial ceremonies, café-concert policies, and the policing of street commerce, music could also shape the aesthetics of urbanization. Scholars working at the intersections of sound, space, and city should continue to untangle the hegemonic narratives that dictated urban identity on the behalf of others. The notion of a singular "urban soundscape," like the regulative work-concept familiar to historical musicologists, obscures the richness of musical activity in an urbanizing city. Rather than focus on a singular sound world, *Fanfare for a City* has presented a range of musical events, spaces, and communities, from the elite to the mundane.

Splintered as the city's theatrical infrastructure became in the aftermath of 1870, the overdue completion of a boulevard could jolt the city back to its love affair with public spectacle and an expansive view. The inaugurations of the boulevards Prince-Eugène and Haussmann, separated by six decades, reveal the extent to which Paris's urban culture is tied to civic ceremony. It reveals a city of not one soundscape but many, framed by differing conceptions, representations, and lived experiences of an urbanizing world. It reveals a populace that enjoyed acoustic richness as much as it enjoyed seeing and being seen. Paris in those years vibrated with new sounds, each leaving a legible trace of the myths and realities of the metropolis.

NOTES

All translations in this book are my own unless otherwise noted.

INTRODUCTION

1. Haussmann's and Napoléon's speeches were reprinted in *Le Moniteur universelle,* December 9, 1862.
2. *Le Ménestrel,* December 7, 1862.
3. "Salut! Boulevard si splendide,/ Qui porte un nom bien glorieux;/ Pour te voir, une foule avide,/ Vient encor le front radieux." Eugène Baumester, "Inauguration du nouveau boulevard: Au souvenir du Prince Eugène" (Paris: Vert frères, 1862).
4. "Honneur à toi, femme toute angélique,/ Nul ne pourrait renier tes vertus." Arthur Halbert d'Angers, "Le Prince Eugène et l'impératrice Joséphine" (Paris: Vert frères, 1862).
5. Joseph Desbrières, "Paris nouveau: Le boulevard du Prince-Eugène" (Paris: L. Tinterlin, 1862).
6. "Encore une nouvelle et merveilleuse artère/ Qui va du vieux Paris secouer la poussière,/ Et qui suffirait seule à la célébrité/ Du premier magistrat de la grande cité."
7. Two handwritten copies of the cantata text, with light line edits by censors, can be found in AN F/18/739.
8. "Sur les débris de l'antique Lutèce/ Chaque jour le nouveau Paris/ Vaillamment déroule les plis/ De son manteau plein de richesse/ Dans l'un de ces plis on découvre/ Un splendide et grand boulevard/ Qui abrite déjà l'étendard/ Que l'on voit flotter sur le louvre/ De la cité régénérée/ Que tous les cœurs reconnaissans/ Fassent de leurs joyeux accents/ Retentir la voûte azurée."
9. Nicholas Papayanis, *Planning Paris before Haussmann* (Baltimore: Johns Hopkins University Press, 2004), 181.
10. Colin Jones, *Paris: Biography of a City* (New York: Penguin Books, 2006), 10–12.

11. Jean des Cars and Pierre Pinon, *Paris-Haussmann. Le pari d'Haussmann* (Paris: Picard, Édition du Pavillon de l'Arsenal, 1991), 147.

12. Anselm Gerhard, *The Urbanization of Opera,* trans. Mary Whittall (Chicago: University of Chicago Press, 1998). Gerhard's book originally appeared in German as *Die Verstädterung der Oper.*

13. Two book-length studies that I view as foundational for my argument here are François Caradec and Alain Weill, *Le Café-concert: 1848–1914* (Paris: Hachette, 2007), and Derek B. Scott, *Sounds of the Metropolis: The Nineteenth-Century Popular Music Revolution in London, New York, Paris and Vienna* (New York: Oxford University Press, 2008).

14. Jennifer Stoever, *The Sonic Color Line: Race and the Cultural Politics of Listening* (New York: New York University Press, 2016), 6.

15. Nadar, *Quand j'étais photographe* (Paris: Flammarion, 1900), 118.

16. Jones, *Paris,* 352.

17. David P. Jordan, "The City: Baron Haussmann and Modern Paris," *The American Scholar* 61, no. 1 (1992): 105.

18. Esther da Costa Meyer, *Dividing Paris: Urban Renewal and Social Inequality, 1852–1870* (Princeton: Princeton University Press, 2022), 186.

19. Walter Benjamin, "Paris, Capital of the Nineteenth Century," in *The Arcades Project,* trans. Howard Eiland and Kevin McLaughlin (New York: Belknap Press, 2002), 86. For a vivid reading of Paris via Benjamin, see Marshall Berman, *All That Is Solid Melts Into Air: The Experience of Modernity* (New York: Penguin Books, 1982), esp. 131–72.

20. Anna-Louise Milne, ed. *The Cambridge Companion to the Literature of Paris* (New York: Cambridge University Press, 2013).

21. Honoré de Balzac, *La Peau du chagrin* (Paris, 1831), 63.

22. Charles Augustin Saint-Beuve, *Correspondance générale* (Paris, 1843), 5:286.

23. Charles Baudelaire, "The Salon of 1846," in *The Mirror of Art: Critical Essays by Charles Baudelaire,* trans. Jonathan Mayne (New York: Doubleday Anchor Books, 1956), 46.

24. "Sous un ciel chagrin, des fanfares étranges/Passent, comme un soupir étouffé de Weber."

25. See Michel Foucault, *Abnormal: Lectures at the Collège de France, 1974–1975,* trans. Graham Burchell (New York: Verso, 2003), 233. My italics.

26. See Andrea Bohlman, "Solidarity, Song, and the Sound Document," *Journal of Musicology* 33, no. 2 (Spring 2016): 232–69.

27. T. J. Clark, *The Painting of Modern Life: Paris in the Art of Manet and His Followers* (Princeton: Princeton University Press, 1982).

28. See Patricia Mainardi, *Art and Politics of the Second Empire: The Universal Expositions of 1855 and 1867* (New Haven: Yale University Press, 1987); Priscilla Parkhurst Ferguson, *Paris as Revolution: Writing the Nineteenth-Century City* (Berkeley: University of California Press, 1997); Christopher Prendergast, *Paris and the Nineteenth Century* (London: Wiley-Blackwell, 1995); and Aimée Boutin, *City*

of Noise: Sound and Nineteenth-Century Paris (Urbana-Champaign: University of Illinois Press, 2015).

29. See Kanishka Goonewardena, "The Urban Sensorium: Space, Ideology and the Aestheticization of Politics," *Antipode* 37 (2005): 46–71.

30. Eugen Weber, *Peasants into Frenchmen: The Modernization of Rural France, 1870–1914* (Palo Alto: Stanford University Press, 1976).

31. See Samuel Llano, *Discordant Notes: Marginality and Social Control in Madrid, 1850–1930* (New York: Oxford University Press, 2018).

32. Ana María Ochoa Gautier, *Aurality: Listening and Knowledge in Nineteenth-Century Colombia* (Durham: Duke University Press, 2014), 28.

33. Annegret Fauser, *Musical Encounters at the 1889 Paris World's Fair* (Rochester: University of Rochester Press, 2005), 10.

34. On the historiography of inclusion and exclusion in the French Revolutionary archives, especially as it relates to music, see Rebecca Dowd Geoffroy-Schwinden, *From Servant to Savant: Musical Privilege, Property, and the French Revolution* (New York: Oxford University Press, 2022), esp. 10–15.

35. Lawrence Kramer, *The Hum of the World: A Philosophy of Listening* (Berkeley: University of California Press, 2018), 86–88.

36. Tim Carter, "The Sound of Silence: Models for an Urban Musicology," *Urban History* 29, no. 1 (May 2002): 8–18. More recently, Carter has also called into relief the relative overuse of the "historical soundscape" idea: "The idea of the 'soundscape' is all well and good," he argues, "but whether there is some kind of continuum from the sounds of the street to those of the church or chamber is another matter." See Tim Carter, "Listening to Music in Early Modern Italy: Some Problems for the Urban Musicologist," in *Hearing the City in Early Modern Europe*, ed. Tess Knighton and Ascensión Mazuela-Anguita (Turnhout: Brepols, 2018), 32. For a broader conceptualization of "sound studies" within the realm of Early Modern musicology, See Alexander J. Fisher, *Music, Piety, and Propaganda: The Soundscapes of Counter-Reformation Bavaria* (New York: Oxford University Press, 2014), esp. 1–29.

37. Jonathan Sterne, "Soundscape, Landscape, Escape," in *Soundscapes of the Urban Past*, ed. Karin Bijsterveld (Bielefeld: Transcript Verlag, 2013), 184.

38. See Stephen Graham and Simon Marvin, *Splintering Urbanism: Networked Infrastructures, Technological Mobilities and the Urban Condition* (London: Routledge, 2001).

39. Jann Pasler, *Composing the Citizen: Music as Public Utility in Third Republic France* (Berkeley: University of California Press, 2009), 26.

40. See Adam Krims, *Music and Urban Geography* (New York: Routledge, 2007).

41. Gascia Ouzounian has adopted Lefebvre's writing on urban space to examine how sound artists in twentieth- and early twenty-first centuries have challenged "Euclidean concepts of space," namely the hegemonic, abstract forms of urban placemaking imposed on users and unrelated to the material, lived needs of those users. See *Stereophonica: Sound and Space in Science, Technology, and the Arts* (Cambridge, MA: The MIT Press, 2020), esp. 116–23.

42. Henri Lefebvre, *Rhythmanalysis: Space, Time and Everyday Life,* trans. Stuart Elden and Gerald Moore (London: Continuum, 2004), 87. Lefebvre was not the only urban thinker to consider the city as a musical vessel or instrument. As Jesse H. Ausubel and Robert Herman write, "Cities are the summation and densest expressions of infrastructure, or more accurately a set of infrastructures, working sometimes in harmony, sometimes with frustrating discord, to provide us with shelter, contact, energy, water and means to meet other human needs" (*Cities and Their Vital Systems: Infrastructure Past, Present, and Future* [Washington, DC: National Academy Press, 1988], 1). For an extended musical metaphor applied to the future city's role in environmental justice, see Jonathan F. P. Rose, *The Well-Tempered City: What Modern Science, Ancient Civilizations, and Human Nature Teach Us About the Future of Urban Life* (New York: Harper Wave, 2016).

43. Henri Lefebvre, "The Right to the City," in *Writings on Cities,* trans. and ed. Eleonore Kofman and Elizabeth Lebas (London: Blackwell, 1996), 147–59.

44. See Ouzounian, *Stereophonica,* 125–49.

45. On the networks of political power that informed the management of the Opéra during the Second Empire, see Mark Everist, *The Empire at the Opéra: Theatre, Power, and Music in Second Empire Paris* (Cambridge: Cambridge University Press, 2021).

46. Lydia Goehr, *The Imaginary Museum of Musical Works: An Essay in the Philosophy of Music* (New York: Oxford University Press, 1993), 102.

47. For a French Revolutionary-centered rereading of the "seismic" date of 1800, see Geoffroy-Schwinden, *From Servant to Savant.*

48. Henri Lefebvre, *The Production of Space,* trans. Donald Nicholson-Smith (London: Wiley Blackwell, 1992), 38.

CHAPTER I

1. *Le Ménestrel,* March 26, 1854.

2. Élisabeth Bernard, "Jules Pasdeloup et les Concerts Populaires," *Revue de musicologie* 57, no. 2 (1972): 153.

3. Bernard, "Jules Pasdeloup," 153.

4. See Nicole Vilkner, "Re-Examining Salon Space: Structuring Audiences and Music at Parisian Receptions," *Journal of the Royal Musical Association* (March 2022): 1–28.

5. *Revue et gazette musicale de Paris,* March 8, 1857. On musical festivities surrounding the Congrès de Paris, see Mark Everist, *The Empire at the Opéra: Theatre, Power and Music in Second Empire Paris* (Cambridge: Cambridge University Press, 2021), 30.

6. *Le Ménestrel,* July 8, 1854.

7. *Le Ménestrel,* May 3, 1857.

8. Mark Everist, *Genealogies of Music and Memory: Gluck in the 19th-Century Parisian Imagination* (New York: Oxford University Press, 2021), 88–89.

9. Philip G. Nord, *The Politics of Resentment: Shopkeeper Protest in Nineteenth-Century Paris* (Princeton: Princeton University Press, 1986), 100.

10. In French the word is *haussmannisation,* which was italicized in the nineteenth-century press; in English, it is either Haussmannization or haussmannisation. I have chosen the uppercase spelling throughout. Louis Althusser, "Ideology and Ideological State Apparatuses," in *Lenin and Philosophy and Other Essays,* trans. Ben Brewster (New York: Monthly Review Press, 1971), 86–87.

11. *Paris désert. Lamentations d'un Jérémie haussmannisé* (Paris: G. Towne, 1868). See Michel Carmona, *Haussmann: His Life and Times, and the Making of Modern Paris,* trans. Patrick Camiller (Chicago: Ivan R. Dee, 2002), 435.

12. W. M. Torrens, "Localism and Centrism," *The Contemporary Review* 17 (1871), 413.

13. David Turnock, *The Historical Geography of Scotland Since 1707: Geographical Aspects of Modernisation* (Cambridge: Cambridge University Press, 2005), 165.

14. Colin Jones, *Paris: Biography of a City* (New York: Penguin Books, 2006), 345.

15. Haussmann's conservative views on apartment buildings as bourgeois "shelters" from city life betray a traditionalist strain in his urbanistic thinking. See Sharon Marcus, "Haussmannization as Anti-Modernity: The Apartment House in Parisian Urban Discourse, 1850–1880," *Journal of Urban History* 27, no. 6 (September 2001): 723–45.

16. Quoted in Carmona, *Haussmann,* 13.

17. Georges-Eugène Haussmann, *Mémoires du Baron Haussmann* (Paris: Victor-Havard, 1890), 1:34.

18. Haussmann, *Mémoires,* 1:23.

19. Haussmann, *Mémoires,* 1:24.

20. Quoted in translation in Katharine Ellis, *Interpreting the Musical Past: Early Music in Nineteenth Century France* (New York: Oxford University Press, 2008), 6.

21. Ellis, *Interpreting the Musical Past,* 29.

22. Haussmann, *Mémoires,* 1:32.

23. Georges Laronze, *Le Baron Haussmann* (Paris: F. Alcan, 1932), 24.

24. Haussmann, *Mémoires,* 1:31.

25. Quoted in translation in David P. Jordan, *Transforming Paris: The Life and Labors of Baron Haussmann* (New York: Free Press, 1995), 51–52.

26. David Cairns, *Berlioz, 1803–1832: The Making of an Artist* (Berkeley: University of California Press, 1999), 219.

27. Haussmann, *Mémoires,* 1:33.

28. Georges Valence, *Haussmann le grand* (Paris: Flammarion, 2000), 49.

29. Laronze, *Le Baron Haussmann,* 24.

30. Jacques Barzun, *Berlioz and the Romantic Century* (New York: Columbia University Press, 1969), 2:228.

31. Quoted in David Cairns, *Berlioz: Servitude and Greatness, 1832–1869* (Berkeley: University of California Press, 1999), 461.

32. CG 6:2474.
33. CG 6:2473 and 2475.
34. CG 3:644. Quoted in translation in Peter Bloom, *Berlioz in Time: From Early Recognition to Lasting Renown* (Rochester: University of Rochester Press, 2022), 196.
35. Bloom, *Berlioz in Time,* 189. See also Katherine Kolb, "Primal Scenes: Smithson, Pleyel, and Liszt in the Eyes of Berlioz," *19th-Century Music* 18, no. 3 (Spring 1995): 232.
36. CG 7:2888.
37. Quoted in translation at "Berlioz in Paris," *The Hector Berlioz Website,* last updated 2011, last accessed April 14, 2023, http://www.hberlioz.com/Paris/BerliozParis.html.
38. Quoted in translation in Hector Berlioz, *New Letters of Berlioz, 1830–1868,* trans. Jacques Barzun (Westport, CT: Greenwood Press, 1974), 229.
39. Emmanuel Reibel, "Carrières entre presse et opéra au XIXe siècle: du mélange des genres au conflit d'intérêts," in *Presse et opéra aux XVIIIe et XIXe siècles,* ed. Olivier Bara, Christophe Cave and Marie-Ève Thérenty, *Médias19: Littérature et culture médiatique* (2012, online).
40. Haussmann, *Mémoires,* 1:xii.
41. Quoted in Stephen Davies et al., eds., *A Companion to Aesthetics* (Oxford, UK: Blackwell, 2009), 129.
42. Walter Benjamin, "Paris, Capital of the Nineteenth Century," in *The Arcades Project,* trans. Howard Eiland and Kevin McLaughlin (New York: Belknap Press, 2002), 11.
43. Annegret Fauser, "Debacle at the Paris Opéra: *Tannhäuser* and the French Critics, 1861," in *Richard Wagner and His World,* ed. Thomas S. Grey (Princeton: Princeton University Press, 2009), 347–48.
44. Jeremy Coleman, *Richard Wagner in Paris: Translation, Identity, Modernity* (Suffolk: Boydell & Brewer, 2019), 7.
45. Coleman, *Wagner in Paris,* 8.
46. Urban historians have long drawn connections between the Wagnerian concept of *Gesamtkunstwerk* and modernist urban planning. See Chris Dähne, Rixt Hoekstra, and Carsten Ruhl, eds., *The Death and Life of the Total Work of Art: Henry van de Velde and the Legacy of a Modern Concept* (Berlin: Jovis, 2014).
47. *Le Ménestrel,* January 3, 1869. Wagner's essay was originally published in *Gazette d'Augsbourg,* December 17, 1868.
48. *Le Ménestrel,* January 3, 1869.
49. Marvin Carlson, "The Theatre as Civic Monument," *Theatre Journal* 40, no. 1 (March 1988): 26.
50. Nicholas Vazsonyi, *Richard Wagner: Self-Promotion and the Making of a Brand* (Cambridge: Cambridge University Press, 2012), 83.
51. Vazsonyi, *Richard Wagner,* 174.
52. Thomas S. Grey, "*Eine Kapitulation:* Aristophanic Operetta as Cultural Warfare in 1870," in *Richard Wagner and His World,* ed. Thomas S. Grey (Princeton:

Princeton University Press, 2009), 96. Peter Mondelli regards Wagner and Offenbach not as opposites, but as a double-sided cultural trope that unsettled traditional French theatrical norms. See "Offenbach's Bouffonnerie, Wagner's Rêverie: The Materiality and Politics of the Ineffable in Second Empire Paris," *The Opera Quarterly* 32, nos. 2–3 (2017): 134–59.

53. Grey, "*Eine Kapitulation,*" 106.

54. Wagner's attempted lampoon of Paris on its knees severely harmed his reputation in French musical circles through the 1870s. See Laurence Senelick, *Jacques Offenbach and the Making of Modern Culture* (New York: Cambridge University Press, 2017), 70.

55. Howard Caygill, *Walter Benjamin: The Colour of Experience* (London: Routledge, 1998), 146.

56. Haussmann, *Mémoires*, 1:v–vi.

57. Christopher Prendergast, *Paris and the Nineteenth Century* (London: Wiley-Blackwell, 1995), 11.

58. Quoted in Donald J. Olsen, *The City as Work of Art: London, Paris, Vienna* (New Haven: Yale University Press, 1988), 53.

59. David Harvey, *Paris, Capital of Modernity* (New York: Routledge, 2005), 149.

CHAPTER 2

1. Burton Benedict, *The Anthropology of World's Fairs: San Francisco's Panama Pacific International Exposition of 1915* (Berkeley: University of California Press, 1983), 23.

2. Donald Reid, *Paris Sewers and Sewermen: Realities and Representations* (Cambridge, MA: Harvard University Press, 1993), 39.

3. Napoléon III was generally apathetic and unknowledgeable when it came to music, but outdoor and festive concerts nonetheless blossomed during the Second Empire. See Danièle Pistone, "La *Fête impériale:* origine et caractéristiques de ses répertoires musicaux dans le Paris de Napoléon III (1852–1870), in *La Musique et le rite sacré et profane,* ed. Marc Honegger and Paul Prévost, 1:132–37 (Strasbourg: Association des Publications près les Universités de Strasbourg, 1986).

4. Walter Benjamin, "Paris, Capital of the Nineteenth Century," in *The Arcades Project,* trans. Howard Eiland and Kevin McLaughlin (Cambridge, MA: Harvard University Press, 2002), 8.

5. Annegret Fauser, *Musical Encounters at the 1889 Paris World's Fair* (Rochester: University of Rochester Press, 2005), 5.

6. See Flora Willson, "Of Time and the City: Verdi's *Don Carlos* and Its Parisian Critics," *19th-Century Music* 37, no. 3 (2014): 188–210.

7. See Nicole Vilkner, "The Opera and the Omnibus: Material Culture, Urbanism and Boieldieu's *La Dame blanche,*" *Cambridge Opera Journal* 32, no. 1 (2020): 90–114. On representations of the omnibus in popular literature, see Masha

Belenky, *Engine of Modernity: The Omnibus and Urban Culture in Nineteenth-Century Paris* (Manchester: Manchester University Press, 2019).

8. See Sudhir Hazareesingh, *The Saint-Napoleon: Celebrations of Sovereignty in Nineteenth-Century France* (Cambridge, MA: Harvard University Press, 2004).

9. Karl Marx, "The Eighteenth Brumaire of Louis Bonaparte (1852)," trans. Saul K. Padover, https://www.marxists.org/archive/marx/works/1852/18th-brumaire.

10. Liza Picard, "The Great Exhibition," *Victorian Britain at the British Library*, October 14, 2009, https://www.bl.uk/victorian-britain/articles/the-great-exhibition.

11. Patricia Mainardi, *Art and Politics of the Second Empire: The Universal Expositions of 1855 and 1867* (New Haven: Yale University Press, 1987), 30.

12. Laborde, "Rapport sur l'application des arts à l'industrie," in *Travaux de la commission française sur l'industrie des nations*. 8 vols. (Paris: Imp. impériale, 1856), 8:234, quoted in Mainardi, *Art and Politics,* 22.

13. Jules Janin, "Les Représentants de la presse parisienne à Londres," *The Illustrated London News en Français*, May 10, 1851, quoted in Mainardi, *Art and Politics,* 26.

14. *Rapport sur l'Exposition universelle de 1855, présenté à l'Empereur par S. A. L. le Prince Napoléon* (Paris: Imprimerie impériale, 1857), 7.

15. Matthew Truesdell, *Spectacular Politics: Louis Napoléon and the Fête Impériale, 1849–1870* (New York: Oxford University Press, 1997), 102.

16. *Journal des débats* (quoting *Le Moniteur*), August 24, 1855.

17. Michel Carmona, *Haussmann: His Life and Times, and the Making of Modern Paris,* trans. Patrick Camiller (Chicago: Ivan R. Dee, 2002), 255.

18. Quoted in David P. Jordan, *Transforming Paris: The Life and Labors of Baron Haussmann* (New York: Free Press, 1995), 305.

19. See Mark Everist, *Genealogies of Music and Memory: Gluck in the Nineteenth-Century Parisian Imagination* (New York: Oxford University Press, 2021); Flora Willson, "Classic Staging: Pauline Viardot and the 1859 *Orphée* Revival," *Cambridge Opera Journal* 22, no. 3 (November 2010): 301–26.

20. Alexander Rehding, *Music and Monumentality: Commemoration and Wonderment in Nineteenth-Century Germany* (New York: Oxford University Press, 2009), 3.

21. Rehding, *Music and Monumentality,* 26.

22. Christopher Mead, "Urban Contingency and the Problem of Representation in Second Empire Paris," *Journal of the Society of Architectural Historians* (1995) 54, no. 2: 138–74.

23. After the 1855 Fair, the Palais de l'Industrie was used as a venue for many Orphéon concerts, as it was one of the few indoor venues in Paris—along with the Cirque de l'Impératrice—that could hold such large-scale musical gatherings. For a discussion of Eugène Delaporte's 1859 Orphéon concerts in light of issues of musical canon formation, see Katharine Ellis, *Interpreting the Musical Past: Early Music in Nineteenth-Century France* (New York: Oxford University Press, 2008), 65–70. See also Donna M. Di Grazia, "Concert Societies in Paris and Their Choral Repertoires, c. 1828–1880" (PhD diss., Washington University in St. Louis, 1993).

24. For an overview, see Carl Thompson, "Nineteenth-Century Travel Writing," in *The Cambridge History of Travel Writing*, ed. Nandini Das and Tim Youngs (Cambridge: Cambridge University Press, 2019), 108–24.

25. See Timothy Mitchell, "The World as Exhibition," *Comparative Studies in Society and History* 31, no. 2 (April 1989): 222.

26. Alexander C. T. Geppert, *Fleeting Cities: Imperial Expositions in Fin-de-Siècle Europe* (London: Palgrave Macmillan, 2010), 4. Antoine Picon argues that the city of Paris became a *véritable ville alternative* when it hosted the Expositions; see "Expositions universelles, doctrines sociales et utopies," in *Les expositions universelles en France au XIXe siècle*, ed. Anne-Laure Carré et al. (Paris: CNRS Éditions, 2012), 44.

27. Such details were published widely and consistently across newspapers and posters, suggesting a popular demand for logistical minutiae surrounding the Expositions universelles. See "Inauguration du Palais de l'Industrie" (Paris: Durand, 1855).

28. *L'Illustration*, May 19, 1855.

29. *Gazette municipale*, July 16, 1853.

30. "Palais de l'Industrie: Vue prise à vol d'oiseau du côté de la grand avenue des Champs-Elysées" (Paris: H. Plon, 1855).

31. Mainardi, *Art and Politics*, 67.

32. Truesdell, *Spectacular Politics*, 102.

33. CG 5:2035.

34. On the arrangements leading up to Berlioz's "monster" concerts in 1844, see David Cairns, *Berlioz, 1832–1869: Servitude and Greatness* (Berkeley: University of California Press, 1999), 299–302. See also David Charlton, ed., *Choral Works with Orchestra II*, vol. 12b of *Hector Berlioz: New Edition of the Complete Works* (Kasel: Bärenreiter, 1993), 219.

35. Lafon wrote another paean to Napoléon III, "Salut impériale," which was set to music by Antoine Elwart in 1856. Charlton, *Choral Works*, xiv. See also "L'Impériale," in *Dictionnaire Berlioz*, ed. Pierre Citron, Cécile Reynaud, Jean-Pierre Bartoli, and Peter Bloom (Paris: Fayard, 2003), 275–76.

36. Hugh Macdonald, *Berlioz* (London: Dent, 1982), 154.

37. CG 4:1773.

38. The work at this stage was renamed *Le Dix décembre*, in honor of Louis-Napoléon's 1848 election as president of the Second French Republic. However, in the letter to the Ministre d'état he continues to call his composition *L'Impériale*. See Charlton, *Choral Works*, xiv, and CG 4: 1866.

39. CG 4:1866.

40. CG 4:1865.

41. Julian Rushton, *The Music of Berlioz* (New York: Oxford University Press, 2001), 214.

42. See Hector Berlioz, "Étude critique des symphonies de Beethoven," in *A travers chants* (Paris: Michel Levy frères, 1862), 50.

43. Rushton, *The Music of Berlioz*, 219. As is well established, Berlioz lifted this opening bass melody from his own 1830 Prix de Rome cantata *Sardanapale*.

Moreover, as Peter Bloom has noted, this festive and militaristic theme may have also served as for the air "Le roi des rois" (The king of kings) in a missing section of the 1830 cantata. See Peter Bloom, "Berlioz and the *Prix de Rome* of 1830," *Journal of the American Musicological Society* 34, no. 2 (Summer 1981): 279–304.

44. Macdonald, *Berlioz,* 154.

45. Hector Berlioz, *The Memoirs of Hector Berlioz,* trans. David Cairns (New York: Everyman's Library, 2002), 483.

46. Detailed information, such as the exact timing and order of the imperial procession, was either copied or lightly paraphrased from source to source. For instance, on November 18, 1855, *La France musicale* listed the program that followed Berlioz's cantata: a chorus of Handel's *Judas Maccabaeus,* the finale of Beethoven's "symphonie triomphale" for chorus and orchestra (presumably the Ninth), scenes from Meyerbeer's *Les Huguenots* and Rossini's *Moïse,* and Mozart's *Ave verum corpus.* However, the wording of the report is conspicuously similar to that of the state newspaper, *Le Moniteur universelle;* it did not mention the interruption nor did it offer any commentary on the musical program.

47. Charles Brainne, "Exposition universelle de 1855," *La Presse,* November 16, 1855.

48. *Journal des débats politiques et littéraires,* November 16, 1855.

49. This account reappears word for word in several published sources.

50. CG 4:188.

51. On the acoustic symbolism of the Saint-Eustache, see Jennifer Walker, *Sacred Sounds, Secular Spaces: Transforming Catholicism Through the Music of Third-Republic Paris* (New York: Oxford University Press, 2021), esp. 133–92.

52. Berlioz, *Memoirs,* 483.

53. *Revue et gazette musicale de Paris,* November 18, 1855.

54. See Inge Van Rij, *The Other Worlds of Hector Berlioz* (Cambridge: Cambridge University Press, 2015), 202.

55. Umberto Eco, "A Theory of Expositions," in *Travels in Hyperreality* (New York: Harvest Books, 1986), 299.

56. *Journal des débats politiques et littéraires,* December 27, 1855.

57. See Oscar Comettant, *La Musique, les musiciens et les instruments de musique chez les différents peuples du monde* (Paris, Michel Lévy, frères, 1869), 21.

58. "Commission impériale," February 24, 1867. Quoted in Comettant, *La Musique,* 23.

59. Comettant, *La Musique,* 28–29.

60. Romain Cornut *fils, Cantate de l'Exposition: Les noces de Prométhée* (Paris: Hachette, 1867), 6.

61. Cornut, *Cantate,* 6.

62. "Le feu, qui fait les Arts et qui fait l'Industrie,/ Qui produit le Génie et qui produit l'Amour,/ Et qui, régénérant notre race flétrie,/ Des mortels étonnés fait des dieux à leur tour."

63. "L'heure de la délivrance,/ Cher amant, vient de sonner./ Sous le beau ciel de la France,/ Vois notre hymen s'ordonner;/ Vois ce palais qui se dresse,/ Et cette

immense richesse /Que mon amour vient t'offrir;/ Vois, dans leur pompe royale,/ Pour la fête nuptiale/ Tous les peuples accourir."

64. Comettant, *La Musique*, 39.

65. Over eight hundred submissions to both the *Hymne* and *Cantate* competitions are housed in four containers at AN, series F/18.

66. Many scores have misplaced or missing identity cards, so it is impossible to identify every entry. Furthermore, several whole entries, such as that of Ernest Guiraud (1837–92), are known to be missing.

67. "Concours de l'hymne. 823 injections de premier ordre. Jury absent. 3 membres ont examiné, ont déclaré que c'était toujours le même. Impossible de décerner le prix. Concours annulé!" Edmond Galabert, *Georges Bizet: Souvenirs et correspondance* (Paris: Michel Lévy, 1877), 115.

68. *Revue des deux mondes,* July 1, 1867.

69. Galabert, *Georges Bizet*, 117–19.

70. Franz Liszt, who wrote to Saint-Saëns following the competition to congratulate him, later performed *Les Noces de Prométhée* during the Tonkünstler-Versammlung festival, held in Weimar between May 26 and 28, 1870. See *Lettres de compositeurs à Camille Saint-Saëns,* ed. Yves Gérard and Eurydice Jousse (Lyon: Symétrie, 2009), 389 and 394.

71. *La Semaine musicale,* September 5, 1867.

72. *Le Ménestrel,* September 8, 1867.

73. Brian Rees, *Camille Saint-Saëns: A Life* (London: Faber and Faber, 2009), 136.

74. Paul Bertagnolli notes that this opening was celebrated both for its ingenious orchestration as well as for its evocation of Greek modality (*Prometheus in Music: Representations of the Myth in the Romantic Era* [Aldershot: Ashgate, 2007], 211). I would disagree, however, that this passage "articulated the Exhibition's agenda" (211) as its subdued character was ultimately deemed inadequate for the performance at the closing ceremony.

75. "Superbes portiques,/ Vos splendeurs magiques/ Enchantent mes yeux;/ Tout n'est que surprise/ Charme, convoitise,/ Pour mes sens joyeux."

76. *Le Ménestrel,* September 8, 1867.

77. *Le Ménestrel,* September 8, 1867.

78. Pacini had previously supplied texts for some of Rossini's *Péchés de vieillesse*. See Joël-Marie Fauquet, ed., *Dictionnaire de la musique en France au XIXe siècle* (Paris: Fayard, 2003), 927.

79. "Sainte Patrie,/ Arts, industrie,/ À ton génie/ Tout rend honneur./ Vive l'Empereur!"

80. For a closer analysis of the *Hymne*'s formal structure, see Martina Grempler, "Rossinis 'politisches Spätwerk': Die *Hymne à Napoléon III* und *La corona d'Italia*," in *Rossini in Paris,* ed. Bernd-Rüdiger Kern and Reto Müller (Leipzig: Leipziger Universitätsverlag, 2002), 181–200.

81. Comettant, *La Musique*, 133.

82. Comettant, *La Musique*, 135.

83. Richard Osborne, *Rossini: His Life and Works* (New York: Oxford University Press, 2007), 163.

84. *Journal des débats politiques et littéraires,* July 2, 1867.

85. *Le Monde illustré,* July 6, 1867, my emphasis.

86. As was the case in 1855, daily newspapers published uncannily similar detailed accounts of the imperial procession, reporting the arrival of key dignitaries down to the minute. The July 3, 1867 issue of *Le Temps* even refers to a "compte-rendu officiel" that detailed events in a manner that was approved by the state.

87. *Le Ménestrel,* July 7, 1867.

88. *La Presse,* July 2, 1867.

89. *Le Figaro,* July 2, 1867.

90. Jann Pasler, *Composing the Citizen: Music as Public Utility in Third Republic France* (Berkeley: University of California Press, 2009), 649. On the collaborations between fin-de-siècle Greek and French scholars whose work bridged antiquity with modernist aesthetics, see Samuel Dorf, *Performing Antiquity: Ancient Greek Music and Dance from Paris to Delphi, 1890–1930* (New York: Oxford University Press, 2018).

91. *Le Constitutionnel,* July 2, 1867.

92. *Le Constitutionnel,* July 2, 1867.

93. *Le Figaro,* July 3, 1867.

94. Benedict, *The Anthropology of World's Fairs,* 5.

95. Benjamin, "Paris, Capital of the Nineteenth Century," 8.

CHAPTER 3

1. Corinne Schneider, "Du Boulevard du Temple à la place du Châtelet, le Théâtre-Lyrique comme 'laboratoire de la musique,'" in *Les Spectacles sous le Second Empire,* ed. Jean-Claude Yon (Paris: Armand Colin, 2010), 214.

2. As quoted in Kelley Conway, *Chanteuse in the City: The Realist Singer in French Film* (Berkeley: University of California Press, 2004), 32–33.

3. AN F/21/1043–1044.

4. Anonymous petition filed in conjunction with urban development around the 1855 Exposition universelle, AN F/21/1157, quoted in translation from Jacques Rancière, "Good Times or Pleasure at the Barriers," in *Voices of the People: The Social Life of 'La Sociale' at the End of the Second Empire,* ed. Adrian Rifkin and Roger Thomas (London: Routledge, 1988), 77; Rancière's italics.

5. Armande Audiganne, *Paris et sa splendeur* (Paris: Henri Charpentier, 1861), 2:25.

6. On the connections of French *opérette* to theatrical canonicity, see Mark Everist, "Jacques Offenbach: The Music of the Past and the Image of the Present," in *Music, Theatre, and Cultural Transfer,* ed. Annegret Fauser and Mark Everist (Chicago: University of Chicago Press, 2009), 72–98.

7. Olivier Bara, "Le Café-concert dans la grande presse, ou la crise du feuilleton dramatique," in *Presse, chanson et culture orale au XIXe siècle* (Paris: Nouveau monde éditions, 2012), 2.

8. "L'Eldorado, café-concert-spectacle," *Nouvelles annales de la construction* 6 (May 1860), 75.

9. Martin Pénet, "Le Café-concert, un nouveau divertissement populaire," in Yon, *Les Spectacles sous le Second Empire*, 356.

10. Audiganne, *Paris dans sa splendeur*, 2:25.

11. *Gazette des tribunaux*, August 27–28, 1860.

12. Richard Sennett, *Building and Dwelling: Ethics for the City* (New York: Farrar, Strauss and Giroux, 2018), 33.

13. E. A.-D., *Les Cafés-concerts en 1866* (Paris: Ch. Égrot, 1866), 139.

14. Patrick O'Connor's brief *Oxford Music Online* entry on the "Café-concert" cites no English sources—or any source after 1992. One reason for this dearth of scholarship is the inordinate emphasis placed on operetta, in particular the operettas of Jacques Offenbach. See Mark Everist, "'Der mächtigste Tanzmeister des Kaiserreiches'? Offenbach at 200," *Journal of the Royal Musical Association* 145, no. 2 (2020): 493.

15. William Weber, *Music and the Middle Class: The Social Structure of Concert Life in London, Paris, and Vienna*, 2nd ed. (Aldershot: Ashgate, 2004), 11.

16. "A *café concert* ... joined the food and beverage service of a café with musical entertainment, usually songs on sentimental, comic, or political topics" (J. Peter Burkholder, Donald J. Grout, and Claude V. Palisca, eds., *A History of Western Music*, 10th ed. [New York: W. W. Norton, 2019], 698). Since political topics were rare in Second Empire cafés-concerts, it is apparent that the authors refer to the establishments of the Third Republic.

17. Jacques Attali, *Noise: A Political Economy of Music*, trans. Brian Massumi (Minneapolis: University of Minnesota Press, 1985), 72.

18. Attali, *Noise*, 76.

19. See Jann Pasler, *Composing the Citizen: Music as Public Utility in Third Republic France* (Berkeley: University of California Press, 2009), 477–78.

20. Hippolyte Hostein, *La Liberté des théâtres* (Paris: Librairie des Auteurs, 1867), 159.

21. Attali, *Noise*, 95.

22. See Derek B. Scott, *Sounds of the Metropolis: The Nineteenth-Century Popular Music Revolution in London, New York, Paris and Vienna* (New York: Oxford University Press, 2008), esp. 49–50.

23. Cited in Conway, *Chanteuse and the City*, 37.

24. Edmond and Jules de Goncourt, *Idées et sensations* (Paris: G. Charpentier, 1877), 68. Quoted in translation in T. J. Clark, *The Painting of Modern Life: Paris in the Art of Manet and His Followers* (Princeton: Princeton University Press, 1984), 34.

25. *Le Siècle*, April 7, 1867.

26. *Le Figaro*, February 1, 1867.

27. *Le Figaro*, February 2, 1867.

28. *Le Figaro*, February 27, 1867.

29. *Le Figaro*, February, 26, 1867.

30. Alicia C. Levin, "A Documentary Overview of Musical Theaters in Paris, 1830–1900," in *Music, Theatre, and Cultural Transfer: Paris, 1830–1914*, ed. Mark Everist and Annegret Fauser (Chicago: University of Chicago Press, 2009), 379.

31. See Katharine Ellis, "Unintended Consequences: Theatre Deregulation and Opera in France, 1864–1878," *Cambridge Opera Journal* 22, no. 3 (November 2010): 327–52.

32. Hostein, *La Liberté des théâtres*, 160.

33. *Le Foyer*, April 6, 1867.

34. Short, well-written English accounts appear in *Grove Music Online* as well as Steven Moore Whiting, *Satie the Bohemian: From Cabaret to Concert Hall* (New York: Oxford University Press, 1999), 11–16, and Conway, *Chanteuse and the City*, 29–31.

35. See Guy Debord, *The Society of the Spectacle*, trans. Ken Knabb (London: Rebel Press, 2005).

36. Eva Kimminich, "Chansons étouffées: Recherche sur les cafés concerts au XIXe siècle," *Politix. Revue des sciences sociales du politique* 14 (1991): 24.

37. Quoted in translation in David Cairns, *Berlioz: Servitude and Greatness, 1832–1869* (Berkeley: University of California Press, 1999), 438.

38. Cairns, *Berlioz: Servitude and Greatness*, 437–38.

39. François Caradec and Alain Weill, *Le Café-concert: 1848–1914* (Paris: Hachette, 2007), 11–12.

40. My thinking here is inspired by Raymond Williams, who contrasted urban and pastoral literary representations to highlight the interdependency of symbolic urban spaces and the "knowable communities" that dwelled in and represented those spaces. See *The Country and the City* (Oxford: Oxford University Press, 1975), 1–9.

41. *Leamington Advertiser*, June 9, 1864.

42. Ross Chambers, *An Atmospherics of the City: Baudelaire and the Poetics of Noise* (New York: Fordham University Press, 2015), 1–2.

43. Baudelaire does mention Paris's *casinos* in his essay on *Tannhäuser*. "There," Baudelaire writes, "the volcanic splendor of [Wagner's] music fell upon the air like thunder in a bawdy-house." See Charles Baudelaire, "Richard Wagner and *Tannhäuser* in Paris," in *The Painter of Modern Life and Other Essays*, trans. Jonathan Mayne (London: Phaidon, 1995), 118. *Casinos* were distinct from cafés-concerts; they were not yet the gambling havens we think of today, but focused more on large-scale ensemble spectacle (orchestral music, dancing) than did cafés-concerts, which focused more on solo and duet entertainment.

44. Charles Baudelaire, "The Eyes of the Poor," in *Paris Spleen: Little Poems in Prose by Charles Baudelaire*, trans. Keith Waldrop (Middletown: Wesleyan University Press, 2009), 51.

45. Aimée Boutin, *City of Noise: Sound and Nineteenth-Century Paris* (Urbana-Champaign: University of Illinois Press, 2015), 100.

46. David Harvey, *Paris, Capital of Modernity* (New York: Routledge, 2005), 221.

47. Chambers, *An Atmospherics*, 9.
48. John Anthony William Galignani, *Galignani's New Paris Guide: For 1862* (Paris: A. and W. Galignani, 1862), 473.
49. Louis Veuillot, *Les Odeurs de Paris* (Paris: J. M. Dent et fils, 1867), 142.
50. Quoted in *L'Eldorado et la question des cafés-concerts* (Paris, L. Hugonis, 1875), 17.
51. André Chadourne, *Les Cafés-concerts* (Paris: E. Dentu, 1889), 2.
52. Chadourne, *Les Cafés-concerts*, 15.
53. Chadourne, *Les Cafés-concerts*, 273–74.
54. See Andrew Israel Ross, *Public City/Public Sex: Homosexuality, Prostitution, and Urban Culture in Nineteenth-Century Paris* (Philadelphia: Temple University Press, 2019), 119.
55. Quoted in Benjamin, *The Arcades Project*, 570.
56. On the aesthetics of gas lighting at the Opéra, see Gabriela Cruz, *Grand Illusion: Phantasmagoria in Nineteenth-Century Opera* (New York: Oxford University Press, 2020), esp. 43–64.
57. Catherine Authier, "La Naissance de la star féminine sous le Second Empire," in Yon, *Les Spectacles sous le Second Empire*, 273–74.
58. See Carol Gouspy, "La Représentation des chanteuses au café-concert: les genres de la romancière comique et de la diseuse," *Volume! La revue des musiques populaires* 2, no. 2 (2003): 27–39.
59. Kimberly White has discussed Thérésa's *Mémoires* in the context of ghostwritten testimonies by popular musicians, arguing the literary genre of *récit de vie de vedette* complemented the commodification of singers' personas. See "Autobiographical Voices: Performing Absence in Singers' Memoirs," *Cambridge Opera Journal* 30, nos. 2–3 (November 2018): 165–85.
60. *Le Figaro*, December 28, 1879.
61. E. A.-D., *Les Cafés-concerts en 1866*, 66.
62. *Le Journal amusant*, March 4, 1865.
63. Naturally, the publication made no mention that the text was not authored solely by Thérésa, as such authorial claims did not play a meaningful role in the memoir genre. Yet I have no doubt that Thérésa shed her own wisdom on various topics, such as behind-the-scenes behaviors of patrons and singers and the material conditions of working-class musicians.
64. *Le Petit journal*, February 18, 1865.
65. *Le Petit journal*, February 18, 1865.
66. Thérésa, *Mémoires de Thérésa, écrits par elle-même* (Paris: E. Dentu, 1865), 43–44.
67. Thérésa, *Mémoires*, 105.
68. Thérésa, *Mémoires*, 176.
69. Thérésa, *Mémoires*, 91.
70. See Louis Chevalier, *Classes laborieuses et classes dangereuses* (Paris: Hachette, 1984), 409–10. See also Esther da Costa Meyer, *Dividing Paris: Urban Renewal and Social Inequality, 1852–1870* (Princeton: Princeton University Press, 2022), 103–104.

71. George Sand, "La Rêverie à Paris," in *Paris-guide* 2: 1196–97, quoted in translation in Costa Meyer, *Dividing Paris*, 103.

72. "Les cafés-concerts gérée par les femmes laissent à désirer sous la rapport de la bonne tenue et de la bonne administration." Letter from the Ministre de la Maison de l'Empereur to the Préfet de Police, December 18, 1866, AN F/21/1044.

73. It is worth remembering that the many public urinals that Haussmann had installed throughout the city—from the workhorse *pissoirs* to the fancier *colonnes*—were for the exclusive use of men. It was not until the 1890s that the Société des Colonnes Doriot designed a *chalet d'aisance*, or public restroom for women. See Costa Meyer, *Dividing Paris*, 129.

74. Patrice Higonnet, *Paris, Capital of the World*, trans. Arthur Goldhammer (Cambridge, MA: Harvard University Press, 2002), 1.

75. *L'Univers musicale,* January 21, 1864.

76. *L'Univers musicale,* January 21, 1864.

77. *Le Café-concert,* March 24, 1867.

78. Roger Price, *A Concise History of France*, 2nd ed. (Cambridge: Cambridge University Press, 2005), 183.

79. See Lydia Goehr, *The Imaginary Museum of Musical Works: An Essay in the Philosophy of Music* (New York: Oxford University Press, 1993).

80. Jane Fulcher, "The Popular Chanson of the Second Empire: 'Music of the Peasants' in France," *Acta Musicologica* 52, no. 1 (January 1980): 27–37.

81. See Scott, *Sounds of the Metropolis,* 34–37.

82. *Le Café-concert,* June 2, 1867.

83. Pénet, "Le Café-concert, un nouveau divertissement populaire," 364.

84. Henri Lefebvre, *The Survival of Capitalism: Reproduction of the Relations of Production,* trans. F. Bryant (London: Allison and Busby, 1976), 35.

CHAPTER 4

1. Charles Nisard, *Des Chansons populaires chez les anciens et chez les Français: Essai historique suivi d'une étude sur la chanson des rues contemporaine,* 2 vols. (Paris: E. Dentu, 1867), 2:1–2.

2. Esther da Costa Meyer, *Dividing Paris: Urban Renewal and Social Inequality, 1852–1870* (Princeton: Princeton University Press, 2022), 131.

3. Quoted in Costa Meyer, *Dividing Paris*, 131.

4. Michel de Certeau, *Heterologies: Discourse on the Other,* trans. Brian Massumi (Minneapolis: University of Minnesota Press, 1986), 121.

5. See Pierre Capelle, ed., *La Clé du caveau: À l'usage de tous les chansonniers français, des amateurs auteurs, acteurs du Vaudeville, et de tous les amis de la Chanson* (Paris: Capelle et Renard, 1811). For a book-length history of the *caveau* singing societies and their relation to contemporary currents in poetry and philosophy, see Brigitte Level, *À Travers deux siècles: Le Caveau, société bachique et chantante, 1726–1939* (Paris: Presses de l'Université de Paris-Sorbonne, 1988).

6. Nisard, *Des Chansons,* 2:2.

7. Romain Benini, "La Chanson, voix publique (Paris, 1816–1881)," *Romantisme* 171, no. 1 (2016) : 40–52.

8. Laura Mason, *Singing the French Revolution: Popular Culture and Politics, 1787–1799* (Ithaca: Cornell University Press, 1996), 3.

9. See James H. Johnson, *Listening in Paris: A Cultural History* (Berkeley: University of California Press, 1995), esp. 35–53.

10. Jacques Rancière, "Good Times or Pleasure at the Barriers," in *Voices of the People: The Social Life of "La Sociale" at the End of the Second Empire,* ed. Adrian Rifkin and Roger Thomas (New York: Routledge, 1988), 50–51.

11. "La Belle polonaise," words by Paul Avenel, music by Marc Chautagne, 1863.

12. Timothée Trimm, "Hé! Lambert!..." in *Le Petit journal,* August 18, 1864.

13. The café-concert was later renamed Éden Comédie, then Nouveau Théâtre du Château d'Eau, before it ultimately closed in 1923.

14. "Vous n'auriez pas vu Lambert/ la gar' du chemin de fer?/ Vous n'auriez pas vu … / Lambert? (5 *fois*)/ S'est-il noyé dans la mer,/ S'est-il perdu dans l'désert?/ Qu'est-c' qu'a vu Lambert?/ Lambert? (4 *fois*)," quoted in Nisard, *Des Chansons,* 2:286–88.

15. "Scie," in *Dictionnaire de la langue française,* ed. Émile Littré (Paris: Hachette, 1863–1872).

16. Trimm, "Hé! Lambert!..."

17. Derek B. Scott, *Sounds of the Metropolis: The Nineteenth–Century Popular Music Revolution in London, New York, Paris and Vienna* (New York: Oxford University Press, 2008), 50.

18. Jean de Tinan, "Cirques, cabarets, concerts," *Mercure de France* (September, 1898), 838, quoted in Steven Moore Whiting, *Satie the Bohemian: From Cabaret to Concert Hall* (New York: Oxford University Press, 1999), 16.

19. See *Almanach chantant: Choix des plus jolies chansons françaises* (Paris: Delarue, 1866), 12–13.

20. "(*Parlé*) Ah ben! Il peut s'vanter d'avoir des connaissances, Lambert. J'l'ai entendu appeler de la Bastille au Champs de Mars, dans toutes les rues, dans tous les coins; il s'était caché, bien sûr.... En achetant le *P'tit journal,* j'dis à la marchande: As-tu vu Lambert ?—En v'a un s'rin, qu'elle me répond.... Décidément on n' s'amuse qu'à Paris."

21. "Our Paris Correspondence," *The New York Times,* September 3, 1864.

22. Guy Debord, "Theory of the *Dérive*" (1956), trans. Ken Knabb, in *Situationist International Anthology,* ed. Ken Knabb (Berkeley: Bureau of Public Secrets, 1981), 62.

23. Some of these names originate from popular chansons. "Poule" was adapted from a song with the opening words "Le pantalon/De Madelon/N'a pas de fond," and "Pastourelle" emerged from a ballad by the cornet player Collinet. See Andrew Lamb, "Quadrille," in *Oxford Music Online.*

24. Edmond and Jules de Goncourt, *Journal: Mémoires de la vie littéraire* (Monaco: Fasquelle and Flammarion, 1956), 6:233. English translation in Scott, *Sounds of the Metropolis,* 49.

25. H. Gourdon de Genouillac, *Les Refrains de la rue* (Paris: E. Dentu, 1879), 101.
26. Nisard, *Des Chansons,* 2:286.
27. "Concerning Lambert," in *Temple Bar: A London Magazine for Town and Country Readers* 12 (November 1864), 417.
28. "Concerning Lambert," 420.
29. "Ohé Lambert," *London Review of Politics, Society, Literature, Art & Science,* August 27, 1864.
30. The journalist is most likely referring to the first King of the Franks, Hugues Capet, who succeeded the last Carolingian King, Louis V.
31. "Ohé Lambert."
32. Helen Abbott, *Baudelaire in Song, 1880–1930* (New York: Oxford University Press, 2017), 178.
33. Genouillac, *Les Refrains,* 8.
34. "Orgue de barbarie," in Marc Vignal, ed., *Larousse de la musique* (Paris: Librairie Larousse, 1982), 2:1165.
35. *Paris-Gagne-Petit, par les auteurs des mémoires de Bilboquet* (Paris: E. Taride, 1854), 40.
36. *La Lanterne,* February 8, 1870.
37. Charles Baudelaire, "The Painter of Modern Life," in *The Painter of Modern Life and Other Essays,* trans. Jonathan Mayne (London: Phaidon, 1995), 11.
38. Charles Yriarte, *Paris grotesque: Les célébrités de la rue* (Paris: Librairie parisienne, 1864), 4–5.
39. François Caradec and Alain Weill, *Le Café-concert* (Paris: Hachette, 2007), 18.
40. In the 1864 volume, Baumester published one of his most celebrated chansons: a parody of the aforementioned "Lambert!" cry, titled "Il est retrouvé Lambert!" (They found Lambert!).
41. *L'Orchestre: Revue quotidienne des théâtres,* October 16, 1869.
42. "En dépit des jaloux, des sots et des méchants,/ Le peuple avec plaisir, écoute encore mes chants."
43. On Béranger's reputation as musician and social critic, see Ralph P. Locke, "The Political Chansons of Béranger: Artistry for Progressive Social Change," in *Musik/Revolution: Festschrift für Georg Knepler zum 90. Geburtstag,* ed. H.-W. Heister (Hamburg: Von Bockel, 1997), 115–32.
44. As Jann Pasler has argued, the Third Republic sought to deploy musical activity as a *utilité publique* to revitalize the country and promote a unified public policy. This practice, as well as the concept of *utilité publique,* was also present during the Second Empire. See *Composing the Citizen: Music as Public Utility in Third Republic France* (Berkeley: University of California Press, 2009), esp. 53–93.
45. "Ordonnance concernant les joueurs d'orgues dans les rues et places publiques," APP, Box DB 201.
46. APP, Box DB 201.
47. Hélène Landron, "Les Musiciens de rue sous l'autorité de la police parisienne," in *Musiciens des rues de Paris,* ed. Michel Colardelle and Florence Gétreau (Paris: Réunion des Musées Nationaux, 1998), 75.

48. Landron, "Les Musiciens de rue," 78.

49. "Ordonnance concernant les saltimbanques, joueurs d'orgue, musiciens ambulants et chanteurs," APP, Box DB 201.

50. The number was necessarily considerably smaller before the 1860 expansion of Paris from twelve arrondissements to twenty.

51. Antoine Granveau, *L'Ouvrier devant la société* (Paris: Hélaine, 1868), 62, quoted in Costa Meyer, *Dividing Paris,* 282–83.

52. See Jacek Blaszkiewicz, "Chez Paul Niquet: Sound, Spatiality, and Sociability in the Paris Cabaret," *19th-Century Music* 44, no. 2 (Fall 2021): 147–66.

53. Haussmann, *Mémoires* 2:177, quoted in Costa Meyer, *Dividing Paris,* 298.

54. This municipal document is still used today in cities in France, Belgium, and Switzerland. Used primarily for job applications, it is a cross between a reference letter and a background check. See, for instance, "Certificat de bonne vie et mœurs, Ville de Nice," https://www.nice.fr/fr/formalites-administratives/certificat-de-bonne-vie-et-moeurs.

55. See, for instance, *Le Carnaval partout,* a vaudeville in four acts by Clairville and Bernard Lopez, which premiered at the Théâtre des Variétés on February 8, 1854.

56. Jeremy Coleman has noted Wagner's ambivalence toward Parisian carnival season, suggesting that Wagner's musical contribution was musical mercenary work. Nevertheless, traces of *Courtille,* such as its buoyant, percussive orchestration, can be detected in his *Liebesverbot,* which Wagner was composing at the time. See *Richard Wagner in Paris: Translation, Identity, Modernity* (Suffolk: Boydell & Brewer, 2019), 34–35.

57. See Alfred Delvau, *Les Cythères parisiennes: Histoires anecdotiques des bals de Paris* (Paris: E. Dentu, 1864), 273.

58. "Vraiment ne point fêter/ Les chœurs de Belleville,/ Serait se comporter/ De façon peu civile./ De la grande cité/ Redoutant l'atmosphère,/ La cordialité/ S'exile à la barrière."

59. Émile de Labedollière, *Le Nouveau Paris: Histoire de ses 20 arrondissements* (Paris: Gustave Barba, 1860), 304.

60. See Donna M. Di Grazia, "Concert Societies in Paris and Their Choral Repertoires, c. 1828–1880" (PhD diss., Washington University in St. Louis, 1993), 93–163.

61. "De ce joyeux dîner/Nous garderons mémoire;/ Mais pour le couronner,/ Empressons-nous de boire;/ Car l'octroi de Paris,/ Étendant sa carrière,/ Compte augmenter le prix/ Des vins de barrière."

62. To Colardelle and Gétreau, songs were in a unique position among cultural artifacts to articulate collective sentiments, opinions, and grievances of citizens. See their preface to Michel Colardelle and Florence Gétreau, eds., *Musiciens des rues de Paris* (Paris: Réunion des Musées Nationaux, 1998).

63. "Adieu, Paris, ville adorée,/ Où mon pauvre cœur fut heureux./ Je vais de ma triste contrée/ Fouler encore le sol poudreux./ Je te quitte, adieu, mon idole,/ Tu vois, mes yeux sont attendris./ Avec toi ma gaité s'envole,/ Et mon bonheur reste à Paris. (*bis*)" (Baumester, *La Chanson des rues,* 10).

64. Antoine Elwart, *Œuvres musicales choisies* (Paris: G. Brandus et Dufour, 1867). Elwart without a doubt published the collection, which includes the cantata "Le pouvoir de l'Harmonie," to coincide with the 1867 Exposition universelle and the intense Parisian and imperial chauvinism that came with the event.

65. "[Paris] ce séjour enchanté/ Où l'âme libre et fière/ Peut, cachant sa misère/ Garder sa liberté."

66. "Le génie, à Paris,/ Reçoit le saint baptême;/ Et son pouvoir suprême/ Rayonne en tous pays!"

67. See Clair Rowden, *Opera and Parody in Paris, 1860–1900* (Turnhout: Brepols, 2020).

68. "La Vie de Paris" was published—with text only—in *La gaudriole de 1860: Chansons et chansonnettes nouvelles* (Paris: Bernardin-Béchet, 1861).

69. "Cité splendide et fière,/ Toujours hospitalière,/ S'il est sur cette terre,/ S'il est un paradis,/ C'est toi, ville bruyante,/ Où la jeunesse ardente/ Travaille, espère et chante... / Oui, c'est toi!... C'est Paris!/ Vive la folie!/ Et que le plaisir/ Laisse à notre vie (*bis.*)/Un gai souvenir. (*bis.*)"

70. "Mais j'entends, à la Ville,/ Sonner l'heure... Ah! Matin./ Pour l'ouvrier agile,/ C'est déjà le matin; Le Marteau, la tenaille/ Commencent à marcher./ On se lève, on travaille... / Vite, allons-nous coucher!/ Oui, voilà, mes amis, voilà, Paris la nuit, etc."

71. Henri Lefebvre, *Rhythmanalysis: Space, Time and Everyday Life*, trans. Stuart Elden and Gerald Moore (London: Continuum, 2004), xii.

72. "Même logis, souvent à la même heure,/ A des sanglots mêlés de joyeux cris./ Vive Paris, où l'on rit ou l'on pleure;/ Quel paradis! quel enfer que Paris!"

73. Gregory Shaya, "The Flâneur, the Badaud, and the Making of a Mass Public in France, circa 1860–1910," *American Historical Review* 109, no. 1 (February 2004): 41–77.

74. Shaya, "The Flâneur," 47. On the notion of "aural flânerie," see Aimée Boutin, *City of Noise: Sound and Nineteenth-Century Paris* (Urbana-Champaign: University of Illinois Press, 2015), esp. 11–34.

75. *La Chanson illustré*, January 1, 1870.

76. Leo Charney and Vanessa R. Schwartz, "Introduction," in *Cinema and the Invention of Modern Life*, ed. Leo Charney and Vanessa R. Schwartz (Berkeley: University of California Press, 1995), 5.

77. See "Ménétrier, Casimir," in *Dictionnaire des girouettes, ou nos contemporains peintent d'après eux-mêmes* (Paris: Alexis Eymery, 1815), 328–31. See also "Ménétrier (Casimir)," in *Dictionnaire des protées modernes, ou Biographie des personnages vivants qui ont figuré dans la Revolution Française, depuis le 14 juillet 1789, jusques et compris 1815, par leurs actions, leur conduit ou leurs écrits* (Paris: Davi et Locard, 1815), 186–87.

78. Casimir Ménétrier, "Le Flâneur," in *Chants et chansons populaires de la France* (Paris: Henri Plon, 1859), 285–87.

79. The idea of Paris as a palimpsest has a long literary history. Championed by Benjamin in his *Arcades Project*, the metaphor relies on the notion that the urbanizing

city mixes old and new edifices, just like a chalkboard often bleeds together new and erased text. For a recent reexamination of the palimpsest as a trope in nineteenth-century Parisian literature, see Amy Wiğelsworth, *Rewriting "Les Mystères de Paris:" The "Mystères Urbains" and the Palimpsest* (London: Routledge, 2016), especially 41–55.

80. See Rebecca Dowd Geoffroy-Schwinden, "Music as Feminine Capital in Napoleonic France: Nancy Macdonald's Musical Upbringing," *Music & Letters* 100, no. 2 (May 2019): 302–34.

81. See Annegret Fauser, "*La Guerre en dentelles:* Women and the *Prix de Rome* in French Cultural Politics," *Journal of the American Musicological Society* 51, no. 1 (Spring 1998): 83–129.

82. See Jerrold Seigel, *Bohemian Paris: Culture, Politics, and the Boundaries of Bourgeois Life, 1830–1930* (Baltimore: Johns Hopkins University Press, 1986), 40–43.

83. "La nuit qui vient m'appelle à l'autre rive;/ Vite, fuyons le travail et l'ennui;/ Gagnons le seuil où chaque soir j'arrive/ Pour m'enivrer de Plaisir et de bruit./ Ah! Quoique belle, jadis je fus sage!/ Mais maintenant, du soir jusqu'au matin,/ Moi, je m'en vais, fol oiseau de passage,/ Boire du punch dans le quartier latin!"

84. Hugh Macdonald, "Delibes, Léo," in *Oxford Music Online*.

85. Frits Noske, *French Song from Berlioz to Duparc* (New York: Dover Publications, 1988), 204.

86. Macdonald, "Delibes, Léo."

87. See Ellen Lockhart, *Animation, Plasticity, and Music in Italy, 1770–1830* (Berkeley: University of California Press, 2017), 9–10.

88. See Philippe Darriulat, *La Muse du peuple: Chansons politiques et sociales en France, 1815–1871* (Rennes: Presses Universitaires de Rennes, 2010), 1–21.

89. "Des gants couleur de paille,/ Un pantalon collant,/ Un habit dont la taille/ Gênerait un enfant;/ Puis, de bottes qui brillent/ D'un vernis éclatant;/ C'est ainsi que s'habillent/ Nos lions d'à présent." English translation by David Tunley, in *Romantic French Songs 1830–1870* (New York: Routledge, 2013), xlvii–xlviii.

90. "[Un *Beau* doit] mener avec addresse,/ Sans aucun embarrass/ Un nègre qui sans cesse/ Se croise les deux bras."

91. "On n'est pas gentilhomme/ Quand on a de bons yeux./ Faut-il voir une toile/ Qu'on expose au Salon,/ Ou bien l'Arc de l'Étoile/ Vite on prend son lorgnon."

92. Unsurprisingly, a slew of songs about industry appeared in the years surrounding the Expositions universelles, and they praise not only the edifices but also the government that erected them. Examples include Léon de Chaumont's "La Rue de Rivoli: Chant national," published in 1856, and Gioachino Rossini's "Le Chemin de fer," which first appeared in censors' reports around 1867.

93. Nisard, *Des Chansons*, 1:237.

94. "Vivons sans chagrin,/ Travaillons tous avec courage/ Par un gai refrain,/ L'ouvrage va toujours son train./ L'on nous voit monter gaiement/ Sur nos échafaudages./ Ensemble chantons/ Vive tous nos joyeux maçons!"

95. "Que d'démolitions/ Dans notre capitale/ Aussi faut des maçons/ Pour refair' des maisons./ À la Grève et au Louvr', même aussi à la Halle,/ L'on ne voit qu'démolir,/ Mais c'est pour rebâtir," quoted in Nisard, *Des Chansons*, 1:238.

96. Jules Ferry, *Les Comptes fantastiques d'Haussmann: Lettre adressée à mm. les membres de la commission du Corps législatif chargés d'examiner le nouveau projet d'emprunt de la ville de Paris* (Paris: Armond Le Chevalier, 1868).

97. Ferry, *Les Comptes fantastiques*, 8, quoted in translation in Costa Meyer, *Dividing Paris*, 87.

98. See Pierre Pinon, "Le Double mythe Haussmann," paper presented at *Le IIIième congrès de la SERD a porté sur La Vie parisienne, une langue, un mythe, un style*, Paris, June 7–9, 2007.

99. "Osman, préfet de Bajazet,/ Fut pris d'un étrange délire:/ Il démolissait pour construire,/ Et pour démolir, construisait./ Est-ce démence? Je le nie,/ On n'est pas fou pour être musulman;/ Tel fut Osman,/ Père de l'Osmanomanie."

CHAPTER 5

1. David Harvey, *Paris, Capital of Modernity* (New York: Routledge, 2005), 3.

2. A few examples of nineteenth-century books about "the old Paris" include Pierre Zaccone, *Les Mystères du vieux Paris*, 3 vols. (Paris: Gabriel Roux et Cassanet, 1854); Amédée de Ponthieu, *Légendes du vieux Paris* (Paris: Bachelin-Deflorenne, 1867); and Victor Fournel, *Les Rues du vieux Paris* (Paris: Firmin-Didot, 1879). On the genealogy of *le vieux Paris* as an antimodern idea, see Ruth Fiori, *L'Invention du vieux Paris: Naissance d'une conscience patrimoniale dans la capital* (Wavre: Mardaga, 2012).

3. Emily Laurance has positioned Kastner as a quintessentially modern "aural flaneur." See "Georges Kastner's *Les Voix de Paris* (1857): A Study in Musical Flânerie," in *Cultural Histories of Noise, Sound and Listening in Europe, 1300–1918*, ed. Ian Biddle and Kirsten Gibson, 53–75 (London: Routledge, 2016).

4. See Gavin Steingo, "Musical Economies of the Elusive Metropolis," in *Audible Empire: Music, Global Politics, Critique*, ed. Ronald Radano and Tejumola Olaniyan (Durham: Duke University Press, 2016), 246–66.

5. See Alev Çinar and Thomas Bender, eds., *Urban Imaginaries: Locating the Modern City* (Minneapolis: University of Minnesota Press, 2007), xi–xxv.

6. As John Milsom has posited, the origins of the *Cries of London* topos are shrouded in mystery. See "Oyez! Fresh Thoughts on the 'Cries of London' Repertory," in *Rethinking Music Circulation in Early Modern England*, ed. Linda Phyllis Austern, Candace Bailey, and Amanda Eubanks Winkler (Bloomington: Indiana University Press, 2017), 67–78.

7. Nicholas Mathew, "Interesting Haydn: On Attention's Materials," *Journal of the American Musicological Society* 71, no. 3 (2018): 661–62.

8. That is, 13 percent of what was *then* Paris, namely the first through the twelfth arrondissements. See Eric Fournier, *Paris en ruines: Du Paris haussmannien au Paris communard* (Paris: Imago, 2008), 19.

9. Colin Jones, *Paris: Biography of a City* (New York: Penguin Books, 2006), 356–57.

10. Esther da Costa Meyer, *Dividing Paris: Urban Renewal and Social Inequality, 1852–1870* (Princeton: Princeton University Press, 2022), 52.

11. My italics. Quoted in Costa Meyer, *Dividing Paris,* 13–14.

12. Pierre Pinon, *Paris détruit: du vandalisme architectural, aux grandes opérations d'urbanisme* (Paris: Parigramme, 2011), 162.

13. Patrice Higonnet, *Paris, Capital of the World,* trans. Arthur Goldhammer (Cambridge, MA: Harvard University Press, 2002), 89.

14. *Paris qui s'en va, Paris qui vient: publication littéraire et artistique,* ed. Léopold Flameng (Paris: Alfred Cadart, 1859).

15. Adolphe Berty, *Les Trois îlots de la cité: Compris entre les rues de la licorne, aux Fèves, de la Lanterne, du Haut-moulin et de Glatigny* (Paris: Didier et Cie., 1860), 8.

16. See Jann Pasler, "Theorizing Race in Nineteenth-Century France: Music as Emblem of Identity," *The Musical Quarterly* 89, no. 4 (Winter 2006): 459–504.

17. See Eric Hobsbawm, "Introduction: Inventing Traditions," in *The Invention of Tradition,* ed. Eric Hobsbawm and Terence Ranger, 1–14 (Cambridge: Cambridge University Press, 1983).

18. English translation by Keith Waldrop in Charles Baudelaire, *Paris Spleen: Little Poems in Prose by Charles Baudelaire* (Middletown, CT: Wesleyan University Press, 2009), 15.

19. See Aimée Boutin, *City of Noise: Sound and Nineteenth-Century Paris* (Urbana-Champaign: University of Illinois Press, 2015), 101.

20. The song is published in *Paris en chansons: sous la direction de Comte* (Paris: P. H. Krabbe, 1855).

21. "Ferraille à vendre! Chiffons! Assurément, pour peu qu'on ait habité Paris, on connaît ce cri à la fois strident et plaintif, qui, se prolongeant pendant quelques secondes, vient frapper le tympan d'une manière si peu agréable."

22. "Mais, voyez donc cette antiquaille,/ Cette éternelle m'ame Ourlier,/ Qui vient ravaler mon métier/ De vieux chiffons et de ferraille./ Sale fricoteuse! allons donc!/ Ton métier a tant de mérite!/ Ah! laisse ferraille et chiffons,/ Vends ta pomme de terre frite./ De cet honneur, je me tiens quitte./ Ferraille à vendre! Chiffons!/ Habits, chapeaux, galons!"

23. Marcel Proust, *Remembrance of Things Past: The Captive,* trans. C. K. Scott Moncrieff (New York: Modern Library, 1929), 166.

24. The poem was republished with an updated translation in the nineteenth century. See Georges-Adrien Crapelet, *Proverbes et dictons populaires: Avec les dits du mercier et des marchands et les crieries de Paris, aux XIIIe et XIVe siècles* (Paris: Imprimerie de Crapelet, 1831).

25. Emma Dillon, *The Sense of Sound: Musical Meaning in France, 1260–1330* (New York: Oxford University Press 2012), 77–81. See also Boutin, *City of Noise,* 37–38.

26. For an extended comparison of Janequin's and Villeneuve's treatments of the *cris de Paris* trope, see Laurent Vissière, "Les Cris de Paris: Naissance d'un genre littéraire et musicale (XII–XVe siècles)," in *Clément Janequin: Un musicien au*

milieu des poètes, ed. Olivier Halévy, Isabelle His, and Jean Vignes (Paris: Publications de la Société Française de Musicologie, 2013), 87–116.

27. Jean-Philippe Rameau, *Le Code de la musique pratique ou méthodes pour apprendre la musique, avec de nouvelles réflexions sur le principe sonore* (Paris: Imprimerie royale, 1760), 14–17.

28. Referenced in Vincent Milliot, *Les Cris de Paris, ou, le peuple travesti: Les représentations des petits métiers parisiens* (Paris: Publications de la Sorbonne, 1995), 283.

29. André-Ernest-Modeste Grétry, *Mémoires, ou essais sur la musique* (Brussels: A. Wahlen, 1829), 2:223.

30. Louis-Sébastien Mercier, *Tableau de Paris* (Neuchâtel: Samuel Fauche, 1781), 2:54.

31. Mercier, *Tableau de Paris,* 6:129.

32. *Les Embarras de Paris: Quel horrible fracas, quel tumulte, quel cris* (Paris: Chez l'Editeur, 1840).

33. *Les Embarras de Paris,* 10.

34. Antoine Le Roux de Lincy, "Rue et faubourg Saint-Martin," in *Paris chez soi. Revue historique, monumentale, et pittoresque de Paris ancien et moderne* (Paris: Paul Boizard, 1855), 257–71.

35. Lincy, "Rue et faubourg Saint-Martin," 271.

36. APP, Box DB 195.

37. APP, Box DB 195.

38. Boutin, *City of Noise,* 36.

39. See Jonathan Sterne, "Sonic Imaginations" in *The Sound Studies Reader,* ed. Jonathan Sterne (New York: Routledge, 2012), 3–4.

40. Jean-Georges Kastner, *Les Voix de Paris: Essai d'une histoire littéraire et musicale des cris populaires de la capitale depuis le Moyen Âge jusqu'à nos jours, suivi par une grande symphonie humoristique vocale et instrumentale* (Paris: Brandus, Dufour, et Cie, 1857), v.

41. Kastner, *Les Voix de Paris,* v.

42. See Svetlana Boym, *The Future of Nostalgia* (New York: Basic Books, 2002), xvi.

43. Kastner, *Les Voix de Paris,* 77.

44. Emily Laurance, "Varieties of Operatic Realism in Nineteenth-Century France: The Case of Gustave Charpentier's *Louise*" (PhD diss., University of North Carolina–Chapel Hill, 2003), 335.

45. "Entendez-vous le coq lointain?/ Un air plus frais rase la terre./ À l'horizon l'ombre s'altère,/ Songes légers, c'est le matin."

46. "Bruits divers. Les boutiques qui s'ouvrent, la trompette du laitier, le forgeron qui bat l'enclume, le chaudronnier qui frappe le cuivre, etc, etc".

47. "Le dormeur: Restez, restez, ô mes songes fidèles! . . .
　　Une voix: La noix! La noix! mangez la noix nouvelle!
　　Le dormeur: Elle m'écoute; elle semblait parler . . .
　　Une voix: couteaux, ciseaux, à repasser!"

48. Neither Kastner nor Thierry leave any indication of whether the "Dona Flor" subject is original or if it derives from another contemporary source; a character named Doña Flor appeared in Alexandre Dumas *père*'s *El Salteador,* a historical novel set in sixteenth-century Spain published in 1854.

49. Kastner's full score can be downloaded from the Petrucci Music Library, https://imslp.org/wiki/Les_voix_de_Paris_(Kastner,_Jean-Georges).

50. Kastner, who prominently featured the E-flat alto saxophone in the first part of *Les Cris de Paris,* was an avid champion of Sax's instruments, promoting them in the press and in his own treatises.

51. "*Les Voix de Paris* a fait naître autant d'étonnement par l'originalité de l'idée que par la patience des recherches." See François–Joseph Fétis, "Kastner, Jean-Georges," in *Biographie universelle des musiciens et bibliographie générale de la musique* (Paris: Firmin Didot frères, 1866–68), 4:484.

52. Antoine Elwart, "Les Voix de Paris!," in *Revue des beaux-arts* 27 (1857): 202–3.

53. *Journal des débats politiques et littéraires,* March 19, 1858.

54. *Journal des débats politiques et littéraires,* March 19, 1858.

55. Thomas Christiansen, *Stories of Tonality in the Age of François-Joseph Fétis* (Chicago: University of Chicago Press, 2019), 114. On the cultural politics around vocal pedagogy and the art of *déclamation* in late nineteenth-century France, see Katherine Bergeron, *Voice Lessons: French Mélodie in the Belle Époque* (New York: Oxford University Press, 2009).

56. Proust, *The Captive,* 151–52. On Proust, Debussy, and Kastner, see Jean-Rémy Julien, "L'Influence des crieurs de rue de Paris sur le récitatif debussyste: Une hypothèse," *International Review of the Aesthetics and Sociology of Music* 152 (1984): 147–57.

57. Proust, *The Captive,* 168–69.

58. See Daniel Karlin, *Street Songs: Writers and Urban Songs and Cries, 1800–1925* (New York: Oxford University Press, 2019), 138–58, and Boutin, *City of Noise,* 57–60.

59. See Jacek Blaszkiewicz, "Street Cries on the Operetta Stage: Offenbach's *Mesdames de la Halle,*" in *Musical Theatre in Europe, 1830–1945,* ed. Michela Niccolai and Clair Rowden (Turnhout: Brepols, 2017), 63–89.

60. See Arman Schwartz, *Puccini's Soundscapes: Realism and Modernity in Italian Opera* (Florence: Olschki, 2016), and Laurance, "Varieties of Operatic Realism in Nineteenth-Century France." On street cries in Delius's *Paris,* see David J. Eccott, "Les Cris de Paris," *The Delius Society Journal* 153 (Spring 2013): 79–88.

61. *Le Parisien,* July 6, 1976.

62. See Ross Cole, *The Folk: Music, Modernity, and the Political Imagination* (Berkeley: University of California Press, 2021).

EPILOGUE

1. "Communications à la presse," *Le Temps,* October 26, 1870; "Communications à la presse," *Le Figaro,* October 26, 1870.

2. John Merriman, *Massacre: The Death and Life of the Paris Commune* (New Haven: Yale University Press, 2014), 242.

3. Vincent d'Indy, *Histoire du 105ième bataillon de la Garde Nationale de Paris en l'année 1870–1871, par un engagé volontaire dudit bataillon âgé de 19 ans* (Paris: Charles Douniol et Cie, 1872), 93. On the reception of war sounds ca. 1870 and their traumatic effects, see Erin Brooks, "Sonic Scars in Urban Space: Trauma and the Parisian Soundscape during *l'année terrible*," *Nineteenth-Century Music Review* (2022): 1–32.

4. Delphine Mordey, "'Dans le palais du son, on fait de la farine': Performing at the Opéra during the 1870 Siege of Paris," *Music and Letters* 93, no. 1 (February 2012): 3.

5. Mordey, "Dans le palais du son," 1.

6. M. Casslant, "Projet sur la réorganisation des théâtres Subventions—Censure—Droit des pauvres—Administration supérieure" (1872), AN F/21/953.

7. "Société entre Paul Renard et Charles Joseph Eléazar Lorge," notary document, August 9, 1871, AN MC/ET/LXXX/465.

8. AN AB/XIX/5203.

9. "Boulevard Haussmann: il y a 90 ans il était (enfin) inauguré," *Le Figaro*, January 13, 2017.

10. *Le Petit journal*, January 16, 1927.

11. See Jann Pasler, *Composing the Citizen: Music as Public Utility in Third Republic France* (Berkeley: University of California Press, 2009), 1–4.

BIBLIOGRAPHY

ABBREVIATIONS

AN   Archives nationales
APP   Archives de la Préfecture de Police
BHVP   Bibliothèque historique de la ville de Paris
BnF   Bibliothèque nationale de France
CG   Hector Berlioz, *Correspondance générale*. Pierre Citron, general editor. Paris: Flammarion, 1972–2003.

NEWSPAPERS AND MAGAZINES

Le Café-concert
La Chanson illustrée
Le Charivari
Le Constitutionnel
Les Coulisses: Journal quotidien
Le Figaro
Le Foyer
La France musicale
Gazette des tribunaux
Gazette municipale
The Illustrated London News
L'Illustration
Le Journal amusant
Journal des débats politiques et littéraires
La Lanterne
Leamington Advertiser

London Review of Politics, Society, Literature, Art & Science
Le Ménestrel
Mercure de France
Le Monde dramatique
Le Monde illustré
Le Moniteur universel
The New York Times
Nouvelles annales de la construction
L'Orchestre: Revue quotidienne des théâtres
Le Parisien
Le Pays
Le Petit journal
La Presse
Revue des beaux-arts
Revue et gazette musicale de Paris
La Semaine musicale
Temple Bar: A London Magazine for Town and Country Readers
Le Temps
L'Univers musicale

BOOKS AND ARTICLES

Abbott, Helen. *Baudelaire in Song, 1880–1930*. New York: Oxford University Press, 2017.

Almanach chantant: Choix des plus jolies chansons françaises. Paris: Delarue, 1866.

Althusser, Louis. "Ideology and Ideological State Apparatuses." In *Lenin and Philosophy and Other Essays,* translated by Ben Brewster, 79–87. New York: Monthly Review Press, 1971.

Attali, Jacques. *Noise: The Political Economy of Music*. Translated by Brian Massumi. Minneapolis: University of Minnesota Press, 1985.

Audiganne, Armande. *Paris et sa splendeur*. 2 vols. Paris: Henri Charpentier, 1861.

Ausubel, Jesse H., and Robert Herman. *Cities and Their Vital Systems: Infrastructure Past, Present, and Future*. Washington, DC: National Academy Press, 1988.

Authier, Catherine. "La Naissance de la star féminine sous le Second Empire." In *Les Spectacles sous le Second Empire,* edited by Jean-Claude Yon, 270–81. Paris: Armand Colin, 2010.

Bara, Olivier. "Le Café-concert dans la grande presse, ou la crise du feuilleton dramatique." In *Presse, chanson et culture orale au XIXe siècle: La parole vive au défi de l'ère médiatique,* edited by Marie-Ève Thérenty and Élisabeth Pillet, 1–14. Paris: Nouveau monde éditions, 2012.

Barzun, Jacques. *Berlioz and the Romantic Century*. 2 vols. New York: Columbia University Press, 1969.

Baudelaire, Charles. *The Painter of Modern Life and Other Essays.* Translated by Jonathan Mayne. London: Phaidon, 1995.

———. *Paris Spleen: Little Poems in Prose by Charles Baudelaire.* Translated by Keith Waldrop. Middletown, CT: Wesleyan University Press, 2009.

———. *The Mirror of Art: Critical Essays by Charles Baudelaire,* edited and translated by Jonathan Mayne, 38–130. New York: Doubleday Anchor Books, 1956.

Belenky, Masha. *Engine of Modernity: The Omnibus and Urban Culture in Nineteenth-Century Paris.* Manchester: Manchester University Press, 2019.

Benedict, Burton. *The Anthropology of World's Fairs: San Francisco's Panama Pacific International Exposition of 1915.* Berkeley: University of California Press, 1983.

Benini, Romain. "La Chanson, voix publique (Paris, 1816–1881)." *Romantisme* 171, no. 1 (2016): 40–52.

Benjamin, Walter. *The Arcades Project.* Translated by Howard Eiland and Kevin McLaughlin. New York: Belknap Press, 2002.

Bergeron, Katherine. *Voice Lessons: French Mélodie in the Belle Époque.* New York: Oxford University Press, 2009.

Berlioz, Hector. *A travers chants.* Paris: Michel Levy frères, 1862.

———. *The Memoirs of Hector Berlioz.* Translated by David Cairns. New York: Everyman's Library, 2002.

———. *New Letters of Berlioz, 1830–1868.* Translated by Jacques Barzun. Westport, CT: Greenwood Press, 1974.

Berman, Marshall. *All That Is Solid Melts into Air: The Experience of Modernity.* New York: Penguin Books, 1982.

Bernard, Élisabeth. "Jules Pasdeloup et les Concerts Populaires." *Revue de musicologie* 57, no. 2 (1972): 150–78.

Bertagnolli, Paul. *Prometheus in Music: Representations of the Myth in the Romantic Era.* Aldershot: Ashgate, 2007.

Berty, Adolphe. *Les Trois îlots de la Cité: Compris entre les rues de la Licorne, aux Fèves, de la Lanterne, du Haut-Moulin et de Flatigny.* Paris: Didier et Cie., 1860.

Biddle, Ian, and Kirsten Gibson, eds. *Cultural Histories of Noise, Sound and Listening in Europe, 1300–1918.* Farnham: Ashgate, 2016.

Bijsterveld, Karin, ed. *Soundscapes of the Urban Past: Sound as Mediated Cultural Heritage.* Bielefeld: Transcript Verlag, 2013.

Blaszkiewicz, Jacek. "Chez Paul Niquet: Sound, Spatiality, and Sociability in the Paris Cabaret." *19th-Century Music* 45, no. 2 (November 2021): 147–66.

———. "Listening to the Old City: Street Cries and Urbanization in Paris, ca. 1860." *Journal of Musicology* 37, no. 2 (May 2020): 123–57.

———. "Street Cries on the Operetta Stage: Offenbach's *Mesdames de la Halle.*" In *Musical Theatre in Europe, 1830–1945,* edited by Michela Niccolai and Clair Rowden, 63–89. Turnhout: Brepols, 2017.

Bloom, Peter. "Berlioz and the *Prix de Rome* of 1830." *Journal of the American Musicological Society* 34, no. 1 (Summer 1981): 279–304.

———. *Berlioz in Time: From Early Recognition to Lasting Renown.* Rochester: University of Rochester Press, 2022.

Bloom, Peter, ed. *Berlioz: Past, Present, Future*. Rochester: University of Rochester Press, 2003.

Bohlman, Andrea. "Solidarity, Song, and the Sound Document." *Journal of Musicology* 33, no. 2 (Spring 2016): 232–69.

Boutin, Aimée. *City of Noise: Sound and Nineteenth-Century Paris*. Urbana–Champaign: University of Illinois Press, 2015.

Boym, Svetlana. *The Future of Nostalgia*. New York: Basic Books, 2002.

Brooks, Erin. "Sonic Scars in Urban Space: Trauma and the Parisian Soundscape during *l'année terrible*." *Nineteenth-Century Music Review* (2022): 1–32.

Burkholder, J. Peter, Donald Jay Grout, and Claude V. Palisca. *A History of Western Music*. 10th ed. New York: W. W. Norton, 2019.

Cairns, David. *Berlioz, 1803–1832: The Making of an Artist*. Berkeley: University of California Press, 1999.

———. *Berlioz, 1832–1869: Servitude and Greatness*. Berkeley: University of California Press, 1999.

Capelle, Pierre, ed. *La Clé du caveau: À l'usage de tous les chansonniers français, des amateurs, auteurs, acteurs du vaudeville, et de tous les amis de la chanson*. Paris: Capelle et Renard, 1811.

Caradec, François, and Alain Weill. *Le Café-concert: 1848–1914*. Paris: Hachette, 2007.

Carlson, Marvin. "The Theatre as Civic Monument." *Theatre Journal* 40, no. 1 (March 1988): 12–32.

Carmona, Michel. *Haussmann: His Life and Times, and the Making of Modern Paris*. Translated by Patrick Camiller. Chicago: Ivan R. Dee, 2002.

des Cars, Jean, and Pierre Pinon, eds. *Paris-Haussmann. Le Pari d'Haussmann. Ouvrage publié à l'occasion de l'exposition au pavillon de l'Arsenal inaugurée le 19 septembre 1991*. Paris: Picard-Pavillon de l'Arsenal, 1991.

Carter, Tim. "Listening to Music in Early Modern Italy: Some Problems for the Urban Musicologist." In *Hearing the City in Early Modern Europe*, edited by Tess Knighton and Ascensión Mazuela-Anguita, 25–54. Turnhout: Brepols, 2018.

———. "The Sound of Silence: Models for an Urban Musicology." *Urban History* 29, no. 1 (May 2002): 8–18.

Caygill, Howard. *Walter Benjamin: The Colour of Experience*. London: Routledge, 1998.

de Certeau, Michel. *Heterologies: Discourse on the Other*. Translated by Brian Massumi. Minneapolis: University of Minnesota Press, 1986.

Chadourne, André. *Les Cafés-concerts*. Paris: E. Dentu, 1889.

Chambers, Ross. *An Atmospherics of the City: Baudelaire and the Poetics of Noise*. New York: Fordham University Press, 2015.

Chants et chansons populaires de la France. Paris: Garnier Frères, 1854.

Charlton, David, ed. *Choral Works with Orchestra II*. Vol. 12b, *Hector Berlioz: New Edition of the Complete Works*. Kasel: Bärenreiter, 1993.

Charney, Leo, and Vanessa R. Schwartz, eds. *Cinema and the Invention of Modern Life*. Berkeley: University of California Press, 1995.

Chevalier, Louis. *Classes laborieuses et classes dangereuses: A Paris, pendant la première moitié du XIXe siècle*. Paris: Hachette, 1984.

Christiansen, Thomas. *Stories of Tonality in the Age of François-Joseph Fétis*. Chicago: University of Chicago Press, 2019.

Çinar, Alev, and Thomas Bender, eds. *Urban Imaginaries: Locating the Modern City*. Minneapolis: University of Minnesota Press, 2007.

Citron, Pierre, Cécile Reynaud, Jean-Pierre Bartoli, and Peter Bloom, eds. *Dictionnaire Berlioz*. Paris: Fayard, 2003.

Clark, T. J. *The Painting of Modern Life: Paris in the Art of Manet and His Followers*. Princeton: Princeton University Press, 1984.

Colardelle, Michel, and Florence Gétreau, eds. *Musiciens des rues de Paris*. Paris: Réunion des Musées Nationaux, 1998.

Cole, Ross. *The Folk: Music, Modernity, and the Political Imagination*. Berkeley: University of California Press, 2021.

Coleman, Jeremy. *Richard Wagner in Paris: Translation, Identity, Modernity*. Suffolk: Boydell & Brewer, 2019.

Comettant, Oscar. *La Musique, les musiciens et les instruments de musique chez les différents peuples du monde*. Paris: Michel Lévy, frères, 1869.

Condemi, Concetta. *Les Cafés-concerts: Histoire d'un divertissement (1849–1914)*. Paris: Quai Voltaire, 1992.

Conway, Kelley. *Chanteuse in the City: The Realist Singer in French Film*. Berkeley: University of California Press, 2004.

Cornut *fils*, Roman. *Cantate de l'Exposition: Les noces de Prométhée*. Paris: Hachette, 1867.

da Costa Meyer, Esther. *Dividing Paris: Urban Renewal and Social Inequality, 1852–1870*. Princeton: Princeton University Press, 2022.

Crapelet, Georges-Adrien. *Proverbes et dictons populaires: Avec les dits du mercier et des marchands et les crieries de Paris, aux XIIIe et XIVe siècles*. Paris: Imprimerie de Crapelet, 1831.

Cruz, Gabriela. *Grand Illusion: Phantasmagoria in Nineteenth-Century Opera*. New York: Oxford University Press, 2020.

Dähne, Chris, Rixt Hoekstra, and Carsten Ruhl, eds. *The Death and Life of the Total Work of Art: Henry van de Velde and the Legacy of a Modern Concept*. Berlin: Jovis, 2014.

Darriulat, Philippe. *La Muse du peuple: Chansons politiques et sociales en France, 1815–1871*. Rennes: Presses Universitaires de Rennes, 2010.

Debord, Guy. *The Society of the Spectacle*. Translated by Ken Knabb. London: Rebel Press, 2005.

———. "Theory of the *Dérive*." Translated by Ken Knabb. In *Situationist International Anthology*, edited by Ken Knabb, 62–66. Berkeley: Bureau of Public Secrets, 1981).

Delvau, Alfred. *Les Cythères parisiennes: Histoires anecdotiques des bals de Paris.* Paris: E. Dentu, 1864.

Dictionnaire des girouettes, ou nos contemporains peints d'après eux-mêmes. Paris: Alexis Eymery, 1815.

Dictionnaire des protées modernes, ou Biographie des personnages vivants qui ont figuré dans la Révolution française, depuis le 14 juillet 1789, jusques et compris 1815, par leurs actions, leur conduit ou leurs écrits. Paris: Davi et Locard, 1815.

Di Grazia, Donna M. "Concert Societies in Paris and Their Choral Repertoires, c. 1828–1880." PhD diss., Washington University in St. Louis, 1993.

Dillon, Emma. *The Sense of Sound: Musical Meaning in France, 1260–1330.* New York: Oxford University Press, 2012.

Dorf, Samuel. *Performing Antiquity: Ancient Greek Music and Dance from Paris to Delphi, 1890–1930.* New York: Oxford University Press, 2018.

E. A.-D. *Les Cafés-concerts en 1866.* Paris: Ch. Égrot, 1866.

L'Eldorado et la question des cafés-concerts. Paris: L. Hugonis, 1875.

Eccott, David J. "Les Cris de Paris." *The Delius Society Journal* 153 (Spring 2013): 79–88.

Eco, Umberto. *Travels in Hyperreality.* New York: Harvest Books, 1986.

Ellis, Katharine. *French Musical Life: Local Dynamics in the Century to World War II.* New York: Oxford University Press, 2021.

———. *Interpreting the Musical Past: Early Music in Nineteenth Century France.* New York: Oxford University Press, 2008.

———. "Unintended Consequences: Theatre Deregulation and Opera in France, 1864–1878." *Cambridge Opera Journal* 22, no. 3 (November 2010): 327–52.

Elwart, Antoine. *Œuvres musicales choisies.* Paris: G. Brandus et Dufour, 1867.

Les Embarras de Paris: Quel horrible fracas, quel tumulte, quel cris. Paris: Chez l'Editeur, 1840.

Everist, Mark. *The Empire at the Opéra: Theatre, Power and Music in Second Empire Paris.* Cambridge: Cambridge University Press, 2021.

———. *Genealogies of Music and Memory: Gluck in the 19th-Century Parisian Imagination.* New York: Oxford University Press, 2021.

———. "Jacques Offenbach: The Music of the Past and the Image of the Present." In *Music, Theatre, and Cultural Transfer,* edited by Annegret Fauser and Mark Everist, 72–98. Chicago: University of Chicago Press, 2009.

———. "'Der Mächtigste Tanzmeister Des Kaiserreiches'? Offenbach at 200." *Journal of the Royal Musical Association* 145, no. 2 (November 2020): 485–94.

Fauquet, Joël-Marie, ed. *Dictionnaire de la musique en France au XIXe siècle.* Paris: Fayard, 2003.

Fauser, Annegret. "Debacle at the Paris Opéra: *Tannhäuser* and the French Critics, 1861." In *Richard Wagner and His World,* edited by Thomas S. Grey, 347–71. Princeton: Princeton University Press, 2009.

———. "*La Guerre en dentelles:* Women and the *Prix de Rome* in French Cultural Politics." *Journal of the American Musicological Society* 51, no. 1 (Spring 1998): 83–129.

———. *Musical Encounters at the 1889 Paris World's Fair*. Rochester: University of Rochester Press, 2005.

Ferguson, Priscilla. *Paris as Revolution: Writing the Nineteenth-Century City*. Berkeley: University of California Press, 1994.

Ferry, Jules. *Les Comptes fantastiques d'Haussmann: Lettre adressée à mm. les membres de la commission du Corps législatif chargés d'examiner le nouveau projet d'emprunt de la ville de Paris*. Paris: Armond Le Chevalier, 1868.

Fétis, François-Joseph. *Biographie universelle des musiciens et bibliographie générale de la musique*. 8 vols. Paris: Firmin Didot Frères, 1866–88.

Fiori, Ruth. *L'invention du vieux Paris: Naissance d'une conscience patrimoniale dans la capital*. Wavre: Mardaga, 2012.

Fisher, Alexander J. *Music, Piety, and Propaganda: The Soundscapes of Counter-Reformation Bavaria*. New York: Oxford University Press, 2014.

Flameng, Léopold, ed. *Paris qui s'en va, Paris qui vient: publication littéraire et artistique*. Paris: Alfred Cadart, 1859.

Foucault, Michel. *Abnormal: Lectures at the Collège de France, 1974–1975*. Translated by Graham Burchell. New York: Verso, 2003.

Fournel, Victor. *Les Rues du vieux Paris: Galerie populaire et pittoresque*. Paris: Firmin-Didot, 1879.

Fournier, Eric. *Paris en ruines: Du Paris haussmannien au Paris communard*. Paris: Imago, 2008.

Fulcher, Jane. "The Popular Chanson of the Second Empire: 'Music of the Peasants' in France." *Acta Musicologica* 52, no. 1 (January–June 1980): 27–37.

Galabert, Edmond. *Georges Bizet: souvenirs et correspondence*. Paris: Michel Lévy, 1877.

Galignani, John Anthony William. *Galignani's New Paris Guide: For 1862*. Paris: A. and W. Galignani, 1862.

La gaudriole de 1860: Chansons et chansonnettes nouvelles. Paris: Bernardin-Béchet, 1861.

Gautier, Ana María Ochoa. *Aurality: Listening and Knowledge in Nineteenth-Century Colombia*. Durham: Duke University Press, 2014.

de Genouillac, H. Gourdon. *Les Refrains de la rue*. Paris: E. Dentu, 1879.

Geoffroy-Schwinden, Rebecca Dowd. *From Servant to Savant: Musical Privilege, Property, and the French Revolution*. New York: Oxford University Press, 2022.

———. "Music as Feminine Capital in Napoleonic France: Nancy Macdonald's Musical Upbringing." *Music & Letters*. 100, no. 2 (May 2019): 302–34.

Geppert, Alexander C. T. *Fleeting Cities: Imperial Expositions in Fin-de-Siècle Europe*. London: Palgrave Macmillan, 2010.

Gérard, Yves, and Eurydice Jousse, eds. *Lettres de compositeurs à Camille Saint-Saëns*. Lyon: Symétrie, 2009.

Gerhard, Anselm. *The Urbanization of Opera: Music Theater in Paris in the Nineteenth Century*. Translated by Mary Whittall. Chicago: University of Chicago Press, 1998.

Goehr, Lydia. *The Imaginary Museum of Musical Works: An Essay in the Philosophy of Music*. New York: Oxford University Press, 1993.

de Goncourt, Edmond, and Jules de Goncourt. *Idées et sensations*. Paris: G. Charpentier, 1877.

———. *Journal: Mémoires de la vie littéraire*. Monaco: Fasquelle and Flammarion, 1956.

Goonewardena, Kanishka. "The Urban Sensorium: Space, Ideology and the Aestheticization of Politics." *Antipode* 37 (2005): 46–71.

Gouspy, Carol. "La Représentation des chanteuses au café-concert: Les genres de la romancière comique et de la diseuse." *Volume!: La revue des musiques populaires* 2, no. 2 (2003): 27–39.

Graham, Stephen, and Simon Marvin. *Splintering Urbanism: Networked Infrastructures, Technological Mobilities and the Urban Condition*. London: Routledge, 2001.

Granveau, Antoine. *L'Ouvrier devant la société*. Paris: Hélaine, 1868.

Grempler, Martina. "Rossinis 'politisches Spätwerk': Die *Hymne à Napoléon III* und *La corona d'Italia*." In *Rossini in Paris*, edited by Bernd-Rüdiger Kern and Reto Müller, 181–200. Leipzig: Leipziger Universitätsverlag, 2002.

Grétry, André-Ernest-Modeste. *Mémoires, ou essais sur la musique*. 3 vols. Brussels: A. Wahlen, 1829.

Grey, Thomas S. "*Eine Kapitulation:* Aristophanic Operetta as Cultural Warfare in 1870." In *Richard Wagner and His World*, edited by Thomas S. Grey, 87–122. Princeton: Princeton University Press, 2009.

Haine, W. Scott. *The World of the Paris Café: Sociability among the French Working Class, 1789–1914*. Baltimore: Johns Hopkins University Press, 1998.

Harvey, David. *Paris: Capital of Modernity*. New York: Routledge, 2005.

Haussmann, Georges-Eugène. *Mémoires du Baron Haussmann*. 3 vols. Paris: Victor-Havard, 1890.

Hazareesingh, Sudhir. *The Saint-Napoleon: Celebrations of Sovereignty in Nineteenth-Century France*. Cambridge, MA: Harvard University Press, 2004.

Higonnet, Patrice. *Paris, Capital of the World*. Translated by Arthur Goldhammer. Cambridge, MA: Harvard University Press, 2002.

Hobsbawm, Eric. "Introduction: Inventing Traditions." In *The Invention of Tradition*, edited by Eric Hobsbawm and Terence Ranger, 1–14. Cambridge: Cambridge University Press, 1983.

Hostein, Hippolyte. *La Liberté des théâtres*. Paris: Librairie des Auteurs, 1867.

d'Indy, Vincent. *Histoire du 105ième bataillon de la Garde Nationale de Paris en l'année 1870–1871, par un engagé volontaire dudit bataillon âgé de 19 ans*. Paris: Charles Douniol et Cie, 1872.

Johnson, James H. *Listening in Paris: A Cultural History*. Berkeley: University of California Press, 1995.

Jones, Colin. *Paris: Biography of a City*. New York: Penguin Books, 2006.

Jordan, David P. "The City: Baron Haussmann and Modern Paris." *The American Scholar* 61, no. 1 (Winter 1992): 99–106.

———. *Transforming Paris: The Life and Labors of Baron Haussmann*. New York: Free Press, 1995.

Julien, Jean-Rémy. "L'Influence des crieurs de rue de Paris sur le récitatif debussyste: Une hypothèse." *International Review of the Aesthetics and Sociology of Music* 15.2 (1984): 147–57.

Karlin, Daniel. *Street Songs: Writers and Urban Songs and Cries, 1800–1925.* New York: Oxford University Press, 2018.

Kastner, Jean-Georges. *Les Voix de Paris: Essai d'une histoire littéraire et musicale des cris populaires de la capitale depuis le Moyen Âge jusqu'à nos jours, suivi par une grande symphonie humoristique vocale et instrumentale.* Paris: Brandus, Dufour, et Cie, 1857.

Kimminich, Eva. "Chansons étouffées. Recherche sur les cafés concerts au XIXe siècle." *Politix. Revue des sciences sociales du politique* 4, no. 14 (1991): 19–26.

Kolb, Katherine. "Primal Scenes: Smithson, Pleyel, and Liszt in the Eyes of Berlioz." *19th-Century Music* 18, no. 3 (Spring 1995): 211–35.

Kramer, Lawrence. *The Hum of the World: A Philosophy of Listening.* Berkeley: University of California Press, 2018.

Krims, Adam. *Music and Urban Geography.* New York: Routledge, 2007.

de Labedollière, Émile. *Le Nouveau Paris: Histoire de ses 20 arrondissements.* Paris: Gustave Barba, 1860.

Landron, Hélène. "Les Musiciens de rue sous l'autorité de la police parisienne." In *Musiciens des rues de Paris,* edited by Michel Colardelle and Florence Gétreau, 74–79. Paris: Réunion des Musées Nationaux, 1998.

Laronze, Georges. *Le Baron Haussmann.* Paris: F. Alcan, 1932.

Laurance, Emily. "Georges Kastner's *Les Voix de Paris* (1857): A Study in Musical Flânerie." In *Cultural Histories of Noise, Sound and Listening in Europe, 1300–1918,* edited by Ian Biddle and Kirsten Gibson, 53–75. London: Routledge, 2016.

———. "Varieties of Operatic Realism in Nineteenth-Century France: The Case of Gustave Charpentier's *Louise.*" PhD diss., University of North Carolina–Chapel Hill, 2003.

Lefebvre, Henri. *The Production of Space.* Translated by Donald Nicholson-Smith. London: Wiley Blackwell, 1992.

———. *Rhythmanalysis: Space, Time and Everyday Life.* Translated by Stuart Elden and Gerald Moore. London: Continuum, 2004.

———. *The Survival of Capitalism: Reproduction of the Relations of Production.* Translated by F. Bryant. London: Allison and Busby, 1976.

———. *Writings on Cities.* Translated and edited by Eleonore Kofman and Elizabeth Lebas. London: Blackwell Publishing, 1996.

Level, Brigitte. *À Travers deux siècles: Le Caveau, société bachique et chantante, 1726–1939.* Paris: Presses de l'Université de Paris-Sorbonne, 1988.

Levin, Alicia C. "A Documentary Overview of Musical Theaters in Paris, 1830–1900." In *Music, Theatre, and Cultural Transfer: Paris, 1830–1914,* edited by Mark Everist and Annegret Fauser, 379–402. Chicago: University of Chicago Press, 2009.

Littré, Émile, ed. *Dictionnaire de la langue française.* Paris: Hachette, 1863–72.

Llano, Samuel. *Discordant Notes: Marginality and Social Control in Madrid, 1850–1930.* New York: Oxford University Press, 2018.

Locke, Ralph. "The Political Chansons of Béranger: Artistry for Progressive Social Change." In *Musik/Revolution: Festschrift für Georg Knepler zum 90. Geburtstag,* edited by H.-W. Heister, 115–32. Hamburg: Von Bockel, 1997.

Lockhart, Ellen. *Animation, Plasticity, and Music in Italy, 1770–1830.* Berkeley: University of California Press, 2017.

Macdonald, Hugh. *Berlioz.* London: Dent, 1982.

———. *Bizet.* New York: Oxford University Press, 2014.

Mainardi, Patricia. *Art and Politics of the Second Empire: The Universal Expositions of 1855 and 1867.* New Haven: Yale University Press, 1987.

Marcus, Sharon. "Haussmannization as Anti-Modernity: The Apartment House in Parisian Urban Discourse, 1850–1880." *Journal of Urban History* 27, no. 6 (September 1, 2001): 723–45.

Mason, Laura. *Singing the French Revolution: Popular Culture and Politics, 1787–1799.* Ithaca, NY: Cornell University Press, 1996.

Mathew, Nicholas. "Interesting Haydn: On Attention's Materials." *Journal of the American Musicological Society* 71, no. 3 (2018): 661–62.

Mead, Christopher. "Urban Contingency and the Problem of Representation in Second Empire Paris." *Journal of the Society of Architectural Historians* 54, no. 2 (1995): 138–74.

Mercier, Louis-Sébastien. *Tableau de Paris.* 12 vols. Neuchâtel: Samuel Fauche, 1781.

Merriman, John. *Massacre: The Death and Life of the Paris Commune.* New Haven: Yale University Press, 2014.

Milliot, Vincent. *Les Cris de Paris, ou, le peuple travesti: Les représentations des petits métiers parisiens.* Paris: Publications de la Sorbonne, 1995.

Milne, Anna-Louise, ed. *The Cambridge Companion to the Literature of Paris.* New York: Cambridge University Press, 2013.

Milsom, John. "Oyez! Fresh Thoughts on the 'Cries of London' Repertory." In *Rethinking Music Circulation in Early Modern England,* edited by Linda Phyllis Austern, Candace Bailey, and Amanda Eubanks Winkler, 67–78. Bloomington: Indiana University Press, 2017.

Mitchell, Timothy. "The World as Exhibition." *Comparative Studies in Society and History* 31, no. 2 (April 1989): 217–36.

Mondelli, Peter. "Offenbach's Bouffonnerie, Wagner's Rêverie: The Materiality and Politics of the Ineffable in Second Empire Paris." *The Opera Quarterly* 32, no. 2–3 (2017): 134–59.

Mordey, Delphine. "'Dans le palais du son, on fait de la farine': Performing at the Opéra during the 1870 Siege of Paris." *Music and Letters* 93, no. 1 (February 2012): 1–28.

Nadar. *Quand j'étais photographe.* Paris: Flammarion, 1900.

Nisard, Charles. *Des Chansons populaires chez les anciens et chez les Français: Essai historique suivi d'une étude sur la chanson des rues contemporaine.* 2 vols. Paris: E. Dentu, 1867.

Nord, Philip G. *The Politics of Resentment: Shopkeeper Protest in Nineteenth-Century Paris.* Princeton: Princeton University Press, 1986.

Noske, Frits. *French Song from Berlioz to Duparc.* New York: Dover Publications, 1988.

Olsen, Donald J. *The City as Work of Art: London, Paris, Vienna.* New Haven: Yale University Press, 1988.

Osborne, Richard. *Rossini: His Life and Works.* New York: Oxford University Press, 2007.

Ouzounian, Gascia. *Stereophonica: Sound and Space in Science, Technology, and the Arts.* Cambridge, MA: The MIT Press, 2020.

Papayanis, Nicholas. *Planning Paris before Haussmann.* Baltimore: Johns Hopkins University Press, 2004.

Paris chez soi. Revue historique, monumentale, et pittoresque de Paris ancien et moderne. Paris: Paul Boizard, 1855.

Paris en chansons: sous la direction de Comte. Paris: P. H. Krabbe, 1855.

Paris–Gagne–Petit, par les auteurs des mémoires de Bilboquet. Paris: E. Taride, 1854.

Paris-Guide: Par les principaux écrivains et artistes de la France, la science, l'art. 2 vols. Paris: Librairie international, 1867.

Pasler, Jann. *Composing the Citizen: Music as Public Utility in Third-Republic France.* Berkeley: University of California Press, 2009.

———. "Theorizing Race in Nineteenth-Century France: Music as Emblem of Identity." *The Musical Quarterly* 89, no. 4 (Winter 2006): 459–504.

Pénet, Martin. "Le Café-concert, un nouveau divertissement populaire." In *Les Spectacles sous le Second Empire,* edited by Jean-Claude Yon, 349–65. Paris: Armand Colin, 2010.

Picon, Antoine. "Expositions universelles, doctrines sociales et utopies." In *Les expositions universelles en France au XIXe siècle,* edited by Anne-Laure Carré, Marie-Sophie Corcy, Christiane Demeulenaure-Douyère, and Liliane Hilaire-Pérez, 37–47. Paris: CNRS Éditions, 2012.

Pinon, Pierre. "Le Double mythe Haussman." Paper presented at *La vie parisienne, une langue, un mythe, un style,* Paris, June 7–9, 2007. http://etudes-romantiques.ish-lyon.cnrs.fr/wa_files/Pinon.pdf.

———. *Paris détruit: Du vandalisme architectural, aux grandes opérations d'urbanisme.* Paris: Parigramme, 2011.

Pistone, Danièle. "La *Fête impériale:* Origine et caractéristiques de ses répertoires musicaux dans le Paris de Napoléon III (1852–1870)." In *La Musique et le rite sacré et profane: Actes du XIIe congrès de la Société internationale de musicologie, Strasbourg, 29 août–3 septembre 1982,* edited by Marc Honneger and Paul Prévost, 1:132–37. Strasbourg: Association des Publications près les Universités de Strasbourg, 1986.

de Ponthieu, Amédée. *Légendes du vieux Paris.* Paris: Bachelin-Deflorenne, 1867.

Prendergast, Christopher. *Paris and the Nineteenth Century.* London: Wiley-Blackwell, 1995.

Price, Roger. *A Concise History of France.* 2nd ed. Cambridge: Cambridge University Press, 2005.

Proust, Marcel. *Remembrance of Things Past: The Captive.* Translated by C. K. Scott Moncrieff. New York: Modern Library, 1929.

Rapport sur l'Exposition universelle de 1855, présenté à l'Empereur par S. A. L. le Prince Napoléon. Paris: Imprimerie impériale, 1857.

Rameau, Jean-Philippe. *Le Code de la musique pratique ou méthodes pour apprendre la musique, avec de nouvelles réflexions sur le principe sonore.* Paris: Imprimerie royale, 1760.

Rancière, Jacques. "Good Times, Or, Pleasure at the Barriers." In *Voices of the People: The Politics and Life of "La Sociale" at the End of the Second Empire*, edited by Adrian Rifkin and Roger Thomas, 203–52. London: Routledge, 1988.

Rees, Brian. *Camille Saint-Saëns: A Life.* London: Faber and Faber, 2009.

Rehding, Alexander. *Music and Monumentality: Commemoration and Wonderment in Nineteenth-Century Germany.* New York: Oxford University Press, 2009.

Reibel, Emmanuel. "Carrières entre presse et opéra au XIXe siècle: du mélange des genres au conflit d'intérêts." In *Presse et opéra aux XVIIIe et XIXe siècles*, ed. Olivier Bara, Christophe Cave and Marie-Ève Thérenty. *Médias19: Littérature et culture médiatique,* 2012. https://www.medias19.org/publications/presse-et-opera-aux-xviiie-et-xixe-siecles/carrieres-entre-presse-et-opera-au-xixe-siecle-du-melange-des-genres-au-conflit-dinterets.

Reid, Donald. *Paris Sewers and Sewermen: Realities and Representations.* Cambridge, MA: Harvard University Press, 1993.

Rose, Jonathan F. P. *The Well-Tempered City: What Modern Science, Ancient Civilizations, and Human Nature Teach Us About the Future of Urban Life.* New York: Harper Wave, 2016.

Ross, Andrew Israel. *Public City/Public Sex: Homosexuality, Prostitution, and Urban Culture in Nineteenth-Century Paris.* Philadelphia: Temple University Press, 2019.

Rowden, Clair. *Opera and Parody in Paris, 1860–1900.* Turnhout: Brepols, 2020.

Rushton, Julian. *The Music of Berlioz.* Oxford: Oxford University Press, 2001.

Sala, Emilio. *The Sounds of Paris in Verdi's* La traviata. Translated by Delia Casadei. New York: Cambridge University Press, 2013.

Schneider, Corinne. "Du Boulevard du Temple à la place du Châtelet, le Théâtre Lyrique comme 'laboratoire de la musique.'" In *Les Spectacles sous le Second Empire*, edited by Jean-Claude Yon, 213–25. Paris: Armand Colin, 2010.

Schwartz, Arman. *Puccini's Soundscapes: Realism and Modernity in Italian Opera.* Florence: Olschki, 2016.

Scott, Derek B. *Sounds of the Metropolis: The Nineteenth-Century Popular Music Revolution in London, New York, Paris and Vienna.* New York: Oxford University Press, 2008.

Seigel, Jerrold. *Bohemian Paris: Culture, Politics, and the Boundaries of Bourgeois Life, 1830–1930.* Baltimore: Johns Hopkins University Press, 1986.

Senelick, Laurence. *Jacques Offenbach and the Making of Modern Culture.* New York: Cambridge University Press, 2017.

Sennett, Richard. *Building and Dwelling: Ethics for the City.* New York: Farrar, Straus and Giroux, 2018.

Shaya, Gregory. "The Flâneur, the Badaud, and the Making of a Mass Public in France, circa 1860–1910." *American Historical Review* 109, no. 1 (February 2004): 41–77.
Steingo, Gavin. "Musical Economies of the Elusive Metropolis." In *Audible Empire: Music, Global Politics, Critique,* edited by Ronald Radano and Tejumola Olaniyan, 246–66. Durham: Duke University Press, 2016.
Sterne, Jonathan. "Sonic Imaginations." In *The Sound Studies Reader,* edited by Jonathan Sterne, 1–19. New York: Routledge, 2012.
———. "Soundscape, Landscape, Escape." In *Soundscapes of the Urban Past,* edited by Karin Bijsterveld, 181–93. Bielefeld: Transcript Verlag, 2013.
Stoever, Jennifer. *The Sonic Color Line: Race and the Cultural Politics of Listening.* New York: New York University Press, 2016.
Thérésa. *Mémoires de Thérésa, écrits par elle-même.* Paris: E. Dentu, 1865.
Thompson, Carl. "Nineteenth-Century Travel Writing." In *The Cambridge History of Travel Writing,* edited by Nandini Das and Tim Youngs, 108–24. Cambridge: Cambridge University Press, 2019.
Truesdell, Matthew. *Spectacular Politics: Louis Napoléon and the Fête Impériale, 1849–1870.* New York: Oxford University Press, 1997.
Tunley, David, ed. *Romantic French Songs 1830–1870.* New York: Routledge, 2013.
Turnock, David. *The Historical Geography of Scotland Since 1707: Geographical Aspects of Modernisation.* Cambridge: Cambridge University Press, 2005.
Valence, Georges. *Haussmann le grand.* Paris: Flammarion, 2000.
Van Rij, Inge. *The Other Worlds of Hector Berlioz.* Cambridge: Cambridge University Press, 2015.
Vazsonyi, Nicholas. *Richard Wagner: Self-Promotion and the Making of a Brand.* Cambridge: Cambridge University Press, 2012.
Veuillot, Louis. *Les Odeurs de Paris.* Paris: J. M. Dent et fils, 1867.
Vignal, Marc, ed. *Larousse de la musique.* 2 vols. Paris: Librairie Larousse, 1982.
Vilkner, Nicole. "The Opera and the Omnibus: Material Culture, Urbanism and Boieldieu's *La Dame blanche*." *Cambridge Opera Journal* 32, no. 1 (March 2020): 90–114.
———. "Re-Examining Salon Space: Structuring Audiences and Music at Parisian Receptions." *Journal of the Royal Musical Association* (March 2022): 1–28.
Vissière, Laurent. "Les Cris de Paris: Naissance d'un genre littéraire et musicale (XII–XVe siècles)." In *Clément Janequin: Un musicien au milieu des poètes,* edited by Olivier Halévy, Isabelle His, and Jean Vignes, 87–116. Paris: Publications de la Société française de musicologie, 2013.
Walker, Jennifer. *Sacred Sounds, Secular Spaces: Transforming Catholicism Through the Music of Third-Republic Paris.* New York: Oxford University Press, 2021.
Weber, William. *Music and the Middle Class: The Social Structure of Concert Life in London, Paris, and Vienna.* 2nd ed. Aldershot: Ashgate, 2004.
White, Kimberly. "Autobiographical Voices: Performing Absence in Singers' Memoirs." *Cambridge Opera Journal* 30, nos. 2–3 (November 2018): 165–85.

Whiting, Steven Moore. *Satie the Bohemian: From Cabaret to Concert Hall.* New York: Oxford University Press, 1999.

Wigelsworth, Amy. *Rewriting "Les Mystères de Paris:" The "Mystères Urbains" and the Palimpsest.* London: Routledge, 2016.

Williams, Raymond. *The Country and the City.* Oxford: Oxford University Press, 1975.

Willson, Flora. "Classic Staging: Pauline Viardot and the 1859 *Orphée* Revival." *Cambridge Opera Journal* 22, no. 3 (November 2010): 301–26.

———. "Of Time and the City: *Don Carlos* and its Parisian Critics." *19th-Century Music* 37, no. 3 (Spring 2014): 188–210.

Yriarte, Charles. *Paris grotesque: Les célébrités de la rue.* Paris: Librairie parisienne, 1864.

Zaccone, Pierre. *Les Mystères du vieux Paris.* 3 vols. Paris: Gabriel Roux et Cassanet, 1854.

INDEX

Abbott, Helen, 121
accessibility: access to food for workers, 128; of cafés-concerts, 19; Haussmann on access to light, 6; of Second Empire song, 115
Adalbert of Bavaria, Prince, 46
Adam, Adolphe, 7, 122
Aeschylus, 61
aesthetics: of Haussmann, 10–11, 35–41, 47; Haussmannization as program of, 10; Kantian, 34, 47–48; monumentality and, 79; Napoléon III on, 3; street songs and, 114; of Wagner, 35–36, 37
Agence centrale artistique, 109, 124
À la recherche du temps perdu (Proust), 147, 176
Albert, Prince Consort of Victoria, 46
Alcazar (café-concert), 78, 80, 94, 98, 100
Alphand, Jean-Charles Adolphe, 9
Althusser, Louis, 23–24
Amblie, Charles, 64
annexed towns: Charonne, 3, 9; Ménilmontant, 3, 9, 109; Montmartre, 9, 103, 183. *See also* Belleville
Apothéose (Berlioz), 186
aqueduct system, 8
Arago, Étienne, 180
The Arcades Project (Benjamin), 99, 208n79
arcs de triomphes, 1, 58, 72, 141, 184
Ardoin et Compagnie, 49
Arènes de Lutèce, 6
Armide (Gluck), 22, 58

arrondissements (administrative districts): Paris' 1860 expansions of, 207n50. *See also* île de la Cité; Latin Quarter
L'Art musical (periodical), 60
Attali, Jacques, 84–86
Auber, Daniel François Esprit, 7, 22, 60, 64–65, 100
Ausubel, Jesse H., 192n42
Avenel, Paul, 116, 205n11
avenue des Champs-Elysées, 1, 49, 71, 72, 92f, 93, 98, 99, 182
avenue Magenta, 9
avenue Richard Lenoir, 9
avenue Victoria, 46
Ave verum corpus (Mozart), 58, 198n46

badauds (gawkers), 9, 136
Baltard, Victor, 1, 178
Balzac, Honoré de, 5, 11, 18, 97, 102
banlieue, 79
Barbier, Henri Auguste, 53
Il barbiere di Siviglia (Rossini), 8, 105
bards, 90, 91, 107, 125, 132. *See also* Béranger, Pierre-Jean de; Darcier, Joseph (Joseph Lemaire); Dupont, Pierre; Elwart, Antoine; Lhuillier, Edmond
Barrault, Alexis, 49
barrel organists, 20, 122, 123f, 125, 127, 128
Barrière, Théodore, 139
Bartholdi, Frédéric Auguste, 50
Barzun, Jacques, 30
Bataclan, 78

229

Baudelaire, Charles: cafés-concerts and, 94–95; on *casinos* of Paris, 202n43; on everyday visual phenomena of Paris, 11; *flâneurs* and, 124, 136, 137, 142; *Les Fleurs du mal,* 12; language usage and, 12, 121; "Le Mauvais vitrier" ("The Bad Glazier") (poem), 147, 152, 176; on modernity, 121; on new café, 94–95; "The Painter of Modern Life," 121, 124; pessimism of, 178; "Les Phares" (The Beacons), 12; "Salon of 1846," 12; on urban industrial modernity, 37; urban influence on, 152, 153, 157, 176; urban narrative of, 18; use of fanfare (term), 12; "Les Yeux des pauvres" (The eyes of the poor) (poem), 94–95

Bauer, E., 72

Baumann, Emmanuel, 175

Baumester, Eugène, 4, 124–25, 126f, 131–33, 206n40

Beauty: Cousin on, 34; Haussmann's conception of, 35

Beethoven, Ludwig von, 18, 47, 53, 55, 58, 198n46

Belgrand, Eugène, 9

Belle Époque, 8, 74

"La Belle polonaise" (Avenel and Chautagne), 205n11

Belleville: annexation of, 9, 129; Café de la Réunion, 109; Carnaval celebrations in, 129; *descente de la Courtille,* 129–30; Grand Café-concert de Calliope, 78; *guinguettes* in, 78; *Hommage au choral de Belleville* (1858 street song), 130. See also twentieth arrondissement

Bellini, Vincenzo, 122

Belorget, Arthur "the Countess," 98

Benedict, Burton, 75

Benini, Romain, 114

Benjamin, Walter: *The Arcades Project,* 99, 208n79; on cafés-concerts, 99; *flâneurs* and, 136, 137; on Haussmann, 34–35; on master narrative, 35; on nineteenth-century Parisian urbanism, 39; on operettas, 76; Paris as palimpsest metaphor, 37, 137, 208–9n79; on Second Empire politics, 10–11; on world exhibitions, 43, 44, 76

Béranger, Pierre-Jean de, 90, 107, 125, 135

Bergson, Henri, 116

Berlioz, Hector: airs, 198n43; *Apothéose,* 186; cantatas, 54, 197–98n43, 198n46; Church of Saint-Eustache concerts, 58; Comité de la composition musicale, 60; on *coup d'état* of 1851, 32; as a crossed career, 33; on Darcier, 91–92; *Le Dix décembre,* 197n38; *Euphonia, ou la ville musicale,* 32; *Les Francs-juges* (Berlioz), 28, 29; Gluck and, 29, 53, 58; *Grande symphonie funèbre et triomphale,* 186; Harriet Smithson and, 31; Haussmann and, 18, 19, 23, 27–32, 184; *Hymne à la France* (cantata) (Berlioz and Barbier), 53; *L'Impériale,* 33, 43, 52–59, 71, 197n38; *Mémoires,* 29, 31, 56; modernity and, 23; "monster" concert in 1844, 53; morbid nostalgia, 33; Palais de l'Industrie and, 53, 54, 55; *Sardanapale* (1830 cantata), 197–98n43; during Second Empire, 31, 33; Théâtre Lyrique and, 31–32; *Les Troyens,* 31

Bertagnolli, Paul, 199n74

Berty, Adolphe, 151

Les Bêtes savantes (Dartois), 136

Beudant, François Sulpice, 28

Biographie universelle des musiciens (Fétis), 175

Bizet, Georges, 7, 63, 64, 138, 181

Bloom, Peter, 198n43

Blum, Ernst, 100

La Bohème (Puccini), 138, 178

Boieldieu, François-Adrien, 7

Bois de Vincennes, 116, 118

Bonaparte, Louis-Napoléon: 1848 election of, 197n38; cafés-concerts and, 92–93; conversion of Paris by, 45; *coup d'état* of 1851, 19, 32; rise of, 91. See also Napoléon III, Emperor of France

Bonaparte, Napoléon. See Napoléon I, Emperor of France

Bonaparte, Prince Napoléon-Jérôme "Plon-Plon," 45, 46, 52–53, 56, 57, 60

Bonaparte, Princesse Mathilde, 22, 46

Bonapartism, 24, 74

Bonnehée, Marc, 21

Bouffes-Parisiens: of Offenbach, 38, 98, 139, 177; Thérésa at, 100

boulevard des Italiens, 120, 185
boulevard de Strasbourg, 50, 79
boulevard du Prince-Eugène: broadening of, 9; costs of, 47; expansion of 1860, 77; Haussmann on, 3; inauguration of, 1–3, 2f, 6–7, 187; renaming of, 180, 181
boulevard du Temple, 8, 10–11, 31, 77, 100, 102
boulevard Haussmann, 10, 184–85, 185f, 187
boulevards: expansion of, 9; theatrical culture of, 38
boulevard Saint-Germain, 9
boulevard Saint-Michel, 9
boulevard Sébastopol, 9
boulevard Voltaire, 180, 181
Bourbon Restoration, 27, 127, 136
Boutin, Aimée, 13, 95
Boyer, Léopold, 106
Brandus, G., 175
Bruant, Aristide, 108
Burani, Paul, 106, 107–8
Bury, Ange-Henri Blaze de, 64
Busio, Mme, 21

Cabaret de Paul Niquet, 128
cabarets, 128
cabarets artistiques, 108, 183
caf-conç, 97. *See also* cafés-concerts
café-chantant, 77. *See also* cafés-concerts
Le Café-concert: Journal hebdomadaire (newspaper), 106–8
cafés-concerts: during 1860s, 100; atmospherics of, 93–99; Baudelaire and, 94–95; behind the scenes, 99–104; Benjamin on, 99; bourgeois criticism of, 94; *casinos* as distinct from, 202n43; Casslant on, 182–83; censorship and, 109; as center of Parisian popular culture, 77–78; *chanson* repertoire and, 113; classicism and, 87–91; costumes, 89–90; critics of, 105; cross-dressing, 98; as cultural palimpsest, 82; defined, 77, 201n16; as democratic alternative to imperial urbanism, 19–20; early cafés-concerts, 91–93; Éden Comédie, 205n13; the Eldorado and, 182; embourgeoisement and, 99; foreigners and, 94; gendered norms and, 96–97, 103–4;

geographic and socioeconomic differences in, 19; geographic/temporal nature of, 19; guidebooks and, 95–96; historicizing of, 82–87; liberating of, 183; *liberté des théâtres* legislation, 104–8; Nouveau Théâtre du Château d'Eau, 205n13; O'Connor on, 201n14; odes to Paris in revues, 133; operettas at, 19; outdoor urban phenomenon and, 98–99; petition against, 78; same-sex sociability, 98; as social space, 97–98; as social wilderness, 97; sociospatial divide and, 78; uniqueness of, 78; urban planning and, 19, 77–82, 108–10. *See also* Kelm, Joseph; Lagier, Susanne; Thérésa
Les Cafés-concerts (Chadourne), 97–98
café culture: Chadourne on, 97–98; manmade technologies and, 99; natural imagery in, 99
Café de l'Annexion, 109
Café de la Réunion, 109
Café des Géants, Thérésa at, 100
Café du Cirque, 102
Café Moka, Thérésa at, 100
cafés, sonic and spatial worlds of, 7
café singers, 20
Cairns, David, 29, 92
The Cambridge Companion to the Literature of Paris (Milne, ed.), 11
camelots, 146
Canal Saint-Martin, 3, 9. *See also* tenth arrondissement
canonicity, 23, 48, 110
cantatas: as documentation, 182; media campaigns and, 3–4; on Old Paris, 5; "Le pouvoir de l'Harmonie" (1867 cantata), 208n64; propaganda and, 5
Cantate competition, 199n65
"Cantate de l'exposition," 60–61, 62–63
cantate impériale, 54
Capelle, Pierre, 113
Capet, Hugues, King of the Franks, 206n30
capitalism: canonicity and, 110; colonial capitalism, 14; Exposition universelle of 1855 and, 50; Haussmannian capitalist aesthetics, 95
Carafa, Michele, 60
Carlson, Marvin, 37

Carnaval, 129
Le Carnaval partout (1854 vaudeville act) (Lopez and Lopez), 207n55
Carré, Émile, 116
Carter, Tim, 15, 191n36
cartoons, of street musicians, 20
Carvalho, Léon, 31, 32
La Caserne de la Cité (police headquarters), 150
casinos, defined, 202n43
Casslant, L., 182–83
casualness (*sans-gêne*), 85–86
Cauchy, Augustin-Louis, 28
caveau singing, 108, 112–13
Caygill, Howard, 39
censorship: cafés-concerts and, 109; Casslant's calls for, 183; street songs and, 114; urbanism and debates about, 7; urban soundscapes and, 14
censors' reports, "Le Chemin de fer" (1867 song) (Rossini), 209n92
ceremonial music, modernist narratives of *le nouveau Paris* and, 7, 19
Certificat de bonne vie et mœurs (municipal document), 207n54
Chadourne, André, 97–98
chalet d'aisance, 204n73
Chambers, Ross, 94, 95
Champs-Élysées, Palais de l'Industrie and the, 49
Des Chansons populaires chez les anciens et chez les Français (Popular songs ancient and French) (Nisard), 111, 142
La Chanson des rues (Baumester), 125, 126f
chansonnette industry, 81, 87, 107, 108, 121, 134. *See also* Darcier, Joseph (Joseph Lemaire); Hervé (Florimond Ronger); Villebichot, Auguste de
chansonniers, 130, 138
chanson populaire genre, 107, 108
chansons réalistes, 183
La Chapelle, 109
Charlton, David, 53
Charonne, annexation of, 3, 9
Charpentier, Gustave, 178–79, 185, 186
Charpentier, Victor, 185
Château d'Eau (tenth arrondissement), 3, 78; Concerts du XIXe Siècle in, 115;

urbanization of, 78. *See also* tenth arrondissement
Chat Noir (*cabarets artistiques*), 183
Chaumont, Léon de, 135, 209n92
Chautagne, Marc, 205n11
"Le Chemin de fer" (1867 song) (Rossini), 209n92
Cherubini, Luigi, 18, 29, 30, 184
Cheval Blanc, 78
choral concerts. *See* Orphéon concerts
Choron, Alexandre-Étienne, 18, 27
Chouquet, Gustave, 60, 62, 63
Christiansen, Thomas, 176
Church of Saint-Eustache concerts, 58
Cirque de l'Impératrice, large-scale musical gatherings at, 196n23
cirque d'Hiver, 124
Cirque Impérial, 120
cities, as sets of infrastructures, 192n42
city space: idealized, homogenized uses of, 6; sonic and spatial worlds of, 7
civic heritage, urbanism and debates about, 7
Claretie, Jules, 96–97
Clark, T. J., 13
classicism: cafés-concerts and, 87–91; obsession with, 23
Clé du caveau anthology, 112–13
clowns, 128; as legal category of street performer, 127
"Le Code fashionable" (1857 song) (Vialon and Delibes), 140–42
Code Napoléon, 138
Colardelle, Michel, 131, 207n62
Cole, Ross, 179
Coleman, Jeremy, 35, 207n56
Colet, Hippolyte, 136
Collinet (cornet player), 205n23
Colombian archives, 14
colonial enslavement, 140
colonization, 39
colonnades, boulevard du Prince-Eugène, 1
la Colonne (popular tune), 4
colonnes, 112, 204n73
colporteur, 146
Comédie-Française, 89
Comettant, Oscar, 69–72
Comité de la composition musicale, 60, 62

commodification: *récit de vie de vedette* literary genre and, 203n59; of singers' personas, 203n59

Communards, 180, 181

composers, 17, 162; ambient soundscapes and, 17; *descente de la Courtille* celebration and, 129; at the Eldorado, 182; imperial canata competition and, 60, 62–63; laboring class and, 148–49; in National Guard, 181; power over sensory experience of, 18; Second Empire materialism and, 139; street hawkers and, 162; street vendors and, 178. See also *specific composers*

Les Comptes fantastiques d'Haussmann (The fantastic accounts of Haussmann) (pamphlet) (Ferry), 143, 183

conceived space, 18, 19, 32

Concert des Oiseaux, 109

Le Concert à la cour (1824 opéra-comique) (Auber), 22

concert programs, as documentation, 182

concerts, disrupted schedule of, 3

concerts, outdoor and festive, during Second Empire, 195n3

Concerts du XIXe Siècle, 115

Concerts populaires, 3, 21

Congrès de Paris, 22

Considerant, Victor, 149–50

Le Constitutionnel (periodical), 74

Contes fantastiques d'Hoffmann (The fantastic tales of Hoffmann), 143–44

contredanse movement, 118

Coppée, François, 60, 62

Coppélia (ballet) (Delibes), 139

Cormon, Eugène, 134

Corneille, Pierre, 22, 87, 89, 97

Cornélie, 87–90, 97, 99, 101, 104, 106, 108, 182

Cornut, Romain, *fils*, 60–62, 66

Così fan tutte (Mozart), 22

costumes, 89–90, 104, 109

Coubertin, Pierre de, 74

coup d'état of 1851, 1

Cousin, Victor, 12, 28, 34

Craig, William Marshall, 148

Crémieux, Hector, 139

crescendo, law of, 55

"Les Crieries de Paris" (poem) (Villeneuve), 157

les cris de Paris (cries of Paris). See cries of Paris (*les cris de Paris*)

Cries of London, 210n6

cries of Paris (*les cris de Paris*), nostalgic counternarratives and, 20

crieurs, 146

crieurs de Paris, defined, 146

Crimean War, 22, 107

cris de Paris: bourgeois fascination with, 148; disappearance of, 151–52; as noise pollution, 147; perceived/policed soundscape and, 147

Les Cris de Paris (Kastner), 213nn49–50

cris de Paris trope, 157, 163. See also street cries of 1860s Paris

cross-dressing, 98, 103

Cruvelli, Sophie, 21

Crystal Palace, 42, 44, 49, 50

cultural diversity, of Paris, 148

cultural politics, 24

cultural representations of Second Empire urbanization, visual phenomena defining, 11

culture

La Curée (The Kill) (Zola), 150

curfew, 128

Dahlhaus, Carl, 84

La Dame blanche (Boieldieu), 7

dandies, 136, 139, 140, 141, 142

Darboy, Georges, 181

Darcier, Joseph (Joseph Lemaire), 91–92, 107

Darriulat, Philippe, 139

Dartois, Armand, 136

Daumier, Honoré, 122, 123f, 125

David, Félicien, 7, 60

Davioud, Jean-Antoine-Gabriel, 9

Debord, Guy, 117

de Certeau, Michel, 112

declamation, 173, 176

Degas, Edgar, 82–84, 104

Delacour, Alfred, 134

Delacroix, Eugène, 12

Delibes, Léo, 139–42

de Lincy, Antoine Le Roux, 159

Delius, Frederick, 178
Delvau, Alfred, 129
demolition: displacements from, 9, 10; Haussmann as *artiste-démolisseur* (demolition-artist), 28, 30, 35, 40, 144, 184; as Second Empire phenomena, 11; street hawkers and, 20
"Les Démolitions de Paris, ou les joyeux maçons" (Paris demolition, or the happy masons) (song) (Pecquet), 142–43
Dentzel, Georges Frédéric, 25–26
dérive (drifting) (Debord), 117–18
Desbrières, Joseph, 4
Descendons gaiement la Courtille (Wagner), 129, 207n56
descente de la Courtille, 129–30
Desgranges, Émile, 174
Dillon, Emma, 157
d'Indy, Vincent, 181
discord, of city infrastructures, 192n42
displacements: from demolition, 9, 10; passing over, 18
Le Dix décembre (Berlioz), 197n38. See also *L'Impériale* (Berlioz)
Le Domino noir (Auber), 7
"Dona Flor" subject, 173, 213n48
Don Carlos (Verdi), 60
Donizetti, Gaetano, 7, 8
d'Ortigue, Joseph, 59, 175, 176
Doucet, Camille, 89–90, 104, 106
Doumergue, Gaston, 184–86
drag performers, 98
Dubos, 80
Duchesne, Alphonse, 87–88
Dufour, S., 175
Dulong, Pierre Louis, 28
Dumas, Alexandre (*père*), *El Salteador*, 213n48
Dumersan, Théophile Marion, 129, 136
Dupeuty, Charles-Désiré, 129, 134
Dupont, Pierre, 107
Duval, Charles, 79

L'Echo (newspaper), 106
eclecticism, 34
Eco, Umberto, 58–59
École Royale de Musique et de Déclamation, 18

economics, commentary on, 20
Éden Comédie, 205n13
"Eh! Lambert!!" (piano quadrille) (Marx), 118
Eiffel Tower, 43, 50–51
eighteenth arrondissement, 9, 103, 128, 161, 183
1812 Overture (Tchaikovsky), 71
eighth arrondissement, 128, 161
Eine Kapitulation, Lustspiel in antiker Manier (Capitulation: Comedy in the antique style) (operetta libretto) (Wagner), 38
the Eldorado: atmospherics of, 93–99; cafés-concerts and, 183; Claretie on, 96–97; Cornélie at, 87; costumes, 89–90, 104, 109; foreigners and, 94; during Franco-Prussian War, 182; gendered norms and, 96–97; Goncourt brothers on, 86; Haussmannization and, 97; Jockey-Club at, 82; Lorge and, 85, 182; monumentality of venue, 80; prestige of, 79; spectatorship at, 87–89; staging, 109; Thérésa at, 100; Veuillot on, 96
eleventh arrondissement: cafés-concerts in, 78; designated public performance spaces in, 128; medallions for, 161; renaming of boulevard du Prince-Eugène, 180, 181
Ellis, Katharine, 27
El Salteador (Dumas), 213n48
Elwart, Antoine, 208n64; on Kastner, 175; *Oeuvres musicales choisies*, 132, 208n64; "Paris!" (chanson), 132–33; "Le pouvoir de l'Harmonie," 208n64; "Salut impériale" (Lafon and Elwart), 197n35
Les Embarras de Paris (booklet) (Lanterelu), 158–59
embourgeoisement, 93, 94, 99
"Empire Means Peace" slogan, 60
L'Enfance du Christ (Berlioz), 53–54
Enlightenment, 29
entertainment sector. See cafés-concerts; theater industry
Ernani (Verdi), 22
espace conçu (conceived space), 18, 19, 32
L'Estaminet lyrique (venue), 91–92

Été movement of quadrille, 118
ethnography, 97, 151, 163, 179
Euclidean concepts of space, challenges to, 191n41
Eugène de Beauharnais, Prince, 4
Euphonia, ou la ville musicale (short story) (Berlioz), 32
Everist, Mark, 22, 47
exhibition/exhibiting city, 49
exhibition gaze, 48–49, 59
exhibition halls, within urban network, 17
Expositions universelles, 49–52; *Apothéose* (Berlioz) during, 186; attendance and advertisement, 42; Berlioz and, 33; as celebration of urban reforms, 19, 39, 42–43; first, 45; functions of, 42; hierarchies of spectatorship at, 48–49; overview, 43–47; popular demand for details about, 197n26; sensory manipulation in, 43, 48; as showcase of imperial achievements, 19, 39, 42–43; songs about industry and, 209n92; sonic monumentality and, 19. *See also specific expositions*
Exposition universelle of 1855, 196n23; admission fees, 49–50; attendance and advertisement, 42; Berlioz's *L'Impériale*, 52–59; chief administrator of, 45, 46; exhibition ball for Queen Victoria, 46; Haussmann and, 9; Haussmannization and, 159; as microcosm of Haussmannian urban planning, 46–47; monumentality and, 49–52, 72; posters, 50; Prince Napoléon and, 45, 52–53, 56, 57, 60; Salle Lacaze and, 98; showcasing Paris, 19. *See also* Palais de l'Industrie
Exposition universelle of 1867, 19, 61, 63, 208n64; attendance and advertisement, 42; cantata competition, 59–62, 63–69; ceremonial sound and, 75; closing ceremonies, 72f; Comité de la composition musicale, 60, 62; *commissaire générale* of, 65; Haussmann and, 9; "Hymne de la paix" competition, 60, 62–63; language usage and, 63; as microcosm of Haussmannian urban planning, 46–47, 76, 77, 97; monumentality and, 65–66, 68, 72–73, 80, 97; Napoléon III's speech at, 73–76; "Les Noces de Prométhée" (Cornut, fils) and, 60–62; opening and closing ceremony performance, 199n74; Parisian and imperial chauvinism, 208n64; "Le pouvoir de l'Harmonie" (1867 cantata) (Elwart), 208n64; Rossini's *Hymne à Napoléon III*, 64, 69–73; Saint-Saëns's *Les Noces de Prométhée*, 63–69
Exposition universelle of 1889, 43
Exposition universelle of 1900, Palais de l'Industrie and, 182

fanfare: Expositions universelles and, 19; Lambert as sort of, 116; *Les Noces de Prométhée* (Saint-Saëns)'s failure as, 69; for Old Paris, 19; opening fanfare of *L'Impériale*, 55; term usage, 11–14
fanfare impérial, 13
The Fantastic Tales of Hoffmann (*Contes fantastiques d'Hoffmann*), 143–44
faubourg, 79
Fauser, Annegret, 15, 35, 43, 138
Faust (Gounod), 8
La Favorite (Donizetti), 7
Ferguson, Priscilla Parkhurst, 13
Ferry, Jules, 143–44, 144
Festspielhaus, 37–38
fête impériale: amplifying spirit of, 59; Bauer on monumentality of, 72; ceremonial fanfare of, 44; classical beauty and, 74; cultural continuity and, 186; defined, 13, 182; end of, 182; reporting on, 72–73; Rossini and, 69–73
Fétis, François-Joseph, 175
fifteenth arrondissement, 9, 128, 161
fifth arrondissement, 78, 128, 161. *See also* Latin Quarter
Fifth French Republic, 182
Fifth Symphony (Beethoven), 58
Le Figaro (newspaper), 135; as critic of Paris, 87, 88; on Napoléon III's speech, 74; on renaming of boulevard du Prince-Eugène, 180; Wolff's 1879 article in, 100
filles de maisons, 102
Finale movement of quadrille, 118
fin de siècle: Greco-Roman popularity at, 73–74; music halls, 19; republicanism of, 14; spaces of spectacle and, 95, 182

first arrondissement: boulevard Haussmann and, 184; designated public performance spaces in, 128; medallions for, 161
First Empire, imperial guard veterans, 1
Flameng, Léopold, 151
Flan, Alexandre, 136
flânerie concept: aural flânerie, 173; Baudelaire on, 11, 124, 136, 137, 142; capitalism and, 148; in "Le Code fashionable" (1857 song) (Vialon and Delibes), 140–42; defined, 136; Kastner and, 169, 173, 174, 210n3; literary, 124, 139; palimpsest metaphor and, 136, 137; theatrical, 136–37
"Le Flâneur" (1816 song) (Ménétrier), 136, 136–37
le Flâneur, J. C. M. (pen name of Lanterelu), 159
"Fleur des Alpes" (song), 100
Les Fleurs du mal (Baudelaire), 12
Florimond Ronger (Hervé), 90. *See also* Hervé (Florimond Ronger)
Folies-Nouvelles, 139
folklore, 177–79, 185
Fonvielle, Arthur de, 180
foreigners, urban environment transformations and, 20
Foucault, Michel, 12–13
Fourier, Charles, 149, 150
fourteenth arrondissement, 9, 128, 161
fourth arrondissement, 78, 128, 143, 161. *See also* île de la Cité
Le Foyer (newspaper), 90, 106
Fra diavolo (Auber), 7
"France Crowning Art and Industry" (statue) (Robert), 50, 182
La France musicale (periodical), 60, 64, 69, 198n46
Franco-Prussian War, 25, 149, 180–82
Les Francs-juges (Berlioz), 28, 29
Der Freischütz (Weber), 58
"Frenchness" notion, 151, 177
French opera, 22–23. *See also* Opéra
French *opéras-comiques,* barrel organists and, 122
French *opérette. See* Offenbach
French Revolution of 1789, 5, 114, 120, 164
Frisch, Walter, 84

gagne-petits, 146
Gaîté, Thérésa at, 100
Galabert, 64
Galerie des machines, 51
Galignani's New Paris Guide for Travelers, 96
Gambetta, Léon, 38
gandins, 136
Garnier, Charles, 182
garnis, 128
Gautier, Ana María Ochoa, 14–15
gawkers (*badauds*), 9, 136
Gay-Lussac, Joseph Louis, 28
gendered norms, 96–97, 103–4
Genouillac, Henri Gourdon de, 105, 119, 122
genre: debate over, 108. *See also* chansonnette genre; *chanson populaire*
Geppert, Alexander, 49
Gerhard, Anselm, 190n12
German opera: influence of, 7. *See also* Wagner, Richard
Gesamtkunstwerk concept, 194n46
Gétreau, Florence, 131, 207n62
Gibbons, Orlando, 148
Gille, Charles, 130
Girard, Paul, 100
Gluck, Christoph Willibald: *Armide*, 22, 58; Berlioz and, 29, 53, 58; Haussmannian aesthetics and, 22–23, 47; *Orphée* revival, 47; repertory of, 7
Goehr, Lydia, 17–18
goguette(s), 79, 82, 91, 93, 98, 136
Goncourt brothers, 86, 96, 118–19
Goria, Alexandre Édouard, 21
Gounod, Charles, 7, 8, 60
Graham, Stephen, 16
Grand Café-concert de Calliope, 78
grande croisée, 9
Grande symphonie funèbre et triomphale (Berlioz), 186
grand opéra, 7
Grand Palais, 51, 182
grands boulevards: lived experiences of, 103; Parisians view of self and, 11
grands théâtres, 8, 79, 86, 87, 89, 96, 98, 182
Granveau, Antoine, 128

Great Exposition of 1851 (London), 42, 44, 45, 50
Greco-Roman antiquity, 73–74, 79, 93, 182, 199n74
greenspace, redesigning of, 9
Grétry, André-Ernest-Modeste, 148, 158
Grey, Thomas S., 38
"La Grisette du quartier Latin" (chanson) (Pégand), 138
grisettes, 136, 138, 139
Grove Music Online, 202n34
guidebooks: cafés-concerts and, 95–96; as curated catalogues, 48–49; *Mémoires de Thérésa* (Thérésa, Rochefort, Wolff, and Blum) as, 100–101; mythologizing in, 122; on Paris, 131, 134; *Paris et sa splendeur*, 79; on street hawkers, 146, 158; of street musicians, 20; for working-class pedestrians, 122
Guilbert, Yvette, 108
Guillaume Tell (Rossini), 70
guinguettes, 78, 79
Guiraud, Ernest, 199n66

Halbert d'Angers, Arthur, 4
Halévy, Ludovic, 53, 139
Handel, Georg Friedrich, 58, 198n46
harmony, of city infrastructures, 192n42
Harvey, David, 40, 95
Haussmann, Georges-Eugène "Baron": aesthetics of, 10–11, 35–41, 47; ancestors of, 25–26; anti-romanticism of, 29–30; as *artiste-démolisseur* (demolition-artist), 28, 30, 35, 40, 144, 184; Berlioz and, 18, 23, 27–32, 184; boulevard du Prince-Eugène inauguration, 3; boulevard de Strasbourg, 50; as catalyst of progress, 4; classicism and, 23, 48; colleagues and allies of, 9; control of musical circulation, 114–15; critics of, 47; debt financing of, 24, 47, 144; early life, 26–27; education of, 26–28; exhibition ball for Queen Victoria, 46, 47; as Grand Officer of the Légion d'honneur, 46; Haussmannizing by, 24; legacy of, 23; *Mémoires*, 26, 28–29, 31, 101, 128, 144, 183; modernity and, 23, 25, 101; musical influences and interests of, 18,

21–23, 40; as musician, 18, 26–35; music parties at Hôtel de Ville, 21–22; Napoléon III and, 24, 31, 40–41; Pasdeloup and, 21–22; poem dedicated to, 4; politics of spectacle, 19; as Prefect of the Seine, 3, 18, 26, 31–34, 46–47, 127, 183; public urinal installation, 204n73; rezoning the listeners and, 114; rise during Second Empire, 30–31; romanticism and, 18–19, 28–30, 40; sensory curation by, 111–12; speech at inauguration of the boulevard du Prince-Eugène, 3; systematic demolition plans of, 9; traditionalist strain of, 193n15; on urbanization of Second Empire Paris, 6; use of "Baron," 26; Wagner and, 23, 24–25, 35–41; wife of, 184. *See also* Haussmannization
Haussmann, Nicolas, 25
Haussmann, Octavie de Laharpe, 46
Haussmannian aesthetics: Gluck and, 47; Meyerbeer, Giacomo and, 47
Haussmannisation, 193n10
Haussmannism, 25
Haussmannization: as aesthetic program, 10, 98; ambivalence toward, 20; Berlioz and, 32; cafés-concerts and, 19–20, 79, 97; defined, 23–25, 24; Exposition universelle of 1855 and, 9, 159; Exposition universelle of 1867 and, 9, 97; Lambert craze and, 121; musical activity emerging from, 7; sentiment against, 122; as socioeconomic segregation, 148; theater deregulation, 104–10; utopian ideals of, 19, 76, 178. *See also* Haussmann, Georges-Eugène "Baron"; urbanization of Paris
hawkers, 147
"Hé Lambert!" (Baumaine), 115–21
"Hé! Lambert!" (Trimm), 116
Herman, Robert, 192n42
Herman Severin, Expositions universelles and, 77
Hervé (Florimond Ronger): *chansonnette* genre and, 107; as Eldorado's music director, 90, 104, 106; Folies-Nouvelles, 139; French *opérette*, 7; *Le Retour d'Ulysse* of, 90, 108, 182

Heugel, J. L., 21, 22, 36–37, 64, 68
Higonnet, Patrice, 104, 151
Histoire des livres populaires et de la littérature du colportage (History of popular books and peddled literature) (Nisard), 111
historical musicology, abstract mapping and, 17
historical soundscapes, 14, 15; Carter on, 191n36; category of, 14–15; of Paris, 15; silence, 15; urban historical musicology and, 15–16
historicity, 179
historiography, regulative work concept and, 17
History of Western Music (Norton), 82, 84
Hogarth, William, 148
homage, 130, 165, 179, 186
Hommage au choral de Belleville (1858 street song), 130
L'Hôpital des Enfants-Trouvés (orphanage), 150
Hopkins, Jerome, 33
Hostein, Hippolyte, 85
Hôtel de Ville, 18, 21–22, 33, 46, 47, 184
L'Hôtel-Dieu (hospital), 150, 151
housing, after Haussmann's renewals, 128
Hugo, Victor, 38, 138
Les Huguenots (Meyerbeer), 58, 198n46
Hymne à la France (cantata) (Berlioz and Barbier), 53
Hymne à Napoléon III et à son vaillant peuple (Rossini), 43, 64, 68, 69–71, 75
Hymne de la paix (Hymn of Peace) competition, 62, 199n65
"Hymne de la paix" competition, 62–63, 65

identity issues: of café-concert champions and detractors, 19; identity cards, 125, 199n66; identity politics, 35; imperial identity, 43; national identity, 16, 151, 186; Parisian identity, 115, 151; urban identity, 14, 18, 92, 93, 186–87
île de la Cité, 127, 149–52
"Il est retrouvé Lambert!" (1864 chanson) (Baumester), 206n40
illumination, 11
L'Illustration (periodical), 49–50
illustrations: as documentation, 182; envisioning uses of city space through, 6
imaginary space, production through art of, 18
imperial cantata competition of 1867, 59–62
imperial chauvinism, Exposition universelle of 1867 and, 208n64
L'Impériale (Berlioz), 33, 43, 52–59, 71, 197n38
imperialism, 104; Bonapartism as, 24
imperial processions: boulevard du Prince-Eugène inauguration, 1; reporting on, 200n86; reporting on order and timing of, 198n46
imperial Rome, urban reforms and, 10
imperial urbanism: cafés-concerts as democratic alternative to, 19–20; popular song industry and, 113
Impressionism, 13, 104
inaugurations: as aesthetic experience, 39; boulevard du Prince-Eugène, 1–5, 2f, 6–7, 10, 180–81, 184, 187; boulevard Haussmann, 10, 184–85, 187; concert disruptions and, 3; demolition and, 9, 10; fanfare over, 1, 12, 14, 18, 180, 181; Haussmann and, 30, 47; Napoléon III and, 19
industriels nomads, 146
infrastructure network, power structures of, 6
Introduction et rondo capriccioso op. 28 (Saint-Saëns), 68
Italian opera: barrel organists and, 122; influence of, 7. *See also* Donizetti, Gaetano; Rossini, Gioachino; Verdi, Giuseppe

Janequin, Clément, 157, 163
Janin, Jules, 45
Jardin des Tuilieries, 72
Jean de Paris (Boieldieu), 7
Jockey-Club, 82
Johnson, James, 114
Jones, Colin, 25
Josephine, Empress of France, 4
Journal des débats (newspaper), 46, 56, 71
"Judaism in Music" (Wagner), 38

Judas Maccabaeus (Handel), 58, 198n46
July Monarchy, 53, 127, 129

Kálmán, Emmerich, 138
Kant, Immanuel, 34, 47
Kastner, Jean-Georges: as aural flânerie, 210n3; Comité de la composition musicale, 60; *Les Cris de Paris,* 147, 165–77, 213nn48–51; *Les Voix de Paris,* 163–65; *Mesdames de la Halle* (opérette-bouffe) (Offenbach and Lapointe) and, 177–79; preservation of urban noise, 148
Kelm, Joseph, 124
"knowable communities," interdependency of symbolic urban spaces and, 202n40
Kolb, Katherine, 32
Kramer, Lawrence, 15
Krims, Adam, 16

Laborde, Léon de, 45
Lacaze, Salle, 98
Lafon, Achille-Louis, 53–54, 197n35
Lagier, Susanne, 124
Laharpe, Octavie de, 184
Lakmé (opera) (Delibes), 139
Lalla Roukh (*opéra-comique*) (David), 7
"L'amant d'Amanda" (Carré and Robillard), 116
Lambert cry, 118–20, 206n40. *See also* "Eh! Lambert!!" (piano quadrille) (Marx); "Hé Lambert!" (Baumaine)
Lanterelu (J. C. M. le Flâneur—pen name), 159
La Lanterne (periodical), 122
Lapointe, Armand, 177
Laronze, Georges, 28, 29–30
Latin Quarter, 28, 138
Laurance, Emily, 210n3
Le Café-concert aux Ambassadeurs (Degas), 82–84
Lecharpentier, 80
Lefébure-Wély, Alfred, 21
Lefebvre, Henri, 20; lived space, 20; representation of space, 18, 19, 20, 32–33, 104, 110; rhythmanalysis metaphor, 135; on urban spaces, 16–17, 109, 191n41, 192n42
Left Bank: Arènes de Lutèce, 6; as off limits to street performers, 127

Lefuel, Hector-Martin, 51–52
Legrand, Alexandre, 115, 118
Léhar, Franz, 138
Lehmann, Mme, 103
Lemaire, Joseph. *See* Darcier, Joseph (Joseph Lemaire)
"Le pied qui r'mue" (Avenel), 116
Lépine, Ernest, 60
Le Play, Pierre Guillaume Frédéric, 65
Lhuillier, Edmond, 107
liberalism, 104
liberté des théâtres (1864 policy), 89, 104–10
"Liberty Enlightening the World" (sculpture) (Bartholdi), 50
libretti, 17, 38, 90, 162, 186
librettists, 33, 69, 90, 139, 162, 177. *See also* Delibes, Léo
licensing, 127
Liebesverbot (Wagner), 207n56
Limayrac, Paulin, 74
liminal spaces, 7, 72, 94, 103–4, 146, 182
Liszt, Franz, 37, 54, 58, 199n70
literary elites, on street songs, 20
lived spaces, 20
Llano, Samuel, 14
Lockhart, Ellen, 139
logos, 79
London: *Cries of London* (Hogarth and Craig), 148; Gibbons, Orlando, 148; Mathew, Nicholas, 148
London Exhibition. *See* Great Exposition of 1851
London Review of Politics, Society, Literature, Art & Science (periodical), 120
Lorge, Charles Joseph Éleazar, 80, 85, 87, 89–91, 97, 108, 110, 182
Louise (opera) (Charpentier), 179, 184, 185
Louis XVIII, King of France, 136
Løvenskiold., Herman Severin, 21
Lucia di Lammermoor (Donizetti), 8
Lucie de Lammermoor (Donizetti), 7
Ludwig II of Bavaria, 37, 41
Lully, Jean-Baptiste, 22
Die lustige Witwe (Léhar), 138
Lutèce, 5–6
lyrics, as economic and political commentary, 20

Macdonald, Hugh, 53, 55, 139
Madrid, 14
magazines, mythologizing in, 122
Magda (*grisette*), 138
Magnan, Bernard Pierre, 1
Mailliard, Georges, 87
Mainardi, Patricia, 13
Manet, Édouard, 13, 18
Mangeant, Sylvain, 134
marchand de chansons, 113
marchand de contremarques, 146
marchand de fraises, 146
marchand de journaux, 146
marchand de robinets, 146
marchands ambulants, 146
marchands des comestibles, 160
Marché des Innocents, 177–78
Marcus, Sharon, 25
La Marseillaise, 186
Marvin, Simon, 16
Marx, Henry, 118, 118–19
Marx, Karl, 10, 44
Marxism, Haussmannization and, 6
Massé, Victor, 8
Massenet, Jules, 63, 181
master urban plan, 3
Mathew, Nicholas, 148
Maupassant, Guy de, 99, 100
"Le Mauvais vitrier" (The Bad Glazier) (poem) (Baudelaire), 147, 152, 176
Mead, Christopher, 48
media campaigns: cafés-concerts and, 19; empire's investment in, 3–4; idealized uses of city spaces and, 6; as narration of urban history, 7; sound documents, 13. *See also* newspaper announcements
medieval troubadour tradition, 107
Mellinet, Émile Henry, 60
Mémoires (Berlioz), 29, 31, 56
Mémoires (Grétry), 158
Mémoires (Haussmann), 26, 28–29, 31, 128, 144, 183
Mémoires de Thérésa (Thérésa, Rochefort, Wolff, and Blum), 100–104, 203n59, 203n63
memoirs: as economic and political commentary, 20; ghost-written testimonies of popular musicians, 203n59, 203n63;
mythologizing in, 122; on Paris, 131; of street musicians, 20
Le Ménestrel (periodical), 21, 36, 64, 72, 181
Ménétrier, Casimir, 136–37
Ménilmontant, 3, 9, 109
Mercadante, Saverio, 36
Mercier, Louis, 112, 148, 158
Mercure de France (periodical), 116
Mermet, Auguste, 60
Mesdames de la Halle (opérette-bouffe) (Offenbach and Lapointe), 178
Meyer, Esther da Costa, 111
Meyerbeer, Giacomo: Berlioz and, 53; Haussmannian aesthetics and, 47; *Les Huguenots*, 58, 198n46; *opéras-comiques* of, 7; Wagner and, 38
Milsom, John, 210n6
Ministère de la Maison de l'Empereur et des Beaux-Arts, theater division of, 78
Mitchell, Timothy, 49
M. Musard (Picard), 136
modernity: Berlioz and, 23; cafés-concerts and, 86; as creative-destructive, 11; Haussmann and, 23, 24–25, 94, 146; imperial notions of, 20; Lambert craze and, 120–21; Nisard on, 143; urban industrial modernity, 37; visual culture of, 13; Wagner and, 23, 24–25
modernization: nostalgia and, 10; street songs and, 114
Moïse (Rossini), 22, 58, 70, 198n46
Moke, Marie, 32
Le Monde illustré (periodical), 71
Mondelli, Peter, 195n52
Le Moniteur (newspaper), 46, 198n46
Montagne, Édouard, 90
Montmartre (eighteenth arrondissement), 9, 103, 183
Montpellier Codex, 157
monumentality: architectural monumentality, 73; Berlioz and, 31, 32; of cafés-concerts, 19; contingency and, 47–49, 59, 65; costs of community, 102; Exposition universelle of 1867 and, 61, 75; *fête impériale* and, 182; Haussmann's prioritization of, 27, 34, 144; morality and, 27; musical monumentality, 65–66; performance venues and, 77, 80, 94, 98;

social space and, 40; sonic monumentality, 19, 69; spatial monumentality, 49–52; urban monumentality, 31, 34
moral order: Carnaval and, 129; urban space and, 128–29
Mordey, Delphine, 182
Morel, Auguste, 32
Mozart, Wolfgang Amadeus, 22, 58, 198n46
municipal documents, Certificat de bonne vie et mœurs (municipal document), 207n54
Murger, Henri, 138, 150
Musard concert series, 174
musical institutions: urban policy and, 7. *See also* cafés-concerts; operettas
Musetta (*grisette*), 138
music
musical compositions, envisioning uses of city space through, 6
musical entertainment: cafés-concerts, 201n14, 201n16, 202n43; *casinos*, 202n43. *See also* musicians, working-class; patrons; singers
musical genres: of 1850s and 1860s, 7; revival of older repertoires, 7
musical history, intersecting of urban history and, 7
musical monumentality, 65–66
musical press: on canonicity, 23; during Franco-Prussian War, 181; on Haussmann's concerts, 18. *See also specific periodicals*
musical scores, tracing social construction of urban space through, 17
music geography, 16. *See also* urban historical musicology
music halls, 108; cafés-concerts as prequel to, 19
musicians, urban policy debates and, 7
musicians, working-class: conditions of, 203n63; lived experiences of, 17. *See also* street musicians
Music of the Nineteenth Century (Frisch), 84
musicology: on Haussmannization, 25. *See also* urban historical musicology
mythmaking: cafés-concerts and, 104; double myth, 144; Exposition universelle of 1867 and, 61; *grisette* and, 138; Haussmann and, 36, 40, 144; of "new Paris, 13; of Old Paris, 151; Parisian modernity and, 179; of Paris/London competition, 45; *Scènes de la vie de bohème* (Murger) and, 150; of Second Empire's prosperity, 144; street performers and, 122–24, 145; urban historical musicology and, 8, 15; Wagner and, 35–36

Nadar, 9
Nadaud, Gustave, 37, 144–45
Napoléon I, Emperor of France: Bonapartism and, 24; *Code Napoléon*, 138; decrees on licensed theaters, 89; Dentzel and, 26; first wife of, 4; Marx on, 44; Ménétrier's songs celebrating, 136; stepson of, 1
Napoléon III, Emperor of France: boulevard inauguration during Second Empire of, 1–2; capture of, 180; "Empire Means Peace" slogan, 60; end of reign, 39; at exhibition ball for Queen Victoria, 46; Exposition universelle of 1855 and, 45, 46; Haussmann and, 24, 31, 40–41; Lafon's paean to, 197n35; Marx on, 44; music and, 195n3; Palais de l'Industrie competition, 49; Paris as monument to legacy of, 40; as president, 197n38; Princesse Mathilde as cousin of, 22, 46; as Promethean hero, 61–62; speech at Exposition universelle of 1867, 73–76; speech at inauguration of the boulevard du Prince-Eugène, 3; Thérésa at Tuileries for, 100; urbanism as social good, 150; on urbanization of Second Empire Paris, 3
narrator/city connection, 132
national identity, 16, 151, 186
nationalism, in nineteenth-centure Europe, 16
networked spaces: defining of, 17. *See also* boulevards; cafés; exhibition halls
newspaper announcements, media campaigns and, 3–4
newspaper reviews, of street musicians, 20

newspapers: reports on imperial processions, 200n86. *See also specific newspapers*
New York Times (newspaper), 117
nineteenth arrondissement, 9, 128, 161
Nineteenth-Century Music (Dahlhaus), 84
Ninon (*grisette*), 138
ninth arrondissement: boulevard Haussmann and, 184; cafés-concerts in, 78; designated public performance spaces in, 128; medallions for, 161. *See also* Opéra
Ninth symphony (Beethoven), 198n46
Nisard, Charles, 111–14, 119, 142–43, 205n14
Les Noces de Jeannette (Massé), 8
"Les Noces de Prométhée" (Cornut, fils), 60, 61–62
Les Noces de Prométhée (Saint-Saëns): acoustics and, 75; for closing ceremony, 43; comparison to, 70, 71; as competition winner, 62–69; Liszt performance, 199n70
Noise (Attali), 85
noise pollution, 17
Norblin, Émile, 60
Nord, Philip G., 23
nostalgia: counternarrative to modernity, 147; fantasies of, 39; Haussmann and, 40; *Les Cris de Paris* (Kastner) and, 165; modernity and, 162, 179; morbid nostalgia, 33; for Old Paris, 19, 20, 124, 142–45, 151; songs and, 142–45; street cries and, 20; street musicians and, 124, 133, 151, 165, 179; urbanization and, 124, 142. *See also* Old Paris; preservation
Notre-Dame de Paris, 6, 150
le nouveau Paris: emergence of, 13; Expositions universelles showcase of, 19, 48; modernist narratives of, 7; popular music and, 131; in song, 131–42, 142–45. *See also* Paris
Nouveau Théâtre du Château d'Eau, 205n13
Nouvelle Lutèce district, 6
"La Nuit: Le cauchemar" (The night: Nightmare) (de Maupassant), 99

O'Connor, Patrick, 201n14
Les Odeurs de Paris (Veuillot), 96

Oeuvres musicales choisies (collection) (Elwart), 132, 208n64
Offenbach, Jacques, 177; Benjamin and, 39; Bouffes-Parisiens, 98, 139, 177; French *opérette*, 7; Macdonald on musicological shift of, 139; *Mesdames de la Halle*, (1858 one-act opérette-bouffe), 177–78; Mondelli on, 195n52; operettas of, 201n14; popular theater industry and, 98; Second Empire Paris and, 186; *Tales of Hoffmann* (opera), 143–44; Wagner and, 38, 195n52
Old Paris: arrondissements of, 210n8; as check on Second Empire, 147; disappearance of, 124, 151–52; literary trope of, 4; nostalgia and, 39, 124, 144; remnants predating, 6; social and cultural customs of, 19; in song, 142–45; sweeping away of, 4–5. *See also* nostalgia; Paris; preservation; *le vieux Paris*
Olympic Games, 73, 74
"On n' s'amuse qu'à Paris" (One has the most fun in Paris) (Renard), 117
On the True, the Beautiful, and the Good (*Du vrai, du beau, et du bien*) (Cousin), 34
Opéra, 89; in 1862 season, 7; Berlioz and, 31; Casslant as inspector general of, 182–83; Choron as regisseur of, 27; elite patrons of, 158; grandiosity of, 77; *Hymne à Napoléon III* and, 71; Meyerbeer and, 47; mode of spectatorship of, 88–89; overrepresentation of, 16; Palais Garnier, 9; perennial programming of, 98; political power networks and, 10, 17, 192n42; Royer as director of, 101; singers at, 158; Wagner and, 37
opera: *Les Francs-juges* (Berlioz), 28, 29; urbanization of, 8
opéra bouffe model, of Offenbach, 38
Opéra-Comique, in 1862 season, 7
opera houses: during Franco-Prussian War, 182; within urban network, 17
opera libretti, 38, 162
opéras-comiques: in 1850s and 1860s Paris, 7; barrel organists, 122; *Le Concert à la cour* (1824) (Auber), 22
opera singers, 21

242 · INDEX

operetta, emphasis on, 201n14
opérette-bouffe model, 177
operrettas, at cafés-concerts, 19
L'Opinion nationale (periodical), 64, 96–97
L'Orchestre (periodical), 125
order: Berlioz and, 30; at the Eldorado, 97; habits of, 3; Haussmann's obsession with, 10, 18, 27, 33–34, 39, 40, 41, 144; moral order, 27, 39, 128; vocal clarity and, 74–75
orgue de Barbarie. *See* barrel organists
Orphée (Gluck), 47
Orphéon concerts, 7, 62–63, 130, 196n23
Osborne, Richard, 71
"Osmanomanie" (1868 song) (Nadaud), 144–45
othering, 151–52
Ouzounian, Gascia, 17, 191n41
Oxford History of Western Music (Taruskin), 84

Pacini, Émilien, 69
"The Painter of Modern Life" (Baudelaire), 121, 124
Palais de Beaux-Arts, 51–52
Palais de l'Industrie: acoustics of, 64, 66, 75; Berlioz and, 53, 54, 55, 56; closing ceremonies, 52–59; competition with London, 50; destruction of, 182; documentation on, 182; Exposition universelle of 1855 and, 42; façade, 50, 51f; during Franco-Prussian War, 181; Galerie des machines, 51; Orphéon concerts, 196n23; Palais des Beaux-Arts, 51–52; performance space of, 59; size of, 50; spatial monumentality and, 49–52
Palais des Champs-Élysées, 71
Palais Garnier, 9, 184
palimpsest(s), 37, 137, 143, 208–9n79
pamphlets, envisioning uses of city space through, 6
Pantalon movement of quadrille, 118
Parc de Saint-Cloud, 182
Paris: Ardoin et Compagnie partnership with, 49–50; Benjamin on, 11; British on antisocial social spaces of, 93–94; Chaumon on parallel realities of, 135–36; conceived as work of art, 18; expansion of 1860, 9, 207n50; Haussmann on, 128; modernization of, 131; musical culture of, 20; as noisy, 134; palimpsest metaphor, 37, 137, 208–9n79; rebuilding as showcase and monument, 19; urban identity of literati of, 92–93; visual culture of, 10–11; Wagner's attempted lampoon of, 195n54. *See also* Expositions universelles; *le nouveau Paris*; Old Paris
"Paris!" (chanson) (Elwart), 132–33
"Paris" (song) (Baumester), 131–32
Paris (symphonic nocturne) (Delius), 178
"Paris, Capital of the Nineteenth Century" (Benjamin), 34–35
Paris, Siege of, 180
Paris Commune, 39, 180, 181, 182
Paris en chansons: sous la direction de Comte, 154f
Paris grotesque (Yriarte), 124
Paris-guide (Sand), 103
Parisian chauvinism, 1867 Exposition universelle and, 208n64
Parisian identity, 115, 151
Le Parisien (newspaper), 179
"Paris la nuit" (stage play) (Dupeuty and Cormon), 134–35
"Paris nouveau: Le boulevard du Prince-Eugène" (poem) (Desbrières), 4
"Paris qui rit et Paris qui pleure" (Paris laughing and Paris weeping) (chanson) (Chaumont), 135
Paris qui s'en va, Paris qui vient (periodical), 151
Pasdeloup, Jules, 3, 21, 184
Pasler, Jann, 16, 85, 151, 186, 206n44
Passage Choiseul, 98
pastoral literary representations, contrasts to, 202n40
Pastourelle movement of quadrille, 118, 119, 205n23
pathos, 79
patrons, 114; behavior of, 203n63
Patti, Adelina, 8, 101
La Peau du chagrin (Balzac), 11
Pecquet, Eléonore, 142
peddlers, 159–61

Pégand, Eugène, 138
Pénet, Martin, 109
Penna-Spada, 106, 107
Père Lachaise cemetery, 182
performance venues: gendered norms of, 96–97; recentralization of, 183; within urban network, 17. *See also* exhibition halls
performers, representations of, 20
Perreymond (pseudonym), 149–50
perspective, 11; in Exposition universelle of 1855 and 1867, 46
Le Petit journal (periodical), 116
Petit Palais, 51
petits métiers, 146
petits théâtre, 106
Peuchot, Léon, 152–57, 154f
phantasmagoria, 11, 39
"Les Phares" (The Beacons) (Baudelaire), 12
photos, as documentation, 182
Picard, M. L. B., 136
Picon, Antoine, 197n26
Pinon, Pierre, 144
pissoirs, 111, 204n73
place de Grève, 143
place de la Concorde, 72
place de la Nation (formerly place du Trône), 1, 180
place de la République (formerly place du Château d'Eau), 1, 180
place de l'Hôtel de Ville, 46
place du Château d'Eau (currently place de la République), 1, 3, 9, 115, 180
place du Châtelet, 8, 46
place du Trône (currently place de la Nation), 1, 180
placemaking, 15, 16, 39, 79, 191n41
Pleyel, Camille, 32
poems: envisioning uses of city space through, 6; media campaigns and, 3–4; "Paris nouveau: Le boulevard du Prince-Eugène" (poem) (Desbrières), 4
policing: Casslant's calls for, 183; establishing moral order, 128; *fanfare impérial* and, 13; increase in, 93; peddlers and, 159–61; street music and, 125, 126, 127–31; street musicians and, 20; urban historical musicology and, 16

politics: cafés-concerts and, 201n16; commentary on, 20; cultural politics, 24; Haussmann's politics of spectacle, 19; identity politics, 35; Lambert craze and, 120–21; of mediation, 14; narrator/city connection, 132; of placemaking, 16; regulation and, 18; of representation, 16, 20, 114; Second Empire aesthetics linked with, 10
Poniatowski, Prince Józef Michał, 60
Pont Neuf, 6, 78, 127
popular entertainment: cafés-concerts as, 19. *See also* cafés-concerts
popular music, modernist narratives of *le nouveau Paris* and, 7
popular song industry, 112–13; imperial urbanism and, 113; increasing popularity of, 124; politics and, 20; popular culture and, 113. *See also* "Hé Lambert!" (Baumaine)
posters: envisioning uses of city space through, 6; Exposition universelle of 1855, 50; media campaigns and, 3–4
Le Postillon de Lonjumeau (Adam), 7
Poule movement of quadrille, 118, 205n23
"Le pouvoir de l'Harmonie" (1867 cantata) (Elwart), 208n64
power: fanfare and, 12, 13–14; Haussmannization as cultural power, 24; to produce space, 18; regulation and, 18
power structures, 6, 8
pre-Haussmannian Paris, 5
Prendergast, Christopher, 13
preservation, 6, 122, 145, 148, 151, 162, 179. *See also* Kastner; nostalgia; Old Paris
press: media campaigns and, 3–4; press reviews of Haussmann's soirées, 22–23; term usage of *haussmannisé* by, 24. *See also* musical press; *specific newspapers*
La Presse (newspaper), 56, 72
Prévost, Hippolyte, 64, 69
printed materials, Haussmann's effort to curb unsanctioned, 112
La Prisonnière (Proust), 147, 156–57, 176, 177
Prometheus, 61, 66, 67, 74
Prometheus Bound (Aeschylus), 61–62
Prometheus myth, 61

propaganda, cantatas and, 5
prose descriptions, as documentation, 182
Proust, Marcel, 174, 176–77; *La Prisonnière*, 147, 156–57, 176, 177; urban narrative of, 18
Prussia: Franco-Prussian War, 180, 181; Siege of Paris of 1870, 180
Psyché (Thomas), 22
public policy, Third Republic's use of musical activity to promote, 206n44
public restrooms, 204n73
public urinals, 204n73
Puccini, Giacomo, 138

quadrilles, 118
quai aux Fleurs, 150
quartier(s), 28, 79, 98, 138, 184

Racine, Jean-Baptiste, 87–89, 97
Rameau, Jean-Philippe, 148, 157–58
Ramée, Daniel, 39–40
Ramond, 68
Reber, Napoléon Henri, 60
recentralization of performance venues, Casslant's calls for, 183
récit de vie de vedette literary genre, 203n59
rectilinear urban space: consequences of, 20; *flânerie* concept and, 142; Haussmann and, 6, 10, 18; progress and, 7
Les Refrains de la rue (Genouillac), 119, 122
regulation: political power networks and, 18; urban historical musicology and, 16
regulative work concept, historiography and, 17–18
Rehding, Alexander, 47–48
Reicha, Anton, 18, 28, 184
Renard, Jules, 117
Renard, Paul, 183
representation, of street cries, 20
representation of space (conceived space), 13, 18, 19, 32
representation(s): of cafés-concerts, 99; cultural representations of Second Empire urbanization, 11; Expositions universelles and, 52, 60; Mitchell on, 49; nostalgic representation, 157; politics of, 16, 113–14; soundscapes as, 14–15; of street cries, 163; of street peddlers,

157; symphonic representation, 65; of urban landscape, 14; of urban life, 20, 187, 202n40. *See also* soundscapes
restrooms, for women, 204n73
Le Retour d'Ulysse (Hervé), 90, 108, 182
revolution of 1830, 5, 127, 144
revolution of 1848, 5, 19, 91, 92–93, 144, 182, 197n38
Revue et gazette musicale de Paris (periodical), 22, 58, 60, 175, 181
revues, 133–34
rhythmanalysis metaphor, 135
"Richard Wagner and *Tannhäuser* in Paris, 202n43
Right Bank (Paris): boulevard du Prince-Eugène, 1; cafés-concerts venues on, 78; domestic servant jobs in, 103; the Eldorado, 80; as off limits to street performers, 127; performance spaces of, 77
Le Rire (Bergson), 116
Robert, Élias, 50, 182
Robillard, Victor, 116
Rochefort, Henri, 100
Roger, Gustave-Hippolyte, 21
"Le roi des rois" (The king of kings) (1830 air), 198n43
romanticism: of Berlioz, 28–29; effects on city from, 10; Haussmann and, 18–19, 28–30, 40; music predating, 18–19; narrator/city connection, 132
Roméo et Juliette (Vaccai), 22
La Rondine (Puccini), 138
Ronger, Florimond, 90. *See also* Hervé (Florimond Ronger)
Rossini, Gioachino: *Il barbiere di Siviglia*, 8, 105; "Le Chemin de fer" (1867 song), 209n92; Comettant on, 69–72; Comité de la composition musicale, 60; *Guillaume Tell*, 70; *Hymne à Napoléon III et à son vaillant peuple*, 43, 64, 68, 69–71, 75; *Moïse*, 22, 58, 70, 198n46; *Seriramis*, 70; *Le Siège de Corinthe*, 70; Wagner's essay on, 36, 38
Rousseau, 164
Royer, Alphonse, 100, 101
rue Chanoinesse, 150
rue du Château d'Eau, 115
rue du Faubourg Saint-Honoré, 72

rue de Rivoli, 3, 9, 72, 120
"La Rue de Rivoli" (1856 song) (Chaumont), 209n92
rue de Turbigo, 3, 9
rue Drouot, 185
rue du Cloître Notre-Dame, 150
rue du Faubourg Poissonnière, 98
rue Lafayette, 3, 9
rue Saint-Martin, 159
Rushton, Julian, 55

SACEM (Société des auteurs, compositeurs et éditeurs de musique), 124
Saint-Beuve, Charles Augustin, 12
Saint-Napoléon holiday, 44, 54, 71, 119
Saint-Saëns, Camille: imperial commission's plans and, 75; Liszt's congratulations to, 199n70; in National Guard, 181; *Les Noces de Prométhée*, 43, 62–69, 70, 71, 75, 199n70
"Salon of 1846" (Baudelaire), 12
salons: cafés-concerts and, 86, 93, 94, 98, 100; as controlled urban spaces, 94, 98; embourgeoisement and, 93, 94; gendered norms of, 86; Haussmann and, 22; "Lambert" (cry) in, 118, 121; *Mémoires de Thérésa* and, 100; music and, 8; musicmaking for, 175; "Osmanomanie" (1868 song) (Nadaud) and, 144–45; poetic salons, 22; of Princesse Mathilde Bonaparte, 22, 46; ritualized activities of, 93; "Salon of 1846" (Baudelaire), 12; Vilkner on, 22
"Salut impériale" (Lafon and Elwart), 197n35
same-sex sociability, 98
Sand, George, 102, 103, 138
sans-gêne (casualness), 85–86
Sarasate, Pablo de, 68
Sarcey, Francisque, 89, 99–100
Sardanapale (1830 cantata) (Berlioz), 197–98n43
Sax, Adolphe, 213n50
saxophones, 213n50
Scènes de la vie de bohème (Murger), 150
Schafer, R. Murray, 17
Schaff, P., 90
Schneider, Hortense, 101

scie parisienne or (Parisian saw), 116. *See also* "Hé Lambert!" (Baumaine)
Scott, Derek, 86, 116
Scudo, Paul, 22
seasonal venues, 98
second arrondissement, 128, 161
Second Empire, 10–11; boulevard inauguration during, 1; broader liberalization of, 183; bureaucrats of, 114; cafés-concerts and, 87, 201n16; collapse of, 9, 122; concerts and, 195n3; *coup d'état* of 1851, 1; cultural politics of, 24; Delibes and, 139; the Eldorado and, 182; habits of high society in, 20; Haussmannization during, 24; modernity during, 13; music and, 7; politics and culture of urbanization in, 8, 10–11; rebuilding of Paris and, 19; sensory curation in, 186; *utilité publique* concept during, 206n44
Second French Republic, 91, 93, 197n38
Sedan, Battle of, 180
Seigel, Jerrold, 138
Seine: Department of the, 149–50; Haussmann as Prefect of the, 3, 18, 26, 31–34, 46–47, 127, 183; Palais de l'Industrie and the, 49; Prefecture of the, 47, 128, 150, 179
Sennett, Richard, 81
sensory curation: cafés-concerts and, 19–20; *fête impérial* and, 182
sensual immediacy/silence dichotomy, 15
Seriramis (Rossini), 70
seventeenth arrondissement, 9, 128, 161
seventh arrondissement, 128, 161
sewer system, 8–9, 42, 184
Le Siège de Corinthe (Rossini), 70
Siege of Paris of 1870, musical industry during, 181
silence, sensual immediacy/silence dichotomy, 15
singers: as legal category of street performer, 127; restricted hours for, 128–29
singers' personas: commodification of, 203n59. *See also* Thérésa
sixteenth arrondissement, 9, 128, 161
sixth arrondissement, 128, 161
Smithson, Harriet, 31
social Darwinism, 142

Société des auteurs, compositeurs et éditeurs de musique (SACEM), 124
Société des Colonnes Doriot, 204n73
Société de secours, 181
socioeconomics groups, cafés-concerts and, 19
songs: as documentation, 182; media campaigns and, 3–4; narrating alternative urban experiences, 121; on Paris, 131; *scie parisienne* or (Parisian saw), 116; as sound documents, 13; "Souvenir du Prince-Eugène" (Baumester), 3–4; unique position among cultural artifacts of, 207n62; urban environment transformations and, 20. *See also* popular song industry; street songs
song texts, tracing social construction of urban space through, 17
songwriters, 114, 162
sonic monumentality, 19, 69; Expositions universelles and, 19
sound: documents of, 13; fanfare, 11–14; musical rendering of, 17
sound artists, Lefebvre on, 191n41
soundscapes: Carter on, 191n36; defined, 14; regulation and, 125, 126; as representation, 15; World Soundscape Project, 17. *See also* historical soundscapes; urban soundscapes
sound worlds: during Franco-Prussian War, 182; historical soundscapes, 14, 15; modernist narratives of *le nouveau Paris* and, 7
"Souvenir du Prince-Eugène" (Baumester), 4
spectacle(s): Haussmann's politics of, 19, 40; Haussmann's aesthetic of, 113; Haussmann's hosting of, 21; *Lambert* and, 117–18; Lambert craze and, 120–21; Lorge's recasting of, 97; of *nouveau Paris*, 97; of popular musical industry, 124; street songs as, 111
Spontini, Gaspare, 53, 176
staging, 109
stars. *See* Bruant; Guilbert; Paulus; Piaf
star system: Burani on, 107–8; street musicians and, 124
Statue of Liberty ("Liberty Enlightening the World") (Bartholdi), 50

Steingo, Gavin, 148
straight lines. *See* rectilinear urban space
street commerce, 148
street cries: counternarrative to modernity, 20; *cris de Paris*, 146–49; *Les Cris de Paris* (symphony) (Kastner) and, 165–75; hawkers, 152–57; île de la Cité and, 149–52; Kastner and, 163–77, 179; *Mesdames de la Halle*, (1858 one-act opérette-bouffe) (Offenbach and Lapointe) and, 177–78; musicology of, 147; peddlers and, 159–62; police and, 159–62; as urbanized commodity, 148; *le vieux Paris* and, 157–59, 179; *Les Voix de Paris* (Kastner), 175–77, 178
street cries of 1860s Paris, 175–76. *See also cris de Paris* trope
street hawkers: defined, 146; in poetry, fiction, and song, 152–57, 170; as victims of urban demolition, 20. *See also* street musicians
street instrumentalists: as legal category of street performer, 127; restricted hours for, 128–29
street music, 111–15; cafés-concerts and, 113; *Clé du caveau* anthology, 112–13; collections of, 111–12; "Hé Lambert!" (Baumaine), 115–21; Llano on, 14; *le nouveau Paris* and, 131–42; policing and, 125, 126, 127–31; politics of representation and, 113–14; street musicians, 122–26; *le vieux Paris* and, 142–45
street musicians: barrel organists, 20, 122, 125, 127, 128; effects of urbanization on, 122; as ironic urban heroes, 20; lived experiences of, 17; policing and, 20; representations of, 20; star system and, 124; tourist guidebooks, 20. *See also* Baumester, Eugène
street performers: legal categories of, 127; reforms regarding, 127–28. *See also* barrel organists; singers
street-song industry, exploding of, 13
street songs: *Des Chansons populaires chez les anciens et chez les Français* (Popular songs ancient and French) (Nisard), 111; *Histoire des livres populaires et de la littérature du colportage* (History of

street songs *(continued)*
  popular books and peddled literature) (Nisard), 111; literary elites on, 20; sociopolitical communities and, 114–15
Strohm, Reinhard, 15
Sue, Eugène, 138
Sylvia (ballet) (Delibes), 139
symmetry: Berlioz and, 30; of boulevards, 81; cafés-concerts and, 97–98; Haussmann's obsession with, 10, 18, 28, 30, 175; Western fixations on, 17
"Symphony in D" (Saint-Saëns), 68

Tableau de Paris (Mercier), 112, 158
Tannhäuser (Wagner), 35, 82
Taruskin, Richard, 84
Tchaikovsky, Piotr, 71
Temple Bar (periodical), 119–20
Le Temps (newspaper), 180, 200n86
tenements, demolishing of, 9
tenth arrondissement: cafés-concerts in, 78, 115; designated public performance spaces in, 128; medallions for, 161. *See also* Canal Saint-Martin; Château d'Eau
Texier, Edmond, 86
theater industry: censorship and, 183; compartmentalization in, 77; deregulation of, 104–10; during Franco-Prussian War, 181; liberation from licensing and generic restrictions in 1864, 183; policing and, 183; for recentralization of performance venues, 183; *théâtres secondaires,* 89. *See also* cafés-concerts; *grands théâtres*
Théâtre de l'Ambigu-Comique, 134
Théâtre de la Porte Saint-Martin, 99
Théâtre des Variétés: *Le Carnaval partout* (1854 vaudeville act) (Lopez and Lopez) at, 207n55; *Souvenirs de jeunesse* revue, 134
Théâtre-Italien, 8, 54
Théâtre Lyrique, 5, 8, 21, 31–32, 47, 77
théâtres secondaires, 89
theatrical deregulation, urbanism and debates about, 7
Théaulon, Emmanuel, 136
Thenard, Louis Jacques, 28

Thérésa, 89, 99–104, 107–8, 124, 183, 203n59, 203n63
Thierry, Édouard, 169, 213n48
Thiers, Adolphe, 47
third arrondissement, 128, 161
Third Republic: cafés-concerts and, 85, 87, 183, 201n16; civic spaces of, 16; Delibes and, 139; Greco-Roman tradition and, 73–74; infrastructure network of, 16; sensory curation in, 186; Thiers as president of, 47; urban reforms and, 186; use of musical activity in, 206n44; *utilité publique* concept during, 206n44
thirteenth arrondissement, 9, 128, 161
Thomas, Ambroise, 22, 60
timbres, 113
time: canonicity and, 23. *See also* urban time
Tinan, Jean de, 116
tonality, 67, 132, 173, 175–76
Tonkünstler Versammlung festival, 199n70
Torrens, W. M., 25
tourist guidebooks, on street musicians, 20
Le Tribunal de Commerce (municipal court), 150
Trimm, Timothée, 100–101, 116–17
triumphal arches: *arc de triomphe éphémère* (Baltard), 1; as stage, frame, monument, 1
trottins, 136
troubador tradition, 107
Les Troyens (Berlioz), 31
Truesdell, Matthew, 46, 52
trumpets, underground tunnel tours and, 9
Tuileries Palace, 46, 100
tunnels, as tourist attraction, 8–9, 42, 184
Turnock, David, 25
twelfth arrondissement, 9, 128, 161
twentieth arrondissement, 3, 9, 128, 129, 161. *See also* Belleville
type parisien, 122, 135–36, 139

underground urban spaces, 8–9, 42, 184
Union des artistes lyriques des cafés-concerts, 109
urban aesthetics, 6; extensions of, 10; Haussmannization and, 6, 20
urban amenities, redesigning of, 9

urban demolitions. *See* demolition
urban development: byproducts of, 5; cantatas on, 5
urban historical musicology: categories of analysis, 16–17; defined, 15–16; historical sound studies and, 15; nationalism and, 16; urban space and, 147
urban history, intersecting of musical history and, 7
urban identity, 14, 18, 92, 93, 186–87
urban infrastructure network: boulevards in, 3; Expositions universelles and, 9; studies of, 16
urbanism: Benjamin on, 39; censorship and, 7; civic heritage and, 7; government conceptions of, 17; imperial urbanism, 19–20; regulative work concept and, 17–18; theatrical deregulation and, 7
urbanization, effects on street musicians of, 122
urbanization of Paris, 124; effects on musical life, 20; effects on street performers, 124; Haussmann as chief overseer of, 3; Heugel on demolition and, 37; Napoléon III and, 39; Napoléon III on, 3; palimpsest metaphor and, 37, 208–9n79; poetics of, 8–11; as social Darwinism, 142; as theatrical performance, 1; urban identity and, 18; visual phenomena defining representation of, 11. *See also* Haussmannization; master urban plan
urban labor, moral order and, 128
urban life: Lefebvre on, 17; politics of representing, 20
urban literary representations, contrasts to, 202n40
urban modernity, obsession with classicism and, 23
urban planning: actual use and, 6; cafés-concerts and, 19, 77–82, 108–10; decisions shaping, 7; rectilinear nature of, 20
urban policy: musical institutions and, 7; urban historical musicology and, 15
urban renewal: cantatas glorifying, 5; visual spectacles of, 11

urban renovation, Haussmannization and, 25
urban semiotic, 111
urban soundscapes, 6; censorship and, 14
urban space
urban spaces: defining of networked, 17; Ferry on Haussmann parceling out, 144; Haussmannization and, 6; infrastructure network in, 6; interdependency of "knowable communities" and symbolic, 202n40; Lefebvre on, 16–17, 191n41; Parisians' use of, 11; power to produce, 18; rectilinear and symmetrical design in, 10; regulation of, 120; representations of, 14; right for existence of, 109; salons as controlled, 94, 98; socioeconomics of, 8; underground spaces, 8–9, 42, 184
urban symmetry, Haussmann and, 18
urban time, Haussmannization and, 6
urinals, public, 111, 204n73
utilité publique, concept of, 206n44
utopian ideals: of capitalistic urbanism, 147; of community, 124; Expositions universelles and, 75, 76; Fourier's disciples and, 149; of Haussmannization, 19, 76, 178; public works projects, 142

Vaccai, Nicola, 22
Vacquer, Théodore, 6
Vaillant, Jean-Baptiste Philibert, 103
Valance, Georges, 29
Valencienne (*grisette*), 138
Valentin, Jules, 87
Valladon, Emma, 99. *See also* Thérésa
vaudeville, 7, 82, 88f, 129
Das Veilchen vom Montmartre (Kálmán), 138
veiling, 11
venues, geographic differences in, 19
Verbrugghen, Henri, 58
Verdi, Giuseppe, 7, 22, 60, 87
Véron, Pierre, 71
Veuillot, Louis, 96, 97
Vialon, Antoine, 140–42
Viardot, Pauline, 32
Victoria, Queen of Great Britain, 46
"La Vie de Paris" (Lambert-Thiboust and Delacour), 134, 208n68

Viel, Jean-Marie-Victor, 49
le vieux Paris, 4; emerging idea of, 147; popular music and, 131. *See also* Old Paris
le vieux Paris and, cultural remnants of, 85
Villebichot, Auguste de, 107
Villemain, 28
Villeneuve, Guillaume de la, 157
Vive l'Empereur (chant), 3, 56, 71, 75, 120
vocal pedagogy, 148
Voltaire, 180

Wagner, Richard: aesthetics of, 37; anti-Semitism of, 38; anti-urbanism of, 38; Baudelaire on music of, 202n43; *Descendons gaiement la Courtille,* 129; *Eine Kapitulation, Lustspiel in antiker Manier* (Capitulation: Comedy in the antique style) (operetta libretto), 38; essay on Rossini, 36, 38; *Gesamtkunstwerk* concept, 194n46; Haussmann and, 19, 23, 24–25; Heugel on, 36–37; influence of, 7, 24; "Judaism in Music," 38; *Liebesverbot,* 207n56; Ludwig II of Bavaria and, 37, 41; modernity and, 23; Mondelli on, 195n52; Napoléon III and, 38; nationalism of, 38; Paris and, 35, 37, 38; Parisian carnival season and, 207n56; reputation of, 195n54; *Tannhäuser* premiere, 35, 82
Wagnerism, 23, 24, 36
war(s): cantatas in propaganda on, 5; celebrations of, 69; Crimean War, 22, 107; d'Indy on sounds of, 181; Franco-Prussian War, 25, 149, 180–82; World's Fairs and, 75
water works, redesigning of, 9
Weber, Eugen, 14, 29, 47, 53, 58
Weber, William, 82
Weelkes, Thomas, 148
Williams, Raymond, 202n40
Wolff, Albert, 100
workers: Coppée on toils of, 60; displaced by demolishing of tenements, 9, 149; stratification of social space and, 102–3, 149; working conditions of, 203n63. *See also* street hawkers
World's Fairs, 43, 44, 61. *See also* Expositions universelles; Great Exposition of 1851 (London)
World Soundscape Project, 17

"Les Yeux des pauvres" (The eyes of the poor) (poem) (Baudelaire), 94–95
Yriarte, Charles, 124

Zola, Émile, 18, 102, 150, 178

Founded in 1893,
UNIVERSITY OF CALIFORNIA PRESS
publishes bold, progressive books and journals
on topics in the arts, humanities, social sciences,
and natural sciences—with a focus on social
justice issues—that inspire thought and action
among readers worldwide.

The UC PRESS FOUNDATION
raises funds to uphold the press's vital role
as an independent, nonprofit publisher, and
receives philanthropic support from a wide
range of individuals and institutions—and from
committed readers like you. To learn more, visit
ucpress.edu/supportus.